The Economics of Antitrust

THE ECONOMICS OF ANTITRUST
Cases and Analysis

Don E. Waldman

COLGATE UNIVERSITY

LITTLE, BROWN AND COMPANY
Boston   Toronto

Library of Congress Cataloging-in-Publication Data

Waldman, Don E.
  The economics of antitrust.

  Includes index.
    1. Antitrust law — United States — Cases.   2. Antitrust
law — Economic aspects — United States.   3. Monopolies —
United States.   I. Title.
KF1648.W35   1985   343.73'072   85-24148
                           347.30372
  ISBN 0-316-91791-5

Library of Congress Catalog Card No. 85-24148

ISBN 0-316-91791-5

9 8 7 6 5 4 3 2 1

DON

Published simultaneously in Canada
by Little, Brown & Company (Canada) Limited

Printed in the United States of America

*To my wife, Lynn
And my daughter, Abigail Beth*

Preface

The idea for this book took form a decade ago during my search for an antitrust casebook for my advanced undergraduate students in government and business. The books available at that time were little more than legal casebooks. They contained long legal excerpts from landmark decisions with little economic analysis. My students consistently found them tedious, so much so that many students admitted to me that they simply elected to glance over the assigned casebook. After several years of waiting for someone to combine economic analysis with *tight* editing of the cases that would emphasize the economic aspects, I finally decided to undertake the task myself, and what emerged was a book that reads like a traditional text rather than a legal casebook.

Difficult choices had to be made while writing this book. The first involved the level of economics background required to understand the analysis. Should the book be written for students with only an introductory level of economics background or for advanced undergraduates with an intermediate microeconomics background? I elected to write at a level that would be understandable to any good student with an introductory background, but also of great use to advanced undergraduates. I trust the result will be challenging to either an advanced beginner or an advanced undergraduate economics major. By requiring only a principles background, I believe the text will be useful to business majors, political science majors, and law students as well as economics majors.

The second difficult choice concerned case selection. If too few cases were chosen, students would fail to grasp the important sense of history, as well as economics, involved in antitrust decisions, whereas too many cases would make the book encyclopedic and unacceptable as an auxiliary text. I solved this dilemma by including virtually all the major landmark decisions, but *tightly* editing the case excerpts. Each case discussion includes a detailed introduction of the major facts and economic principles involved in the case, followed by excerpts that emphasize the major *economic* and *legal* lines of reasoning used by the court. This method of editing eliminates the need to meander through page after page of legal writing in order to understand the background of the case.

The third difficult choice involved the correct balance between analysis and excerpts. Because I wanted to write a concise text, I selected excerpts that provided a great deal of economic analysis, supplemented by my own analysis at the end of most cases. In addition I added excerpts from a fairly large number of dissenting opinions, whenever these opinions represented a reasonable alternative in economic reasoning.

The final difficult choice concerned the perspective of the book. Should the analysis present my own opinion about antitrust, or should it present the alternative opinions, leaving to the reader the decision of which opinion makes the most economic sense? In virtually every instance where opposing economic theories exist, I have presented both. In a few cases I have stated explicitly where my sentiments lie, but only after presenting both sides of the picture. Regardless of the opinions expressed, my hope is that the book will result in many lively discussions of the alternative points of view that abound in the field.

Throughout this book I have emphasized economics first and the law second. Chapter 1 presents a brief theoretical overview of the major economic issues involved in antitrust policy. Chapter 2 presents a brief historical background of antitrust policy, and lays out the basic enforcement mechanisms used in present policy. Each of Chapters 3 through 8 examines a different area of antitrust policy: monopolization, mergers, horizontal agreements, price discrimination, patents, and vertical restraints of trade. Each chapter begins with an analysis of the major economic issues involved, continues with a chronological examination of cases, and concludes with a brief summary.

Thanks are due to many for making this book a reality. Without question the greatest thanks are due to Erwin A. Blackstone for first introducing me to the field of antitrust and continuing to guide me through its maze on so many occasions. Many others have contributed to the final product, but three deserve particular praise: W. Lee Baldwin for his painstaking reviews of every chapter; Jeffrey Baldani, a Colgate colleague, for his help and encouragement; and William T. Ethridge, as fine an editor as one could hope to have. Thanks also go to my many students at Colgate who read and commented on earlier drafts, to the Colgate University Research Council for providing release time to complete this project, and to the following reviewers for their very helpful comments:

Bruce T. Allen, Michigan State University
Louis Amato, University of North Carolina–Charlotte
Richard E. Caves, Harvard University
Frances Esposito, Southeastern Massachusetts University
James L. Hamilton, Wayne State University
John Kuhlman, University of Missouri–Columbia
John Lunn, Louisiana State University
John McDowell, Arizona State University
W. F. Mueller, University of Wisconsin–Madison
Richard Peck, University of Illinois–Chicago
Anthony A. Romeo, University of Connecticut

Finally, none of this would have been possible without the constant encouragement of my wife, Lynn, and the love of Lynn and our daughter, Abigail.

Hamilton, New York   Don E. Waldman

Contents

The Economics of Antitrust

CHAPTER
ONE

The Economic Setting for Policy

The antitrust laws of the United States are a unique set of laws. No other country has attempted to legislate the existence of competition in the marketplace on such a grand scale. Because of the unique nature of the American antitrust laws, they can be viewed as a great experiment. There are those who view the experiment as a relative success and those who view the experiment as a total failure. There are few, however, who would argue that the experiment has been boring. The study of antitrust policy in the United States is a fascinating venture because it ties together economic, social, and political issues over almost a century of American history. Over the past nine decades, enforcement efforts have ebbed and flowed; however, the laws have become firmly entrenched as a major part of the American business scene, so much so that it has been said that the ghost of Senator Sherman, whose name is attached to the first federal antitrust act, resides in the boardroom of most American corporations [1].

1

Because the antitrust laws have become such an important part of the American business environment, it is extremely valuable for a student of economics or business to understand the laws and how they have been interpreted by the courts. Furthermore, the antitrust laws have had important economic effects, which must be evaluated so that the positive effects can be reinforced and the negative effects reduced or eliminated. This book analyzes the impact of antitrust law from two perspectives. First, it examines the economic impact of the laws on the American economy. Second, it examines the major legal implications for the behavior of firms.

Economists often disagree about the economic impact of the antitrust laws. Virtually all economists would agree, however, that a major objective of antitrust policy should be a more efficient economic system. An obvious starting point in our evaluation of antitrust policy is an understanding of the concept of economic efficiency.

I   THE MEANING OF ECONOMIC EFFICIENCY

When the first antitrust law was passed in 1890, there was relatively little understanding of the modern concept of economic efficiency. In 1890 there was a belief that monopoly could result in higher prices and restricted output and a fear of the political power of monopolies, but there was virtually no formal argument advanced by economists suggesting that monopoly was necessarily a less efficient market structure than competition. In fact, the economists of the day generally viewed Big Business as a necessary outgrowth of large economies of scale and the Darwinian theory of survival of the fittest. Economists, therefore, tended to oppose the Sherman Act at the time of its passage [2].

Today, even a student in an introductory economics course should have some understanding of the efficiency problems associated with monopoly power. The efficiency or inefficiency associated with monopoly power, however, tends to be an issue more complicated in reality than the way it is typically portrayed in an introductory course. Efficiency has a different meaning depending on whether the term refers to static efficiency or dynamic efficiency. In the context of antitrust policy, it is extremely important to understand the distinction between static and dynamic efficiency.

Static efficiency refers to the *current* relationship between price and cost in an industry. It consists of two basic components: *allocative* efficiency and *productive* efficiency. A market is allocatively efficient if price equals marginal cost; a market is productively efficient (or efficient in production) if total costs are minimized for any given level of output. Productive efficiency, therefore, implies that a firm is operating on its lowest possible average-cost curve.

Perhaps no concept in all of economics is more important than allocative efficiency. A market is allocatively efficient if the price a consumer is willing to pay for the *last* unit sold is equal to the *extra* cost to society of producing that unit. This condition ensures that *every* consumer will be satisfied so long as the consumer is willing to pay a price for an extra unit that is greater than or equal to the cost to *society* (in terms of opportunity costs) of producing that extra unit.

If price equals marginal cost, the *consumers' surplus* or the difference between the *maximum* amount that *all* consumers as a group would be willing to pay for a good and the actual amount they pay is maximized, subject to the constraint that price must always cover *marginal production costs*. In Figure 1-1 if D represents the demand curve for good X and the long-run marginal and average costs (LRMC and LRAC, respectively) of producing good X are constant, then output $Q(1)$ is the allocatively efficient output because price equals marginal cost. The total amount that all consumers would be *willing* to pay for $Q(1)$ units is represented by the area under the demand curve, area $ABQ(1)0$, and the amount they actually pay (price times quantity) is represented by the area $P(1)BQ(1)0$. The shaded area $ABP(1)$, therefore, represents the difference between what consumers would be willing to pay for $Q(1)$ units (if they were somehow forced to pay their maximum acceptable price for each and every unit) and what they actually pay for $Q(1)$ units. This triangle $ABP(1)$ represents the consumers' surplus associated with selling $Q(1)$ units of good X at a price equal to $P(1)$. Note that if output was less than $Q(1)$ units, the consumers' surplus triangle would be smaller. If price equaled $P(2)$ and output equaled $Q(2)$, then the consumers' surplus would be reduced to area $ACP(2)$. If output exceeded $Q(1)$ units, the consumers' surplus would be larger than area $ABP(1)$, but a price below $P(1)$ is *inefficient* because consumers are not paying the

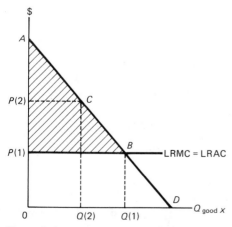

Figure 1–1

extra cost of producing additional units of output beyond $Q(1)$ units. Furthermore, a price below $P(1)$ would result in a price below long-run average total cost and economic losses for the firms in the industry. A price below $P(1)$, therefore, is inefficient and impossible to sustain for long periods of time. It follows that of all *possible* prices that at least cover marginal cost, $P(1)$ yields the largest consumers' surplus.

The consumers' surplus is often regarded as a measure of consumer welfare, and it is often claimed that the output $Q(1)$ maximizes not only the consumers' surplus, but also consumer welfare. In this sense, price equal to marginal cost implies that welfare is maximized and that the socially optimal output is produced [3].

In addition to static efficiency, dynamic efficiency is also very important. *Dynamic efficiency* refers to the performance of a market over time and includes elements of both cost and price performance. If a market is dynamically efficient, the rate of technological advance proceeds at an optimal rate. In order for a market to be dynamically efficient, firms must take advantage of research and development opportunities, and the benefits of these opportunities must be passed on to consumers in the form of higher-quality products and/or lower prices.

II   THE ECONOMIC CASE AGAINST MONOPOLY AND FOR COMPETITION

A close examination of the differences between competitive and monopolistic markets will help to clarify the distinction between static and dynamic efficiency. From a static perspective, competitive markets yield more efficient results than monopolistic markets. In fact, in the long run, perfectly competitive markets must be statically efficient.

Recall the four basic assumptions of the perfectly competitive market:

1. the existence of a large number of buyers and sellers, each with *no* control over price
2. a perfectly homogeneous product, with every producer's product a *perfect* substitute for every other producer's product
3. easy entry and exit from the market (i.e., easy mobility of resources into and out of the market)
4. perfect knowledge on the part of all buyers and sellers

Although few markets exhibit all four characteristics, the perfectly competitive model is a very useful tool for analyzing the behavior of many markets that exhibit most of these characteristics.

Figure 1-2 depicts a long-run equilibrium situation in a perfectly competitive market. Industry demand is represented by the curve D

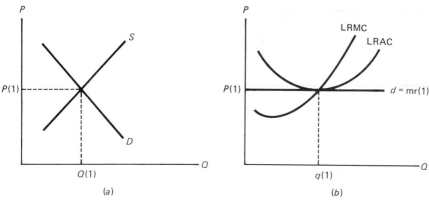

Figure 1–2

in Figure 1-2(a), industry supply is represented by the curve S, and $P(1)$ and $Q(1)$ represent the equilibrium market price and quantity, respectively. Firms take the price $P(1)$ as given and, therefore, have perfectly elastic demand curves represented by d in Figure 1-2(b). Since the firm takes the price as given, price $P(1)$ equals marginal revenue mr(1).

Profit maximization requires a competitive firm to produce an extra unit of output if the marginal revenue it receives from selling that extra unit is greater than the marginal cost (mc) of producing the extra unit. The profit-maximizing firm will produce the output $q(1)$, where $P(1) = \text{mr}(1) = \text{mc}$ and the consumers' surplus is maximized. Profit-maximizing behavior results, therefore, in *allocative efficiency* because price *must* equal marginal cost.

Another implication of the perfectly competitive model is that if short-run economic profits are excessive (above normal) firms will enter the industry in the long run. Entry increases supply, reduces price, and in the long run results in normal economic profits. Furthermore, if short-run economic profits are negative (an economic loss), then firms will leave the market in the long run, thus reducing supply, increasing price, and eventually resulting in zero or normal economic profits. In the long run, firms must earn a profit that is just sufficient to cover the opportunity cost of capital, labor, and other resources invested by the owners of the firm. Since long-run economic profits are normal, price must equal minimum average total cost in the long run.

The competitive market also results in static productive efficiency because firms that fail to produce at the lowest possible average cost will be driven out of the market. In Figure 1-3 if one firm has average costs equal to LRAC(2) while all other firms have average costs equal to LRAC(1) and if the industry price equals $p(1)$, then the high-cost firm will be eliminated from the market. The *high*-cost firm will maximize profits by producing $q(1)$ units and selling each at a price of $p(1)$. (Note: If

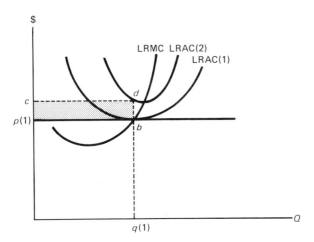

Figure 1–3

the firm tried to raise the price, buyers would flock to cheaper producers.) As a result, the high-cost firm will sustain an economic loss equal to
the shaded area $p(1)bdc$ and will be unable to survive in the long run [4].

Returning to Figure 1-2, three important *long-run* equilibrium
conditions can be noted:

1. Price equals marginal cost; therefore, allocative efficiency is
   achieved.
2. Firms produce on the lowest possible average-cost curve; therefore, productive efficiency is achieved in the static sense.
3. Long-run economic profits are zero (normal).

The competitive market in long-run equilibrium, therefore, results
in static efficiency.

Although the competitive market ensures static efficiency, dynamic efficiency may or may not exist in competitive markets. Since firms in
competitive markets earn only normal economic profits, they may lack
the necessary funds to invest in research and development. Furthermore, since each firm in a competitive market controls a small percentage of the market, from the standpoint of an individual firm the gains
associated with a technological advance may appear small compared
with the total gains to society. It follows that both the ability and the
incentive for firms to engage in research and development may be
lacking in highly competitive industries. Few, if any, farmers have
experimental laboratories in their barns to work on new farm technology. Instead, research and development in agriculture is left almost
entirely in the hands of the government and firms in complementary
industries, such as farm machinery and chemicals. Other competitive
industries that rank low in terms of research and development effort
include natural fiber textiles and apparel, wood products and furniture,

and paper products [5]. The perfectly competitive market, therefore, may result in a slow rate of technological advance and a lack of dynamic efficiency.

Just as there are relatively few American markets that conform to the economist's strict definition of perfect competition, there are few markets that conform to the economist's strict definition of monopoly. The monopoly model, however, can be useful in analyzing situations where one or a few firms dominate a market. Furthermore, any firm that faces a significantly downward sloping demand curve has some degree of control over price and, therefore, some market power. According to the economist's definition of monopoly

1. There is one and only one producer of the product, the price setter.
2. The product is heterogeneous when compared with other products (i.e., there are no close substitutes).
3. Entry is difficult or impossible.

Figure 1-4 represents the equilibrium situation in a typical monopolistic market. The monopolist faces a downward-sloping demand curve that is identical to the industry's demand curve since the monopolist is the industry. The downward-sloping demand curve D results in a marginal revenue curve (MR) that lies everywhere below the demand curve [6]. Profit maximization requires that the monopolist produce an extra unit of output so long as the marginal revenue from selling the extra unit is greater than the marginal cost of producing it. Note that the profit-maximizing rule is the same for the monopolist and the perfectly competitive firm. In Figure 1-4, profit maximization requires that the

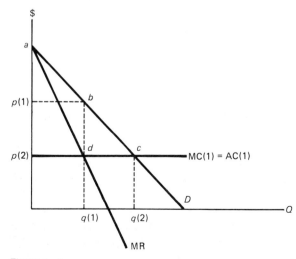

Figure 1–4

monopolist produce an output of $q(1)$ units and charge a price of $p(1)$ to clear the market.

The efficiency implications of monopoly are quite different from those of perfect competition. The monopolist produces an output where price is greater than marginal cost, that is, $p(1)>MC(1)$. The monopolist, therefore, is allocatively *inefficient*. The failure to equate price with marginal cost is typically considered the greatest economic problem associated with monopoly because it ensures that in a static sense the monopolist will not produce the optimal output, where price equals marginal cost [$q(2)$ in Figure 1-4]. The monopolist fails to produce the units between $q(1)$ and $q(2)$ despite the fact that some consumer is willing to pay a price that is greater than the marginal cost of producing each of those units. This is economically inefficient because an extra unit should be produced so long as someone is willing to pay a price for that unit that is greater than the extra cost to society of producing it. The monopolist, therefore, restricts output below the socially optimal level $q(2)$. Furthermore, price is greater than the optimal price $p(2)$.

As a result of monopoly pricing, the consumers' surplus is reduced from the optimal area $acp(2)$ (where price equals marginal cost) to area $abp(1)$. Part of the reduction in the consumers' surplus, however, is transferred to the monopolist in the form of higher profits. The transfer from the consumers' surplus to monopoly profits is represented by the area $p(1)bdp(2)$. Since this area represents an income transfer from one group to another, it can be argued that the area $p(1)bdp(2)$ does *not* represent a complete loss of the consumers' surplus to society, but represents only increased monopoly profits at the expense of a reduction in consumers' surplus [7]. The triangle bcd is lost to consumers but is *not* gained by the monopolist; therefore, it represents a *complete loss* to society associated with monopoly power. The triangle bcd is referred to as the *deadweight loss* associated with monopoly power.

Another efficiency implication of monopoly is that a monopolist may or may not be productively efficient. In Figure 1-4, the monopolist produces an output of $q(1)$ units and earns excess economic profits [equal to area $p(1)bdp(2)$] because price is greater than average cost. Suppose that the curve AC(1) represents the lowest possible average-cost curve associated with producing the monopolist's product. If AC(1) represents the lowest possible cost of production, then the monopolist is productively efficient in the static sense. Suppose, however, that the monopolist becomes complacent about its position and starts to produce its output a bit less efficiently. The monopolist's management may decide to purchase several jet aircraft to carry the managers to several "business" conferences in Hawaii or to use Cadillacs instead of Chevettes as delivery cars even though both cars perform the same function. Suppose that the monopolist's costs begin to rise to a level of AC(2) in Figure 1-5. Despite the rise in costs, the monopolist continues to earn excess profits.

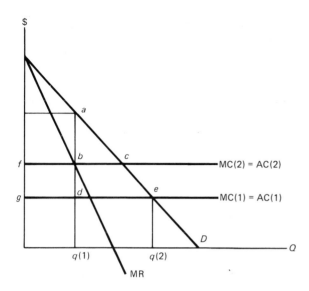

Figure 1–5

True, these profits are less than the maximum possible profits, but they may still be sufficient to keep the firm's owners (stockholders) content. In a competitive market if one firm's costs rise relative to all other firms, it will be driven out of the market. There are few market mechanisms, however, that will quickly discipline an inefficient monopolist. Economists refer to a rise in costs from AC(1) to AC(2) caused by wasted resources as *X inefficiencies* [8]. If *X* inefficiencies exist, productive efficiency will not.

If *X* inefficiencies exist, they will significantly increase the efficiency loss associated with monopoly power. Figure 1-5 illustrates the extra deadweight loss resulting from *X* inefficiencies. Suppose that minimum costs are represented by the curve MC(1) = AC(1) and that because of *X* inefficiencies actual costs are MC(2) = AC(2). A profit-maximizing monopolist *with* X inefficiencies would produce the output q(1) instead of the socially optimal output q(2), and the deadweight loss would equal the triangle *ade plus* the rectangle *fbdg* (the rectangle represents the loss associated with the extra cost of producing the first q(1) units since this area is *not* part of either the consumers' surplus or monopoly profit). A typical study of the deadweight loss due to monopoly power would ignore *X* inefficiencies and *assume* that the profit-maximizing monopolist minimized costs. As a result, a typical study would conclude that the entire deadweight loss is measured by the triangle *abc*. The area *fceg*, therefore, represents the extra deadweight loss associated with *X* inefficiencies. It is clear for Figure 1-5 that theoretically the *X* inefficiency costs can be quite large, and it has been suggested by some economists that the loss due to X inefficiency can be significantly larger than the traditional deadweight loss measure [9].

A monopolist may also earn excess profits. The word *may*, however, must be emphasized because a monopolist may also earn normal profits or even sustain short-run economic losses. Figure 1-4 depicts a situation where the monopolist earns excess profit. Figure 1-6(a), however, depicts a situation where a profit-maximizing monopolist earns only a normal economic profit because price equals average cost. Figure 1-6(b) also indicates that a monopolist can sustain an economic loss if price is below average cost. In fact, it is not difficult to think of real-world monopolists that sustain economic losses. The United States Postal Service is one such example, as is the New York City subway. Furthermore, in recent years Metropolitan Edison, the owner and operator of the Three Mile Island nuclear power plant, has sustained short-run economic losses for rather obvious reasons.

Monopolists, however, often have one major advantage over competitive firms with regard to profitability. If excess profits exist in a competitive market, new firms enter, and established firms expand. As a result industry supply increases, price decreases, and excess profits are eventually eliminated. In a monopolistic market, however, entry is difficult, and excess profits *may* exist for long periods of time.

At this point it may be useful to digress from our efficiency arguments and consider the difference between *positive* and *normative* arguments in economics. It is important to understand that competitive markets are *not* more efficient than monopolistic markets because they result in lower long-run profits. High profits for long periods of time may *indicate* that a market is not performing efficiently. The primary problem with monopoly in a static sense is that price is greater than marginal cost; therefore, monopoly ensures allocative inefficiency. In the short

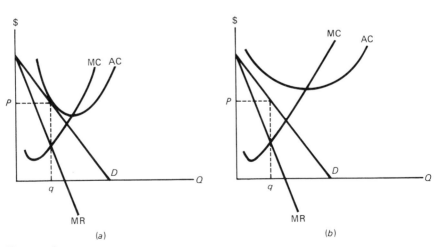

Figure 1–6

run, profits may be normal, excessive, or below normal in either a perfectly competitive or a monopolistic market.

When an economist declares that a monopolistic market results in a higher price and lower output than a competitive market with the same cost and demand conditions, the economist is making a *positive* economic argument. The declaration that there is a profit problem with monopoly is a *normative* argument. A positive argument is one that is based on the tools of economic analysis. By using the tools of economic theory it is possible to show that monopoly results in static inefficiency because price is greater than marginal cost. The statement, "Monopoly results in allocative inefficiency," is a positive statement. Other examples of *positive* economic statements include

1. In a competitive market an increase in demand results in an increase in price, *ceteris paribus* (other things held equal).
2. An increase in the price of oil will result in an increase in the price of gasoline.
3. The recipients of food stamps would either be better off or no worse off if they received a cash grant of equal amount instead of food stamps.

By using the tools of economic analysis each of the above statements can be derived; therefore, they are examples of positive economic statements.

A *normative* statement is one that deals with value judgments. The statement, "A major problem with monopoly power is that it often results in excess profits," is a normative statement. Some readers of this book may agree wholeheartedly with this statement, but others may disagree just as wholeheartedly. For example, one reader, hypothetically named Mr. Marley, might agree with the statement; but another reader, hypothetically named Mr. Scrooge, might disagree. The important thing to realize is that *neither* is right or wrong. They are merely expressing their opinions about the distribution of income in society.

In the context of antitrust policy, normative issues often become extremely important. In 1973–1974, following the Arab oil embargo and a huge increase in oil prices, there was a public outcry against the American oil industry. Even though the price increases resulted primarily from the market power and actions of a foreign cartel and it was unclear how much of an impact the American oil industry had on the price increases of refined products, the Federal Trade Commission (FTC) filed a suit against eight major oil companies. The FTC suit was dropped in 1981, and although there is no direct proof available, it is certainly plausible that the public's ire had as much to do with the filing of the case as economic analysis.

In the United States there are a great many public policies where normative arguments dominate positive arguments. Minimum wage laws exist in part because the normative issue of "fair" wages is politically dominant over the positive issue that minimum wages increase unemployment. Similarly, we have a progressive federal income tax system even though high marginal tax rates on the wealthy may discourage saving and investment. There is nothing wrong with letting normative arguments dominate positive arguments if society so chooses. In fact, the antitrust laws originated in 1890 for largely normative reasons. We should, however, be careful to distinguish positive from normative issues when evaluating antitrust policy. This book concentrates almost exclusively on the positive as opposed to normative issues involved in antitrust policy because only by concentrating on the positive issues can an objective appraisal of the *economic* merits and demerits of antitrust be made.

Returning to the efficiency implications of monopoly power, we can conclude that monopoly generally results in three major outcomes:

1. Price is greater than marginal cost; therefore, static allocative efficiency is not achieved.
2. If X inefficiencies develop, then static productive efficiency will not be achieved.
3. Excess profits *may* exist for long periods of time.

Compared with perfect competition, monopoly is certainly inefficient in a static sense. The competitive model results in allocative efficiency; the monopoly model results in allocative *in*efficiency. The perfectly competitive model results in productive efficiency in the static sense; the monopoly model may result in productive *in*efficiency. The competitive model seems "fairer" from the normative standpoint of equity because profits in the long run will be normal, but even long-run profits may be excessive in monopolistic markets. From a purely static perspective, therefore, competition appears preferable to monopoly.

The dynamic implications of the two models, however, yield a somewhat different conclusion. As noted earlier, the competitive model results in little ability or incentive to invest in research and development. On the other hand, the monopolist may have excess profits for long periods of time, which may be invested in research and development and result in technological advances that lower costs and introduce new and improved products. Furthermore, the monopolist controls the entire market and will obtain all of the benefits derived from any technological advance. A monopolist, therefore, may have both a greater ability and a greater incentive to invest in research and development than a competitive firm has. As a result, the monopolist, although less efficient in a static sense, may be more efficient in a dynamic sense. The case in favor of perfect competition becomes much less clear when both static and dynamic efficiencies are considered.

The dynamic efficiency argument in favor of monopoly must be qualified. It is true that the perfectly competitive model would be expected to result in a relatively slow rate of technological advance, but it does *not* follow that a great deal of monopoly power should result in a rapid rate of technological advance merely because firms have the resources to invest in research and development. An optimal rate of technological advance requires both an ability *and* an incentive to invest in research and development. Although market power may result in a greater ability to invest in research and development, it may also result in a reduced incentive. If entry is very difficult, a monopolist will probably have relatively little incentive to invest large sums in risky research and development because it has relatively little fear of losing its market share to competitive inroads. Theoretically, therefore, neither perfect competition nor monopoly would be expected to result in a very rapid rate of technological advance. Instead, an oligopolistic market structure, where firms have some market power but also face significant competition from other firms with some market power, may be necessary to supply both an ability and an incentive to invest in research and development.

Empirical evidence tends to support the hypothesis that neither very high nor very low degrees of market power are conducive to a rapid rate of technological advance. The most widely accepted opinion among mainstream economists is that the relationship between market power and research and development is likely to be like the one depicted in Figure 1-7. Research and development effort tends to be low when market power is nonexistent, increases to some intermediate level of market power, and then declines as market power increases toward very high levels [10]. If these conclusions are correct, then very high levels of market power should retard the rate of technological advance.

There is another piece of empirical evidence that suggests very high levels of market power are not necessarily conducive to a rapid rate of technological advance. John Jewkes et al. found that most major

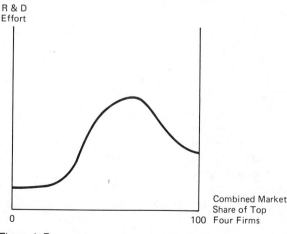

R & D
Effort

0   100   Combined Market
                                                               Share of Top
                                                               Four Firms

Figure 1–7

inventions of the first half of the twentieth century were initially developed by either individual inventors or by researchers at academic institutions [11]. Among the inventions developed outside of the large research and development labs were air conditioning, the automatic transmission, cellophane, the electron microscope, the helicopter, insulin, the jet engine, Kodachrome film, penicillin, the instant camera, the radio, the safety razor, xerography, and the zip fastener. Only twenty-four of seventy inventions examined by Jewkes had their origins in a large research and development laboratory. One of these was DDT, which has proved to be a questionable advance. Jewkes's findings are consistent with the findings of Hamburg that only seven of twenty-seven major inventions between 1946 and 1955 occurred within large research and development labs [12].

The case against the large research and development lab should not be overstated. Relatively few inventions came from these labs, but many of these inventions were *developed* into commercial products by large firms with market power. Cellophane was not invented by Du Pont, but Du Pont greatly improved the commercial viability of cellophane by creating moistureproof cellophane [13]. Similarly, Kodachrome film was not invented by Kodak, but was developed into a commercial product in Kodak labs [14]. Market power and large resources, therefore, may play a more important role in development than in invention. Both stages are important for the introduction of a new commercial product; therefore, very high degrees of monopoly power are probably not conducive to an optimal rate of technological advance.

III   THE MOST COMMON DEFENSE OF MONOPOLY: ECONOMIES OF SCALE

In most instances market power results in some economic inefficiency, but there are cases in which market power is justified because production costs are lower with a monopolistic market structure. In virtually every major monopolization antitrust case, the defense argues that monopoly power is justified because of the existence of large *economies of scale* in production. It is extremely important, therefore, to understand the meaning and significance of economies of scale.

Economies of scale exist for a firm if long-run average total costs decline as output increases. The most common explanation for the existence of economies of scale is the specialization of labor and capital equipment in the production process. All firms experience some economies of scale in production and distribution, but economies of scale will be far more significant in some industries than in others.

Economies of scale tend to result in market power if the following two conditions hold:

1. A firm of *minimum optimal scale* produces a large percentage of total market demand.
2. Suboptimal-scale firms face significantly higher average costs of production compared to optimal-scale firms.

If the first condition holds, then only a limited number of firms can *fit* into the industry. In Figure 1-8 the demand curve D represents total industry demand, and the curve AC represents a typical firm's average-cost curve. Note that at a price $P(1)$ total industry quantity demanded is $Q(t)$. Furthermore, one optimal-scale firm can produce $\frac{1}{4}Q(t)$ units at minimum average cost equal to $P(1)$. In this situation, two optimal-scale firms could produce $\frac{1}{2}Q(t)$ units at AC = $P(1)$, three optimal-scale firms could produce $\frac{3}{4}Q(t)$ units at AC = $P(1)$, and four optimal-scale firms could produce $Q(t)$ units at AC = $P(1)$. If there were four optimal-scale firms each producing $\frac{1}{4}Q(t)$ units (assuming each of the four firms maintained its output at $\frac{1}{4}Q(t)$ units), the addition of another firm would increase output beyond $Q(t)$ units and result in a price reduction below $P(1)$. As a result, all five firms would sustain economic losses since price would be below average cost. In Figure 1-8, therefore, only four optimal-scale firms can fit into the market. If four optimal-scale firms existed, the top four firms would control the entire market.

Economies of scale may result in market power; however, the existence of economies of scale should not be viewed as an economic problem. Quite to the contrary, only by taking advantage of economies of scale can an industry perform efficiently. In Figure 1-8, it would be possible to fit more than four firms into the industry *if* some of the firms produced less than $\frac{1}{4}Q(t)$ units, but this would result in higher average total costs

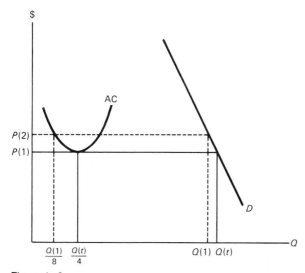

Figure 1-8

of production *and* would require higher prices to cover the higher costs of production. If each firm produced $\frac{1}{8}Q(1)$ units, average costs would equal $P(2)$, and eight firms could fit into the industry, but Price and average cost would both be higher and efficiency would suffer.

Even if an optimal-scale firm produces a large percentage of total industry output, economies of scale will generally not result in market power *unless* suboptimal-scale firms face significantly higher average costs of production. This condition relates to the steepness of the average-cost curve. The steeper the average-cost curve, the more seriously disadvantaged suboptimal-scale firms will be in relation to optimal-scale firms. Very few markets consist of identical firms like the firms depicted in the hypothetical industry in Figure 1-8. Instead, most markets contain a variety of firm sizes and product prices. If suboptimal-scale firms face very significant cost disadvantages, they will have trouble surviving. On the other hand, if an industry's average-cost curve is relatively flat, suboptimal-scale firms will face only minor cost disadvantages, and they will be able to charge prices close to the prices charged by optimal-scale firms.

Figure 1-9 can be used to clarify the significance of the cost disadvantage associated with a suboptimal scale. Suppose the gold-widget industry has an average-cost curve represented by *DE* and the silver-widget industry has an average-cost curve represented by *FE*. If the optimal scale is $Q(1)$ units in each industry, a firm producing at one-half optimal scale in the gold-widget industry will have its average costs increased by 10 percent compared with an optimal-scale gold-widget producer. A silver-widget producer operating at one-half optimal scale will face only a 1 percent cost disadvantage. It will be significantly easier for a suboptimal-scale silver-widget producer to compete against optimal-scale firms than for a suboptimal-scale gold-widget producer to compete against optimal-scale firms. If the average-cost curve is rel-

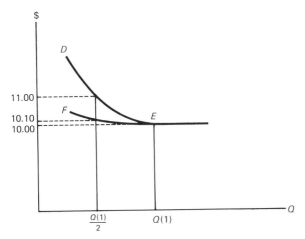

Figure 1–9

atively flat, economies of scale will tend to be less of a justification for market power.

Studies of the significance of economies of scale in American manufacturing indicate that although economies are significant in many industries, they fail to explain completely the high levels of market power found in many markets. Several economists, most notably J. S. Bain, F. M. Scherer, and L. W. Weiss, have studied the degree to which economies of scale at the plant level explain market power in American manufacturing [15].

Table 1-1 summarizes the basic findings of Scherer et al. and Weiss that the two necessary conditions listed above do *not* exist in most markets and that, therefore, economies of scale at the plant level are not significant enough to explain the degree of market power found in many American markets. In Table 1-1, the warranted percent control of the top four firms is obtained by multiplying the percentage of output produced in one optimal-scale plant by 4. The warranted percentage control of the top four firms, therefore, hypothetically measures the share the top four firms would control if each of the top four firms controlled *exactly one* optimal-scale plant. In every market, warranted control is less than actual control. In and of itself this is not surprising since warranted control is the *minimum* possible control consistent with the existence of economies of scale. The ratio of actual control to warranted control, however, tends to be very large in many industries, suggesting that market shares among the top firms are much greater than is necessary to take advantage of plant economies of scale. It should be noted that in a number of markets the market shares of the top firms would be quite high if each firm operated just one optimal-scale plant. For example, warranted control of the top four firms is 92 percent in turbogenerators, 56.4 percent in refrigerators, and 40 percent in aircraft. Even in these markets, however, actual control exceeded warranted control.

It should be emphasized that Table 1-1 refers to economies of scale in production at the *plant* level and there may be economies of scale associated with operating more than one plant in an industry. Even when such multiplant economies are taken into consideration, however, the general conclusion that economies of scale in production usually do *not* completely explain the large market shares found to exist in many American markets holds [16]. In an antitrust case any defense based on the existence of large economies of scale, therefore, should be examined carefully.

IV   CONFLICTING OBJECTIVES OF ANTITRUST POLICY

The broad objective of antitrust policy is to inhibit undesirable business conduct and maintain market structures that are conducive to efficient economic performance. Judges, lawyers, and economists *might* all agree

Table 1–1   THE SIGNIFICANCE OF ECONOMIES OF SCALE IN AMERICAN
MANUFACTURING INDUSTRIES CIRCA 1967

| | Scherer et al. Findings | | | |
Industry	% of U.S. Demand One Optimal-Scale Plant	%Increase in AC at ⅓ Optimal Scale	Warranted % Control, Top Four Firms	Actual % Control, Top Four Firms
Beer	3.4	5.0	13.6	40
Cigarettes	6.6	2.2	26.4	81
Cotton fabrics	0.2	7.6	0.8	36
Paints	1.4	4.4	5.6	22
Petroleum refining	1.9	4.8	7.6	33
Nonrubber shoes	0.2	1.5	0.8	26
Glass bottles	1.5	11.0	6.0	60
Cement	1.7	26.0	6.8	29
Integrated steel	2.6	11.0	10.4	48
Antifriction bearings	1.4	8.0	5.6	54
Refrigerators	14.1	6.5	56.4	73
Automobile batteries	1.9	4.6	7.6	61

with these basic objectives, but their individual objectives may be very different.

Government lawyers often consider quick victory the major objective. This is understandable since a lawyer's reputation is built on victories rather than on positive economic gains to society. If a lawyer wishes to move up the ladder at the Justice Department, it is probably much more important to win cases than to obtain major economic gains [17]. Government lawyers are, therefore, likely to act quickly in response to a relatively minor complaint from a competitor since the complaining firm will supply much of the evidence needed for a court victory, but they are unlikely to respond at all to a major covert oligopolistic price-fixing scheme since evidence will be difficult to obtain and a victory will be questionable at best. In addition, many of the top people at the Justice Department and Federal Trade Commission stay with the government for only a few years and are unlikely to receive credit for a case they began but somebody else finished. A lawyer stopping over at the Justice Department for two years probably prefers to obtain a minor conviction in a year rather than starting a major case that will last ten

Weiss Findings

Industry	% of U.S. Demand, One Optimal-Scale Plant	% Increase in AC at ½ Optimal Scale	Warranted % Control, Top Four Firms	Actual % Control, Top Four Firms
Flour mills	0.7	3	2.8	30
Synthetic rubber	4.7	15	18.8	61
Cellulose synthetic fibers	11.1	5	44.4	86
Detergents	2.4	2.5	9.6	88
Passenger auto tires	3.8	5	15.2	70
Turbogenerators	23.0	NA	92.0	100
Machine tools	0.3	5	1.2	21
Electronic computers	15.0	8	60.0	75
Transformers	4.9	8	19.6	65
Passenger autos	11.0	6	44.0	99
Commercial aircraft	10.0	20	40.0	69

Sources: F. M. Scherer et al., *The Economics of Multi-Plant Operation: An International Comparisons Study* (Cambridge, Mass.: Harvard University Press, 1975), reprinted by permission of Harvard University Press, and L. W. Weiss, "Optimal Plant Size and the Extent of Suboptimal Capacity" in R. T. Masson and P. D. Qualls (eds.), *Essays on Industrial Organization in Honor of Joe S. Bain* (Cambridge, Mass.: Ballinger, 1975).

years. These biases operate to discourage lawyers from filing major cases during their brief tenures with the government.

Judges interpret the laws and actually determine the effectiveness of antitrust policy, yet few are schooled in economics. Their decisions are based on their interpretation of the law, not on the basis of creating a more competitive economy. Historically, judges have interpreted the laws more as a challenge to certain business practices than as a means of directly altering poor market structures or performance. Furthermore, judges have shown a great reluctance to change market structures directly through the use of divestiture, dissolution, and divorcement. This reluctance appears to stem from two fears: (1) the possible loss of economies of scale and (2) the possible unfair punishment of present stockholders for the abuses of past owners and managers [18]. The first fear is justified, for surely economies of scale should not be sacrificed for the sake of trust-busting unless the benefits outweigh the costs. But strong consideration of the second fear would virtually eliminate structural relief from the arsenal of antitrust enforcement because present stockholders almost always suffer a penalty as a result of divestiture or dissolution [19]. Judges have obviously enforced the letter of the law and have been relatively unconcerned about improving economic efficiency.

Where does this leave the economist? The economist's objective is to improve efficiency. The economist is primarily concerned with market power that results in negative efficiency effects. Judges and lawyers are very concerned about the method used to obtain power, but the economist's objective is to eliminate the negative effects of power, regardless of the method used to obtain that power. The objective is efficiency. Price should approach marginal and average costs; technological advances should proceed at a rapid rate; and, perhaps for normative reasons, profits should not be excessive. The economist will favor antitrust action any time the expected welfare gains are greater than the expected costs of litigation.

Since lawyers, judges, and economists have different objectives, conflicts often arise. Lawyers will hesitate to initiate a broad attack on an oligopolistic industry because of a low probability of winning and an even lower probability of winning during their stay with the government. Economists, however, often encourage challenging oligopolists because the potential efficiency gains are great. On the other hand, lawyers may enthusiastically file a price-discrimination case if a firm attempts to enter a new geographic market or attract new customers by selectively lowering prices. The lower prices may result in improved efficiency, and many economists would favor this type of discrimination unless it is an obvious attempt to drive other firms out of the market.

Two conflicts between judges and economists have already been noted. Judges are hesitant to take strong action against oligopolists unless evidence showing collusion is presented in court. Economists, however, realize that there is little reason to expect oligopolists to practice overt collusion because oligopolists often realize their interdependencies and act in unison. According to many economists, therefore, the most effective remedy in oligopoly cases is a change in industry structure. As previously mentioned, however, judges rarely order divestiture or dissolution, even when they find in favor of the government.

Considering these conflicts between the economic objective of increased competition and the objectives of lawyers and judges, is it possible to maintain an effective antitrust policy? If an effective policy requires dramatic convulsive-type changes in market structure, then the present antitrust policy is clearly not effective. If, however, antitrust policy has major direct and indirect effects that lead toward increased effective competition, then perhaps some of the economic objectives are achieved despite the conflicts. The remainder of this book attempts to provide some insight into which of the above two statements comes closer to the truth.

NOTES

1. W. G. Shepherd and C. Wilcox, *Public Policies Toward Business* (Homewood, Ill.: Irwin, 1979), page 87.

2. F. M. Scherer, *Industrial Market Structure and Economic Performance* (Chicago: Rand-McNally, 1980), page 493.

3. This argument is actually based on value judgments because it assumes that price is an accurate measure of marginal utility, an assumption that many economists question.

4. The shaded area $p(1)bdc$ does *not* represent dollar or monetary losses — it represents an *economic* loss in the sense that the firm is not covering its opportunity costs. Since the firm could do better if it transferred its resources to an alternative use, it will leave the industry in the long run.

5. It should be noted that the most important determinant of an industry's research and development effort is the degree to which technological opportunities are available. Since these industries are not technologically progressive, one might expect that their research and development effort would be relatively low. Even after considering opportunities, however, highly competitive industries invest relatively little in research and development.

6. Marginal revenue is everywhere less than price because the monopolist must lower its price on *all* units sold in order to sell an additional unit. When the monopolist sells an additional unit, its revenue gain on the last unit sold is equal to the price *minus* the loss of revenue it sustains on all previously sold units. It follows that the revenue gain from selling the last unit must be less than the price of the last unit and marginal revenue must be less than price.

7. Richard A. Posner has argued that this view is shortsighted because monopoly profits will attract resources to the industry in an effort by sellers to obtain some of the monopoly profits and by consumers to avoid being charged monopoly prices. This process is likely to lead to an increase in nonprice competition and higher production costs, until costs have risen to the level of the monopoly price. According to this view, monopoly power results in an increase in costs rather than in a transfer of consumers' surplus to monopoly profits. If this view is correct, then the area $p(1)bdp(2)$ is primarily an increase in the social costs of production rather than an income transfer from consumers to monopolists. See R. A. Posner, *Antitrust Law: An Economic Perspective* (Chicago: University of Chicago Press, 1976), pages 11–14.

8. H. Leibenstein, "Allocative vs. X-Efficiency," *American Economic Review,* June 1966, pages 392–415.

9. W. S. Comanor and H. Leibenstein, "Allocative Efficiency, X-Efficiency and the Measurement of Welfare Losses," *Economica,* August, 1969: pages 304–309; see also Scherer, *Industrial Market Structure and Economic Performance,* pages 464–466.

10. For an excellent review of the evidence see Scherer, *Industrial Market Structure and Economic Performance,* Chapter 15.

11. J. Jewkes, D. Sawers, and R. Stillerman, *The Sources of Invention* (New York: Norton, 1969).

12. D. Hamburg, "Invention in the Industrial Research Laboratory," *Journal of Political Economy,* April 1963, pages 95–115.

13. *United States v. E. I. Du Pont de Nemours,* 351 U.S. 377 (1956).

14. Scherer, *Industrial Market Structure and Economic Performance,* page 417.

15. J. S. Bain, *Barriers to New Competition* (Cambridge, Mass.: Harvard University Press, 1956); F. M. Scherer, A. Beckenstein, E. Kaufer, and R. D. Murphy, *The Economics of Multi-Plant Operation: An International Comparisons Study* (Cambridge, Mass.: Harvard University Press, 1975); and L. W. Weiss, "Optimal Plant Size and the Extent of Suboptimal Capacity" in R. T. Masson and P. D. Qualls (eds.), *Essays on Industrial Organization in Honor of Joe S. Bain* (Cambridge, Mass.: Ballanger, 1975).

16. J. S. Bain, *Barriers to New Competition;* Scherer et al., *The Economics of Multi-Plant Operation.*

17. J. J. Siegfried, "The Determinants of Antitrust Activity," *Journal of Law and Economics,* October 1975, page 573.

18. See D. Dewey, "Romance and Realism in Antitrust Policy," *Journal of Political Economy,* April 1955, page 93; and K. G. Elzinga and W. Breit, *The Antitrust Penalties: A Study in Law and Economics* (New Haven: Yale University Press, 1976), pages 47–50 and 99–106.

19. D. Dewey, "Romance and Realism in Antitrust Policy," pages 100–102.

CHAPTER
TWO

The Antitrust Laws

I   EARLY HISTORY OF THE ANTITRUST LAWS

Long before the passage of the Sherman Act in 1890, English common law had made contracts in restraint of trade void, and the English courts had even gone so far as to forbid monopoly grants by the crown. Prior to 1890, however, no nation had ever made it part of its legislated public policy to forbid restraints of trade and the act of monopolization.

It is relatively easy to understand the political pressures that led to the passage of the Sherman Act [1]. Prior to the Civil War, the United States was mainly an agrarian society where high transportation costs kept the geographic size of most industrial markets small. After the Civil War, however, the organization of American industry changed dramatically. The rapid growth of national markets in many products developed from a combination of mass production, introduced by the industrial revolution, which resulted in significant economies of scale; a national railroad system, which greatly increased the size of the geographic market in many products; the development of modern capital markets, which enabled firms to raise large amounts of capital in the equity market; and the liberalization of the laws of incorporation in many states. With the growth of national markets, many small regional manufacturers faced competition for the first time. The larger national firms, which took advantage of economies of scale, were often able to invade local markets that were formerly insulated from competition and charge significantly lower prices. As the national producers captured a larger and larger share of many local markets, they threatened to eliminate many local producers.

From the viewpoint of the small local producer, two alternatives were often available: either agreeing to merge with a more efficient national producer or waiting to be eliminated from the market by the more efficient national producer. Needless to say, many local producers chose the first option. These mergers typically took the legal form of a *trust,* in which control of the member corporations was vested in a single board of trustees. Some of the most famous trusts were formed in the petroleum, sugar, tobacco, meat packing, coal, whiskey, and gunpowder industries. During this period, the granddaddy of all trusts, Standard Oil, was established by John D. Rockefeller. By the 1880s, trusts controlled many of the basic necessities of life, and a public outcry against the most powerful trusts began to develop.

One group, farmers, was particularly hard hit by the new industrial order. Throughout the farm belt of the Midwest and West, the railroads held a great deal of monopoly power. As a result, farmers were forced to pay high shipping rates or else watch their grain spoil. In addition, farmers were paying high monopoly prices set by the major trusts to obtain many of the necessities of life. Under such circumstances, the combined power of the railroads and the trusts could sometimes force farmers down to a subsistence standard of living. As a result of these economic pressures, two important political groups arose in America: the Populists and the Grangers. These groups were able to run a candidate for president and also able to win a number of seats in Congress. As the political influence of the Populists and Grangers grew, the two major parties were forced to address the trust problem.

During the elections of 1888, the Democrats and Republicans both offered platform planks to fight the trusts, and right before the election Senator John Sherman (R-Ohio) introduced the first Senate antitrust bill. John Sherman was a distinguished senator. First elected to the House in 1854, and then to the Senate in 1861, he was considered an expert in the areas of public finance and taxation and served as secretary of the treasury, under President Hayes, and secretary of state, under President McKinley. The first Sherman antitrust bill was introduced on August 14, 1888, and was directed at any agreement that tended to "prevent full and free competition" or "to advance the cost to the consumer of any . . . articles." Under the bill, any injured party could sue for double the amount of damages suffered, and a convicted corporation would be required to forfeit its corporate franchise. There was some debate on this first Sherman bill, but it went nowhere in the Fiftieth Congress.

On December 4, 1889, Senator Sherman again introduced his antitrust bill. This time the bill was referred to the Finance Committee. When the Finance Committee reported the bill back to the Senate on March 18, 1890, several amendments had been made to Sherman's original proposal. The Finance Committee's version contained no criminal penalties, but still included equitable relief for injured parties. It has often been contended that the Senate had little interest in the Sherman Act and never seriously debated the bill, but the Finance Committee's bill, which bore some resemblance to the final Sherman Act, was extensively debated in March 1890. Furthermore, it is often argued that Senator Sherman had little to do with the passage of the Sherman Act and was only lukewarm toward its objectives, but Senator Sherman strongly endorsed the Finance Committee's bill during the March debates. At one point the senator stated emotionally, "If we will not endure a king as a political power we should not endure a king over the production, transportation, and sale of any of the necessaries of life. If we would not submit to an emperor we should not submit to an autocrat of trade, with power to prevent competition and to fix the price of any commodity [2]."

These are hardly the words of a lukewarm supporter of the bill. In any event, Sherman's bill was sent to the Judiciary Committee, which proceeded to rewrite the bill completely. On April 2, 1890, the Judiciary Committee reported the new bill back to the Senate. There was virtually no Senate debate on this bill, entitled "A bill to protect trade and commerce against unlawful restraints and monopolies." On April 8, 1890, the Senate voted 52–1 to pass the Sherman Act. The bill then went to the House, and after some debate and a few conferences with the Senate, it passed the House by 242–0 on June 20, 1890. On July 2, 1890, President Harrison signed the measure, an act he probably thought would be little remembered by history. History, of course, proved that it was one of the most significant acts passed by the Fifty-first Congress and signed into law by President Harrison.

Who actually wrote the Sherman Act? It clearly was *not* Senator Sherman, although he deserves credit for introducing the first version of the bill. Historians appear to agree that most of the bill was written by Senator Edmunds (R-Vt.) but that portions of the bill were written by Senators Evarts (R-N.Y.), George (D-Miss.), Ingalls (R-Kan.), and Hoar

(R-Mass.) [3]. In 1890 nobody wanted to take credit for drafting *any* part of the bill; however, by 1910 everybody who had been on the Judiciary Committee wanted to take credit for drafting it *all!*

II   THE CONTENT OF THE ANTITRUST LAWS

Regardless of who wrote the Sherman Act, its major provisions were sections 1 and 2, which read in part:

Section 1: Every contract, combination in the form of a trust or otherwise, or conspiracy, in restraint of trade or commerce among the several states, or with foreign nations, is hereby declared to be illegal. Every person who shall make any such contract or engage in any such combination or conspiracy, shall be deemed guilty of a misdemeanor, and, on conviction thereof, shall be punished by fine not exceeding five thousand dollars, or by imprisonment not exceeding one year, or by both said punishments, in the discretion of the court.

Section 2: Every person who shall monopolize, or attempt to monopolize, or combine or conspire with any other person or persons to monopolize any part of the trade or commerce among the several states, or with foreign nations, shall be deemed guilty of a misdemeanor.

The remaining major sections of the Sherman Act contained the following provisions:

Section 3 simply extended the conditions of section 1 to include actions in any territories held by the United States, as well as the District of Columbia.

Section 4 invested jurisdiction over the Sherman Act in the federal court system and made it the duty of the attorney general of the United States to direct the enforcement of the act. Furthermore, section 4 gave the attorney general the power to "institute proceedings in equity to prevent and restrain . . . violations." This section is very important because it gave the government the power to seek divestiture and dissolution as remedies in civil antitrust proceedings.

Section 6 gave the United States the power to order the "forfeiture, seizure, and condemnation of property" used in any combination in violation of the act. Although this section sounds strong, its sanctions have hardly ever been applied.

Section 7 provided that any person injured by a violation of the act could sue in the federal circuit court for treble damages plus attorney's fees. This section, therefore, cleared the way for private Sherman Act cases.

On a first reading, the Sherman Act may sound quite strong, but certain problems immediately arose with regard to its enforcement. Ironically, the act was first used in 1892 against organized labor to help break the Pullman strike! An even greater problem arose with regard to the legal implications of the wording of section 1. Since section 1 made it *illegal* for competitors to *combine* to fix prices, it created an incentive for firms to get around the law by *merging* with their competitors. The first major merger wave in the United States was at the turn of the century and, ironically, was encouraged and fueled by the Sherman Act.

Another problem developed from the wording of section 2. During the 1890s section 2 of the Sherman Act was completely ineffective in dealing with the monopolization problem. In 1911, however, two major decisions, the *Standard Oil* and *American Tobacco* rulings, provided both hope for enforcement and confusion with regard to what constituted a violation of section 2. In its famous *Standard Oil* decision the Supreme Court ruled that only *unreasonable* attempts to monopolize violated the Sherman Act. This Supreme Court interpretation made only the *verb* "to monopolize" illegal. It permitted the *noun* "monopoly" to exist so long as the monopoly did not result from an aggressive attempt to monopolize. This precedent has come to be known as the *Rule of Reason.*

Partly as a result of the handing down of the Rule of Reason and partly as a result of a lack of clarity in the wording of the Sherman Act with regard to certain types of specific business conduct, by 1912 there was a call for new antitrust legislation. All three presidential candidates in 1912, Wilson, Theodore Roosevelt, and Taft, supported new legislation, and when Woodrow Wilson became president he made antitrust reform part of his comprehensive economic package, which also included the creation of the Federal Reserve System, the reduction of most tariffs, and the establishment of the federal income tax system. What eventually emerged from Congress in 1914 were the next two major pieces of antitrust legislation, the Clayton Act and the Federal Trade Commission Act.

The *Clayton Act* aimed to prevent certain *specific* types of business conduct. It contained the following four substantive sections:

Section 2 forbad price discrimination "where the effect of such discrimination may be to substantially lessen competition or tend to create a monopoly in any line of commerce." The section provided, however, for three defenses: discrimination based on the quantity sold, discrimination based on different costs of selling or transportation, and discrimination based on a need to meet a competitor's lower price. With these defenses, section 2 of the Clayton Act had more holes in it than a piece of swiss cheese.

Section 3 forbad tying contracts (forcing a purchaser to buy good X in order to obtain good Y) and exclusive dealing (forcing a buyer to purchase its entire supply of a commodity from one seller) arrangements "where the effect . . . may be to substantially lessen competition."

Section 7 forbad the acquisition of the *stock* of another corporation if the acquisition would "restrain commerce in any section or community or tend to create a monopoly of any line of commerce." The section was directed at the merger wave that had developed after the passage of the Sherman Act and was limited to *horizontal mergers* between direct competitors. This section was gutted in 1926 when the Supreme Court ruled that corporations could legally avoid section 7 by acquiring simply the *assets* rather than the *stock* of another corporation. It was not until 1950 that this huge loophole was plugged.

Section 8 forbad interlocking directorates between any two *competing* corporations. This prevented the same individual from sitting on the boards of directors of two competing companies.

The *Federal Trade Commission Act* established the Federal Trade Commission as an independent antitrust agency to enforce the Clayton Act. The FTC Act also contained one major substantive provision, section 5, which reads in part:

> The commission is hereby empowered and directed to prevent persons, partnerships, or corporations, except banks, and common carriers subject to the Acts to regulate commerce, from using unfair methods of competition in commerce.

One can hardly imagine a broader mandate! Unfair methods of competition could include just about any business practice. Furthermore, many practices considered "unfair" by competitors may have a positive effect on the competitive process. The FTC had very little power in its early days. In fact, its only available remedy was to issue cease and desist orders.

The next major antitrust statute was the *Robinson-Patman Act* of 1936, which dealt with price discrimination. When Congress passed section 2 of the Clayton Act, it clearly was directed at the *geographic* price discrimination used by the more powerful trusts, such as Standard Oil, to force local competitors out of business. In other words, the Clayton Act was aimed at predatory price discrimination used by powerful firms to increase their market power. Section 2 of the Clayton Act, however, proved to be ineffective, primarily because the quantity defense could be used in almost all cases, and the courts rarely questioned whether or not quantity-based discounts were cost justified. During the Great Depression, however, a different issue emerged: small companies complained that large chain stores, especially in food distribution, were able to increase their market shares by inducing lower prices from suppliers. The small firms argued that these lower prices were out of line with any possible cost savings associated with chain-store purchases, and they pressured Congress for action against the large chains. A study by the FTC seemed to confirm some of the smaller firms' charges, and in 1936 Congress responded by passing the Robinson-Patman Act [4].

The Robinson-Patman Act amended section 2 of the Clayton Act to include the following major provisions:

Section 2(a): That it shall be unlawful for any person engaged in commerce, in the course of such commerce, either directly or indirectly, to discriminate in price between different purchasers of commodities of like grade and quality, where either or any of the purchasers involved in such discrimination are in commerce, . . . and where the effect of such discrimination may be substantially to lessen competition or tend to create a monopoly in any line of commerce, or to injure, destroy or prevent competition with any person who either grants or knowingly receives the benefit of such discrimination, or with customers of either of them:

PROVIDED, That nothing herein contained shall prevent differentials which make only due allowance for differences in the cost of manufacture, sale, or delivery resulting from the differing methods or quantities in which such commodities are to such purchasers sold or delivered:

PROVIDED, HOWEVER, That the Federal Trade Commission may, after due investigation and hearing to all interested parties, fix and establish quantity limits, and revise the same as it finds necessary, as to particular commodities or classes of commodities, where it finds that available purchasers in greater quantities are so few as to render differentials on account thereof unjustly discriminatory or promotive of monopoly in any line of commerce; and the foregoing shall then not be construed to permit differentials based on differences in quantities greater than those so fixed and established. . . .

Section 2(b): Upon proof being made, at any hearing on a complaint under this section, that there has been discrimination in price or services or facilities furnished, the burden of rebutting the prima facie case thus made by showing justification shall be upon the person charged with a violation of this section, and unless justification shall be affirmatively shown, the Commission is authorized to issue an order terminating discrimination:

PROVIDED, HOWEVER, That nothing herein contained shall prevent a seller rebutting the prima facie case thus made by showing that his lower price or the furnishing of services or facilities to any purchaser or purchasers was made in good faith to meet an equally low price of a competitor, or the services or facilities by a competitor. . . .

Section 2(f): That it shall be unlawful for any person engaged in commerce, in the course of such commerce, knowingly to induce or receive a discrimination in price which is prohibited by this section.

The Robinson-Patman Act contained three other sections that declared specific types of price discrimination illegal *per se*. These sections attempted to close potential loopholes in the Robinson-Patman Act and included the following.

Section 2(c) forbad the payment of any brokerage commission "except for services rendered in connection with the sale or purchase of goods, wares or merchandise, either to [another] party to such transactions or to an agent, representative, or other intermediary." This section prevented chains like A&P from setting up their own brokerage agencies that would then charge their suppliers a brokerage fee for the simple act of transferring goods from A&P to A&P. Under section 2(c) only truly *independent* brokers could receive brokerage payments.

Section 2(d) forbad a supplier from *paying* its buyers for promotional services unless the payments were made available to *all* buyers on proportionally equal terms.

Section 2(e) forbad the supplier from *providing* promotional services to any buyer unless the services were made available to *all* buyers on proportionally equal terms.

As we shall see in Chapter 6, the Robinson-Patman Act has become extremely controversial because it has often been used to protect individual competitors rather than the competitive process. The potential problems are easily seen in a careful reading of section 2(a), which extended the words "where the effect of such discrimination may be substantially to lessen competition or tend to create a monopoly" to include the words " . . . or to injure, destroy or prevent competition with any person." The addition of this last clause justified using the Robinson-Patman Act in cases where price discrimination injured just *one* competitor, even if the discrimination actually increased *effective* competition and *improved* economic efficiency.

The final major amendment to the Clayton Act occurred in 1950 with the passage of the *Celler-Kefauver Act*. This act amended section 7 of the Clayton Act to include mergers through *asset* as well as stock acquisition. The Celler-Kefauver Act also extended section 7 to reach *vertical* and *conglomerate* mergers as well as horizontal mergers. With the passage of the Celler-Kefauver Act, section 7 of the Clayton Act finally had some clout in dealing with anticompetitive mergers. Note, however, that it took thirty-six years to plug this loophole!

III   CURRENT MAJOR EXEMPTIONS FROM THE ANTITRUST LAWS

Labor

As soon as the Sherman Act was passed, problems arose regarding the scope and coverage of the act. As previously noted, the first successful use of the Sherman Act was against a labor union, not a trust.

This resulted in lobbying pressure to exclude labor from the reach of the Sherman Act, and section 6 of the Clayton Act specifically excluded labor from the antitrust laws by declaring "that the labor of a human being is not a commodity or article of commerce." The Norris-La Guardia Act of 1932 further extended this exemption, and today any union action directed solely at promoting the interests of its members is beyond the reach of the antitrust laws. It is *illegal,* however, for a union to *combine* with an employer to restrain trade in any way.

Agriculture and Fishing

Agricultural and fishing cooperatives are also exempt from the antitrust laws. The Clayton Act declared that nothing in the laws should prevent agricultural or horticultural cooperatives aimed at mutual help. The *Capper-Volstead Act* of 1922 extended this exemption by permitting agricultural cooperatives to price and market their products collectively. Under the *Fisheries Cooperative Marketing Act* of 1934, fishing cooperatives received the same exemption as farmers. In some markets these exemptions have undoubtedly resulted in higher prices, particularly in regionally concentrated markets for some commodities such as milk.

Export Cartels

The *Webb-Pomerene Act* of 1918 exempted export cartels from antitrust policy. The act required any export cartel to register with the FTC and prohibited collusion that affected markets within the United States, but it clearly authorized business practices that would be illegal if done by firms selling strictly within the United States.

Regulated Industries

Public utilities, banking, and insurance are *partially* exempt from the antitrust laws. The exemption derives from the *primary* jurisdiction granted to the regulatory agencies overseeing these industries, such as the Federal Power Commission, the Federal Communications Commission, the Interstate Commerce Commission, and state banking and insurance commissions. Nevertheless, most regulatory commissions are mandated to consider the antitrust implications of their decisions. Furthermore, a number of cases have suggested that the federal courts may review the antitrust implications of a commission's decision and may overturn a commission's ruling on antitrust grounds. The regulated sectors' exemption from antitrust, therefore, is far from absolute.

Newspapers

In 1970, in response to pressure from the newspaper lobby after a series of court decisions prevented several newspaper mergers, Congress exempted certain joint operating agreements between competing newspapers. The law now permits newspapers to share the same printing and business offices.

IV   ENFORCEMENT PROCEDURES

Antitrust enforcement typically begins with an action by either the Antitrust Division of the Justice Department or the Federal Trade Commission. The Antitrust Division's budget was approximately $44 million in 1982, a trivial sum to oversee the American economy, especially when compared with the legal resources available to America's largest corporations. Most cases are precipitated by either a complaint from a competitor or a report in the business press. Occasionally, a case begins with a staff report from a government agency. After an initial investigation, the staff attorney in charge of the case consults other lawyers and economists in the division and decides whether or not to proceed. Most cases are dropped after the initial investigation; however, some suits eventually work their way up to the assistant attorney general in charge of antitrust. If the assistant attorney general approves, the case is filed in one of ninety federal district courts.

Once a case is in the federal court system, it proceeds to trial and a decision in the district court. Either side can appeal the district court's decision to one of eleven circuit courts of appeal. Once the circuit court rules on a case, either side can appeal to the Supreme Court. The Supreme Court will hear the case (grant *certiorari*) if at least four justices agree that the legal issues warrant a hearing. Otherwise, the Supreme Court refuses to hear the case (*certiorari denied*) and the circuit court's decision stands. The entire process is long and drawn out, with litigation periods averaging over five years and some major cases lasting through several decades.

The workings of the FTC are quite different from the Antitrust Division. Its 1982 budget was approximately $69 million, also a fairly trivial sum. The FTC is headed by five commissioners who are appointed by the president to serve for seven years. It would be nice to be able to say that *all* past and present FTC commissioners have had an excellent understanding of economics. Unfortunately, although some commissioners have been well trained in economics, many others have had a very unsophisticated understanding of economics in theory or practice. Investigations almost always begin with a competitor's complaint, although the FTC staff will sometimes initiate a case. If the staff decides to issue a formal complaint, the respondent has the option of settling the dispute with the FTC staff. In fact, a large majority of cases stop right at this point. If the respondent and the FTC cannot come to an agreement, however, the case goes before an *administrative law judge* who works for the FTC. Based on a hearing that is very similar to a district court trial, the administrative law judge makes a ruling. The judge's opinion can be appealed to the full commission by either the respondent or the FTC staff. The five-member commission hears the appeal and makes a decision, and only the respondent can appeal this decision to the circuit court of appeals. After the circuit court decision, either the FTC or the respondent can appeal to the Supreme Court.

The Justice Department is entirely responsible for the enforcement of the Sherman Act. Furthermore, the department has jurisdiction over Clayton Act cases and has been particularly active in prosecuting mergers under section 7 of the Clayton Act as amended by the Celler-Kefauver Act. The FTC, on the other hand, is concerned with enforcement of the FTC and the Clayton Acts, but has no technical jurisdiction over the Sherman Act. The FTC has *no criminal jurisdiction,* and the commission must leave criminal cases entirely up to the Justice Department. Recently, the line of separation between the two agencies has become blurred as the FTC has convinced the courts that violations of the Sherman Act are unfair methods of competition and, therefore, violate section 5 of the FTC Act. Today, it is fairly safe to say that either agency can attack just about any anticompetitive conduct or structure.

Antitrust suits can also be filed by private parties. In fact, in recent years private antitrust cases have greatly outnumbered government cases. In 1976, 95.6 percent of all antitrust cases were filed by private parties, not the government [5]. Furthermore, for many firms the threat of a large private suit is much greater than the threat of government action because private cases can result in treble damage awards that dwarf the fines imposed by the courts in government cases. Although private cases have become increasingly important in recent years and represent a significant threat to antitrust violators, the major precedents in antitrust law have almost all come from government cases.

V   REMEDIES

In the event of a government victory there are several possible penalties or remedies. In *criminal* cases, fines and jail sentences may be imposed. The original Sherman Act set of maximum fine of $5,000 *per* violation. This limit was increased to $50,000 in 1955 and to $1,000,000 in 1974. Recently, the FTC has been given the power to impose a fine of $5,000 per day on any respondent who refuses to abide by an FTC order. To America's largest and most powerful firms, however, these fines are likely to look insignificant. A $1,000,000 fine imposed on General

Motors is likely to have about as much effect as a $7,500 fine imposed on basketball star Larry Bird (earning over $1 million a year) for hitting Julius Erving. Once a firm is found guilty of an antitrust violation, however, it establishes a prima facie (automatic, literally "first made") case of guilt in private cases. Once a firm loses a major antitrust case, it automatically becomes liable for damages in private treble damage cases as long as the plaintiff can *prove* damages occurred. The fear of private treble damage cases probably explains why so many firms fight so long and so hard to avoid an antitrust conviction.

Until recently, the other criminal penalty, jail sentences, had been imposed only on rare occasions. The use of jail sentences has become somewhat more common during the past decade, and quite a few jail sentences are now handed out each year in criminal price-fixing cases. The most famous sentences ever handed out were in the 1960 electrical-equipment price-fixing cases, when seven executives went to prison.

In *civil cases,* only remedies, *not* penalties, can be imposed. The distinction between a remedy and a penalty is purely a semantic distinction because many antitrust remedies provide more of a threat to violators than the maximum criminal penalties allowed under the law. Civil remedies may include conduct and/or structural changes. In cases where conduct is believed to be the major problem, *injunctions* are often issued forbidding a certain type of conduct (e.g., price discrimination or tying). Injunctions change future behavior without penalizing the defendant for past behavior.

In some extreme cases, the courts may adopt *structural* remedies. Structural remedies include divestiture, dissolution, and divorcement. These remedies have most commonly been used in merger cases, but on a few occasions divestiture has been ordered in monopolization cases under section 2 of the Sherman Act.

It is fairly common for the Justice Department to file concurrent criminal and civil proceedings for one simple reason: Criminal actions can *only* punish a defendant for *past* actions, and civil actions can *only* regulate the *future* behavior and structure of an industry. If the government wishes to both punish past offenses and regulate future conduct, it is forced to file both a criminal and a civil action.

Once a case is filed by the Justice Department, the defendant has several options. In criminal cases, the defendant may plead *nolo contendere* (Latin for "I do not wish to contend"). This plea was made famous by former Vice President Spiro Agnew. The advantage of a nolo contendere plea over a guilty plea is that even though the court can impose penalties just as if the defendant had pleaded guilty, a nolo contendere plea does *not* constitute an admission of guilt; therefore, injured firms cannot automatically receive treble damages based on a nolo contendere plea. Furthermore, since there is no trial record with a nolo contendere plea, private firms cannot use trial facts and testimony as evidence in private suits. The major advantage of the nolo contendere plea, therefore, is that it provides some protection for the defendant from the potential flood of private suits that may follow a major antitrust defeat. Because of this potential advantage to defendants, the Justice Department is not required to accept a nolo contendere plea and may force a trial.

In civil cases, a *consent decree* plays the same basic role as the nolo contendere plea in criminal cases. With a consent decree, the respondent refuses to admit guilt, but agrees to some conduct or structural change. Consent decrees avoid long and costly court battles for both sides and provide the respondent with the same advantages as a nolo contendere plea with regard to potential private suits.

Both nolo contendere pleas and consent decrees are extremely common in antitrust actions. In fact, in a typical year over 80 percent of all antitrust cases end in either a nolo contendere plea or a consent decree [6]. The cases analyzed in the remainder of this book, therefore, represent primarily the major cases fought through the court system. On some issues, such as overt price-fixing, the precedents are now so clear that firms rarely choose to fight in court.

One final point about remedies should be noted. It is often claimed that the government wins most cases in court and loses them when it comes time for the remedies. There is some truth to this statement, but it is important to remember that the antitrust laws, like all laws, are primarily effective because the fear of prosecution prevents violation. Just as traffic laws prevent you from running a red light even when no police officer is around, the antitrust laws prevent firms from sitting down to set prices even when no spy from the government is around. Without this type of self-regulation the antitrust laws would be ineffective. Furthermore, since most business executives do not relish the idea of being taken down to a local police station, being fingerprinted, and being booked for a criminal violation of the Sherman Act, the threat of action, more than actual action, prevents many criminal violations of the Sherman Act. Of course it is fair to assume that if the penalties and remedies in antitrust cases were tougher, the deterrent effect of the antitrust laws would be even greater [7].

Having explored the economic foundations of antitrust law in Chapter 1 and explored the legal foundations in this chapter, we take a detailed look at one aspect of the law in each of the next six chapters. We begin in Chapter 3 with an examination of monopolization.

NOTES

1. The information in this section is based primarily on H. B. Thorelli, *The Federal Antitrust Policy: Origination of an American Tradition* (Baltimore: Johns Hopkins Press, 1955); see also J. D. Clark, *The Federal Trust Policy* (Baltimore: Johns Hopkins Press, 1931); A. H. Walker, *History of the Sherman Law* (New York: Equity Press, 1910); J. W. Markham, "Survey of the Evidence and Findings on Mergers" in National Bureau of

Economic Research, *Business Concentration and Price Policy* (New York: Arno Press, 1975), pages 141–212; S. N. Whitney, *Antitrust Policies: American Experience in Twenty Industries* (New York: Twentieth Century Fund, 1958), Chapter 1; and A. D. Neale and D. G. Goyder, *The Antitrust Laws of the U.S.A.* (Cambridge, England: Cambridge University Press, 1980).

2. Thorelli, *Federal Antitrust Policy,* page 180.

3. Ibid., pages 210–214.

4. Neale and Goyder, *The Antitrust Laws of the U.S.A.,* page 212.

5. W. G. Shepherd and C. Wilcox, *Public Policies Toward Business* (Homewood, Ill.: Irwin, 1979), page 95.

6. R. A. Posner, "A Statistical Study of Antitrust Enforcement," *Journal of Law & Economics,* October 1970, pages 365–419.

7. For an excellent argument along these lines see K. G. Elzinga and W. Breit, *The Antitrust Penalties: A Study in Law and Economics* (New Haven: Yale University Press, 1976).

CHAPTER

THREE

Monopolization

I INTRODUCTION

In Chapter 1 we analyzed the economic inefficiencies associated with
monopoly power. It was shown that monopoly power tends to be associated with static and dynamic inefficiencies. In monopolized markets,
price exceeds marginal cost: therefore, allocative inefficiency exists.
Furthermore, X inefficiencies may exist: therefore technological efficiency may not be achieved. Finally, a lack of incentive to invest in
research and development may result in dynamic inefficiencies. Because of these problems monopoly power is likely to result in significant
economic problems, and public-policy makers should consider antitrust
action if monopoly power lasts for a long period of time.

It was also pointed out in Chapter 1 that monopoly power may be
economically justified if it is based on economies of scale or necessary for

invention and innovation. Public-policy makers, therefore, are faced with the difficult task of trying to distinguish the cases of justified from the cases of unjustified monopoly power.

Within the context of antitrust policy, recall from Chapter 2 that section 2 of the Sherman Act is the primary vehicle for dealing with cases of overwhelming monopoly power. Section 2 reads in part

> Every person who shall monopolize, attempt to monopolize or combine or conspire with any other person or persons to monopolize any part of the trade or commerce among the several States . . . shall be deemed guilty of a misdemeanor.

Upon first reading, section 2 may sound straightforward and easy to interpret, but it has proven to be extremely difficult to enforce. Part of the enforcement problem stems from the section's wording. Another problem stems from the federal courts' interpretation of section 2. In any event, recent cases have often turned into lengthy nightmares for both the government and the defendant firms. Cases tend to be extremely long (e.g., the government's IBM case was filed in 1969 and then dropped in 1982 without a decision), and decisions may be based on obsolete economic facts and circumstances rather than on current economic conditions.

Why have section 2 cases become such legal boondoggles? Perhaps the reason goes back to 1911 when the Supreme Court handed down its famous *Standard Oil* decision and declared that a Rule of Reason must be used to decide monopolization cases. Or, perhaps, the blame should be placed on Congress, which in 1890 failed to specify whether *all* monopolies or only unreasonable monopolies were to be declared illegal.

One point is clear, however, the Sherman Act did not outlaw the *noun* "monopoly," but only the *verbs* "to monopolize" or "attempt to monopolize." The act was not a per se ban on all monopolies. Monopoly power, in and of itself, is not illegal in the United States. From an economic viewpoint this makes sense because much of the monopoly power that exists is based on legitimate economic advantages such as economies of scale or patents. Furthermore, monopoly power often lasts only a few years. It would be inefficient to declare all monopolies illegal, but just because a ban on all monopolies would be inefficient does not imply that current policy is optimal.

Before an analysis of the strengths and weaknesses of antitrust policy toward monopoly can be undertaken, it is crucial to have some understanding of the economic concept of monopoly power. To an economist, monopoly power is the ability to control price. In a technical sense this control should be complete, meaning that the monopolist should control 100 percent of the market. In a realistic, or legal, sense this condition is rarely met, unless a market is defined very narrowly. General Motors is a monopolist in a technical sense in a market defined narrowly as the market for Pontiacs; however, in a market defined more broadly as the market for automobiles General Motors has only limited power. Of these two market definitions, almost everyone would agree that the better economic definition is automobiles since that definition more accurately reflects the true level of competition in the marketplace, but the choice of a market definition is not always this easy.

To better understand the difficulties involved in defining markets correctly, let us consider how the government defines industrial markets. Every five years the Department of Commerce publishes a list of *concentration ratios* in over 400 American manufacturing industries. The most widely used concentration ratio is the percentage of total value of shipments in an industry supplied by the top four firms. This figure is known as the industry's *four-firm concentration ratio*. In addition to the value of shipments, concentration ratios are also published based on value added, employment, capital expenditures, and the cost of materials used. The four-firm concentration ratio based on value of shipments, however, is the most widely used measure of the degree of control by the top firms in an industry.

Concentration ratios provide economists with some information about market structure, but they also suggest several serious problems associated with defining a market. Too often the market definition by the government includes products that are not close substitutes or excludes products that are close substitutes. Since the concentration ratio is supposed to serve as an indirect measure of the degree of competition in a market, either type of error is serious.

If the government's definition contains too many products, it is said to be too broad, and it will overstate the actual degree of competition in the market. A market defined as simply drugs contains aspirin and insulin, yet it is obvious that a diabetic would not be able to substitute aspirin for an insulin injection, and few individuals would consider taking an insulin injection for a headache. The broad definition of drugs includes many nonsubstitute products such as antacids, antibiotics, aspirin, and Preparation H. Since many drugs have few, if any, substitutes, the degree of actual competition is low in many product lines, and the four-firm concentration ratio for drugs would overstate the degree of competition.

Here are other examples of markets that the government defines too broadly, followed by an explanation of the problem with the definition:

1. Newspapers — the government defines concentration on a national level, but newspapers are sold almost exclusively in local or regional markets.
2. Engines and turbines — the government includes large turbine generators in the same market as small appliance motors.
3. Cement — like newspapers, cement is sold in regional markets.

Many Government market definitions are too broad. Others are too narrow because the definition ignores close substitutes. In such cases the concentration ratio will tend to understate the true degree of competition. The market of automobiles includes only domestically produced cars and ignores imports. With imports now making up more than 25 percent of all cars sold in the United States, it is foolish to ignore imports when defining the degree of competition. The 1977 four-firm concentration ratio in the market of motor vehicles and car bodies was 93 percent, which clearly understates the degree of effective competition in the automobile industry.

Other examples of markets defined too narrowly include

1. Metal cans — the government ignores close substitutes such as glass containers and paper containers.
2. Steel — the government ignores substitutes such as aluminum, plastic, scrap metals, and imported steel.
3. Meat products — the government ignores substitutes such as poultry and fish.

In a monopolization case, the correct definition of the market becomes crucial. Virtually all monopolization cases begin with a debate over the proper market definition. A correct definition must include close substitute products and exclude nonsubstitutes. Suppose one firm manufactured almost all of the cellophane produced in the United States. Would that firm necessarily have monopoly power? In 1956 the Supreme Court said no because the producer of cellophane, in this case Du Pont, competed with the producers of other *Flexible Wrapping Materials,* such as waxed paper and aluminum foil. The Court declared that the relevant market for economic purposes was all flexible wrapping materials and consequently acquitted Du Pont. Yet eleven years later, in the *Grinnell case,* the Supreme Court declared that accredited central station protection services did *not* compete with other forms of protection services such as unaccredited central station systems, burglar alarm systems, night-watchdogs, or security guards.

Why did the Supreme Court adopt a broad definition in the *Du Pont* case and a narrow definition in the *Grinnell* case? In an effort to answer this question, we turn now to an examination of the courts' interpretation of section 2.

II   THE EARLY CASES

United States v. E. C. Knight Co. 156 U.S. 1 (1895)   The first major case decided under section 2 of the Sherman Act was the *E. C. Knight* case in 1895. The case dealt with the American Sugar Refining Company, which by 1895 had acquired 97 percent of the sugar refining capacity in the United States. Specifically, the government complaint concerned the purchase of four Philadelphia sugar refineries, with a combined 33 percent market share, which left one independent sugar refiner in the United States, the Revere Sugar Refinery Company.

If ever there was an attempt to monopolize, this was it! American Sugar had acquired all of the sugar refineries in the United States except one. Its market share was close to 100 percent, and it unilaterally set the price of refined sugar throughout the country. The Supreme Court, however, dismissed the government's complaint on the technicality that manufacturing did not involve interstate commerce. The majority reasoned as follows:

> Commerce succeeds to manufacture, and is not a part of it. . . . The fact that an article is manufactured for export to another State does not of itself make it an article of interstate commerce, and the intent of the manufacturer does not determine the time when the article or product passes from the control of the State and belongs to commerce.

The underlying philosophical reason for this decision is probably well stated in the following passage:

> [A]ccording to political economists, aggregation of capital may reduce prices, therefore, the objection to concentration of power is relieved.

In 1895 the Supreme Court believed in the advantages of industrial concentration and was not about to destroy the economic advantages associated with the aggregation of capital.

If the *E. C. Knight* precedent had stood the test of time, section 2 of the Sherman Act would have ceased to have any true meaning, but the lesson of the *E. C. Knight* case was quickly forgotten by a different Supreme Court.

United States v. Northern Securities Co. 193 U.S. 197 (1904)

At the turn of the century two large railway systems dominated the Northwestern part of the United States, the Great Northern Railway Company and the Northern Pacific Railway Company. The Great Northern extended from the cities of Superior, Duluth, and St. Paul to the cities of Everett, Seattle, and Portland; the Northern Pacific ran from Duluth and St. Paul to Spokane, Seattle, Tacoma, and Portland. In the Northwest, these two railroads were the only competitors.

Because of the existence of large economies of scale, it is not surprising that there were only two railroads in the Northwest. Despite their control, the two carriers tended to have serious financial problems during recessions, when low demand and high fixed costs would result in economic losses. In fact, in 1893 the Northern Pacific was on the verge of bankruptcy; its property was taken over by government-appointed receivers. The Great Northern tried, for the first time, to gain control of the Northern Pacific, but the Great Northern's attempt was declared an illegal attempt to monopolize by the State of Minnesota [see *Pearsall v. Great Northern* 161 U.S. 646 (1896)]

In 1901 the Great Northern tried again to gain control of the Northern Pacific. This time a holding company, the Northern Securities Company, was established to acquire the stock of both the Great Northern and the Northern Pacific. As a result of the merger, all of the profits received by the two "independent" companies ended up in the same set of hands.

The government filed a complaint charging the Northern Securities Company with attempting to monopolize rail transportation in the Northwest. In 1904, in a 5-4 decision, the Supreme Court ruled in favor of the United States and ordered the merger dissolved. Justice Harlan spoke for the majority, and early in the decision he went out of his way to clarify the *E. C. Knight* decision by stating that

> Combinations even among *private* manufacturers or dealers whereby *interstate or international commerce* is restained are equally embraced by the act.

Justice Harlan then presented his philosophy with regard to section 2 in the following paragraphs:

> Indeed if the contentions of the defendants are sound why may not *all* the railway companies in the United States, that are engaged, under state charters, in interstate and international commerce, enter into a combination such as the one here in question, and by the device of a holding corporation obtain the absolute control throughout the entire country of rates for passengers and freight, beyond the power of Congress to protect the public against their exactions? . . .
>
> Many suggestions were made in argument based upon the thought that the Anti-Trust Act would in the end prove to be mischievous in its consequences. Disaster to business and wide-spread financial ruin, it has been intimated, will follow the execution of its provisions. . . .
>
> [E]ven if the court shared the gloomy forebodings in which the defendants indulge, it could not refuse to respect the action of the legislative branch of the Government if what it has done is within the limits of its constitutional power. . . . The [defendant's] suggestions imply that the court may and ought to refuse the enforcement of the provisions of the act if, in its judgment, Congress was not wise in prescribing as a rule by which the conduct of interstate and international commerce is to be governed, that every combination, whatever its form, in restraint of such commerce and the monopolizing or attempting to monopolize such commerce shall be illegal. . . .

[I]f the Anti-Trust Act is held not to embrace a case such as is now before us, the plain intention of the legislative branch of the Government will be defeated.

There is nothing in the *Northern Securities* case that suggests the two firms had abused their market power or were aggressive toward competitors. Justice Harlan based his opinion on the simple principle that the combination had monopolized trade in the market of railroads in the Northwestern United States. In fact, Justice Oliver Wendell Holmes based his dissent on the argument that the Northern Securities Company had done nothing to prevent another firm from entering the market. In his opinion there was no violation of the law. An emphasis on behavior in monopolization cases, however, was only a few years away. It began in 1911 with the *Standard Oil of New Jersey* decision.

United States v. Standard Oil Co. of New Jersey 221 U.S. 1 (1911)   The *Standard Oil* case is unquestionably one of the most famous antitrust cases. The case dealt with John D. Rockefeller and associates' control of the oil refining industry during the last quarter of the nineteenth century. All of Standard Oil's actions seemed aimed at one objective: maintaining control over the oil refining business in the United States. It managed to maintain a 90 percent market share for a long period of time by acquiring over 100 competitors through merger; controlling the major oil pipelines, which permitted it to foreclose crude oil supplies from its competitors; obtaining freight rebates from railroads not only on its own shipments, *but also on its competitors' shipments as well;* and *perhaps* using localized price-cutting to drive its more stubborn competitors out of the market. In retrospect it appears that Standard Oil rarely relied on predatory price-cutting as a competitive weapon since it was less costly to buy out competitors by offerring them premium prices for their stock [1]. Despite the fact that Standard Oil usually chose the merger route rather than predatory pricing as a means of acquiring competitors, it still followed policies that can easily be termed aggressive attempts to monopolize.

The Supreme Court unanimously ruled against Standard Oil. In his landmark decision, Chief Justice White (who had sided with the minority in the *Northern Securities* case) laid down the famous Rule of Reason doctrine, which declared that only unreasonable attempts to monopolize violated section 2. Chief Justice White's prose often sounds like poor Shakespearean verse; however, try to identify his major line of reasoning in the following passages:

And as the contracts or acts embraced in [section 2 of the Sherman Act] were not expressly defined, since the [act] addressed itself simply to classes of acts, those classes being broad enough to embrace every conceivable contract or combination which could be made concerning trade or commerce or the subjects of such commerce, and thus caused any act done by any of the enumerated methods anywhere in the whole field of human activity to be illegal if in restraint of trade, it inevitably follows that the provision necessarily called for the exercise of judgment which required that some standard should be resorted to for the purpose of determining whether the prohibition contained in the statute had or had not in any given case been violated. Thus not specifying, but indubitably comtemplating and requiring a standard, it follows that it was intended that the standard of reason which had been applied at the common law and in this country in dealing with subjects of the type embraced by the statute was intended to be the measure used for the purpose of determining whether, in a given case, a particular act had or had not brought about the wrong against which the statute provided. . . .

Undoubtedly, the words "to monopolize" and "monopolize," as used in the section, reach every act bringing about the prohibited results. The ambiguity, if any, is involved in determining what is intended by monopolize. But the ambiguity is readily dispelled in the light of the previous history of the law of restraint of trade to which we have referred and the indication which it gives of the practical evolution by which monopoly and the acts which produce the same result as monopoly, that is, an undue restraint of the course of trade all came to be spoken of as, and to be indeed synonymous with, restraint of trade. In other words, having by the 1st section forbidden all means of monopolizing trade, that is, unduly restraining it by means of every contract, combination, etc., the 2d section seeks, if possible to make the prohibitions of the act all the more complete and perfect by embracing all attempts to reach the end prohibited by the 1st section, that is, restraints of trade by any attempt to monopolize, or monopolization thereof, even although the acts by which such results are attempted to be brought about are not embraced within the general enumeration of the 1st section. And, of course, when the 2d section is thus harmonized with and made, as it was intended to be, the complement of the 1st section, it becomes obvious that the [criterion] to be resorted to in any given case for the purpose of ascertaining whether violations of the section have been committed is the rule of reason guided by the established law and by the plain duty to enforce the prohibitions of the act, and thus the public policy which its restrictions were obviously enacted to subserve . . . [B]y the ommission of any direct prohibition against monopoly in the concrete, it indicates a consciousness that the freedom of the individual right to contract, when not unduly or improperly exercised, was the most efficient means for the prevention of monopoly, since the operation of the centrifugal and centripetal forces resulting from the right to freely contract was the means by which monopoly would be inevitably prevented. . . .

Because the unification of power and control over petroleum and its products which was the inevitable result of the combining in the New Jersey corporation by the increase of its stock and the transfer to it of the stocks of so many other corporations, aggregating so vast a capital, gives rise, in and of itself, in the absence of countervailing circumstances, to say the least, to the *prima facie* presumption of intent and purpose to maintain the dominancy over the oil industry, not as a result of normal methods of industrial development, but by new means of combination which were resorted to in order that greater power might be added than would otherwise have arisen had normal methods been followed, the whole with the purpose of excluding others from the trade, and thus centralizing in the combination a perpetual control of the movements of petroleum and its products in the channels of interstate commerce . . .

Because the *prime facie* presumption of intent to restrain trade, to monopolize and to bring about monopolization, resulting from the act of expanding the stock of the New Jersey corporation and vesting it with such vast control of the oil industry, is made conclusive by considering (1) the conduct of the persons or corporations who were mainly instrumental in bringing about the extension of power in the New Jersey corporation before the consummation of that result and prior to the formation of the trust agreements of 1879 and 1882; (2) by considering the proof as to what was done under those agreements of and the acts which immediately preceded the vesting of power in the New Jersey corporation, as well as by weighing the modes in which the power vested in that corporation has been exerted and the results which have arisen from it . . .

[W]e think no disinterested mind can survey the period in question without being irresistably driven to the conclusion that the genius for commercial development and organization which it would seem was manifested from the beginning soon begot an intent and pupose to exclude others which was frequently manifested by acts and dealings wholly inconsistent with the theory that they were made with the single conception of advancing the development of business power by usual methods, but which, on the contrary, necessarily involved the intent to drive others from their right to trade, and thus accomplish the mastery which was the end in view.

Chief Justice White emphasized Standard Oil's intent and positive drive as being necessary to any conviction under section 2. The significance of the *Standard Oil* decision from a legal standpoint cannot be overstated. It firmly established the precedent that market power, in and of itself, is not sufficient to condemn a firm under section 2. Power must be combined with some effort to obtain that power. Standard Oil violated section 2 because it went beyond the use of normal methods of industrial development, not simply because it controlled 90 percent of the market.

Justice Harlan viewed this interpretation as judicial legislation with the clear intent of changing Congress's purpose when it passed the Sherman Act in 1890. Although concurring with the majority's decision against Standard Oil, Justice Harlan wrote the following dissent:

[By this decision] we are, therefore, asked to hold that the act of Congress excepts contracts which are not in unreasonable restraint of trade, and which only keep rates up to a reasonable price, not withstanding the language of the act makes no such exception. In other words we are asked to read into the act *by way of judicial legislation an exception that is not placed there by the lawmaking branch of the government,* and this is to be done upon the theory that the impolicy of such legislation is so clear that it cannot be supposed Congress intended that natural import of the language it used. . . . This *we cannot and ought not do.*

But my brethren, in their wisdom, have deemed . . . "You may *now* restrain such commerce, provided you are reasonable about it; only take care that the restraint is not undue." The disposition of the case under consideration, according to the views of the defendants, will, it is claimed, quiet and give rest to "the business of the country." On the contrary, I have a strong conviction that it will throw the business of the country into confusion and invite widely-extended and harassing litigation, the injurious effects of which will be felt for many years to come. When Congress prohibited *every* contract, combination, or monopoly, in restraint of commerce, it prescibed a simple definite rule that all could understand, and which could be easily applied by everyone wishing to obey the law, and not to conduct their business in violation of the law. But now, it is to be feared, we are to have, in cases without number, the constantly recurring inquiry — difficult to solve by proof — whether the particular contract, combination, or trust involved in each case is or is not an "unreasonable" or "undue" constraint of trade.

Justice Harlan's premonition has proved to be largely correct. The Rule of Reason has resulted in cases that require proof of both the existence of market power and some effort to obtain that power through other than normal methods of business behavior. As a result, section 2 cases have become longer and longer over the years, and the issues have become more and more complex. If Justice White had required a mere showing of the acquisition and maintenance of market power over a long period of time, instead of some unreasonable effort to acquire power, court cases might be considerably shorter today. If cases were shorter, however, it does not follow that the *economic* outcomes would be better.

As a result of the *Standard Oil* decision, the company was broken up into thirty-four companies by distributing to Standard Oil's stockholders stock in each of the thirty-four firms. As time went by, some of the new companies prospered, and others failed. Within two decades, however, competition developed between Standard Oil of New Jersey (Exxon) and some of the major remnants of the old trust, such as Standard Oil of California (Chevron) and Standard Oil of Indiana (Amaco). By the early 1930s the market had deteriorated into one characterized by its members as being too competitive. When the Great Depression sent oil prices plummeting, the industry no longer had Standard Oil available to stabilize prices, so it turned to the federal government for help. Ironically, beginning in the 1930s, the government began to play the role of the stabilizing force in the oil industry by adopting policies that increased oil prices and, to some extent, reduced some of the positive economic effects of the 1911 breakup of Standard Oil [2]. There is little doubt, however, that the 1911 decree increased the rate at which competition developed in the oil industry.

***United States v. American Tobacco Co.* 221 U.S. 106 (1911)** Immediately following the *Standard Oil* decision, the Supreme Court handed down another important section 2 decision in the *American Tobacco* case. The points of law laid down in the *American Tobacco* case by Justice White were virtually identical to those handed down in the *Standard Oil* case.

From an economic standpoint the *American Tobacco* case is interesting primarily as an example of a very aggressive attempt to monopolize. Prior to 1890, five companies dominated the cigarette segment of the tobacco industry: W. Duke, Allen and Ginter, Kinney Tobacco, W. S. Kimball, and Goodwin. These five firms accounted for 95 percent of domestic cigarette production. In January 1890 the five merged to form the American Tobacco Company. James Duke was the dominant individual behind the consolidation. As one of the corporation's first actions, it *closed down* one of its own members, Goodwin! This move was just the beginning of a series of aggressive acquisitions followed by aggressive dismantlings.

American Tobacco's typical behavior is suggested by its attempt to gain control of the plug market. In 1893 American Tobacco approached several plug manufacturers suggesting possible mergers. When the plug producers refused, American Tobacco embarked on a five-year drive to force them out of the market by selling plug tobacco at prices *below* average total cost. Between 1893 and 1898 American Tobacco lost over $4 million in the plug market, but succeeded in gaining control over the major plug producers. Its aggressive behavior did not stop in 1898; in 1899 alone, it acquired and *shut down* thirty competitors.

American Tobacco used a large variety of aggressive techniques, including predatory pricing, massive advertising campaigns, and the creation of *fighting brands,* which were sold below cost (one fighting brand had the appropriate name of "Battle Axe"). As a result, American Tobacco was able to capture over 90 percent of the market by 1900 and earn a profit of 56 percent on sales in 1899.

Given this evidence it is not surprising that the Supreme Court stated

Indeed the history of the combination is so replete with the doing of acts which it was the obvious purpose of the statute to forbid, so demonstrative of the existence from the beginning of a purpose to acquire dominion and control of the tobacco trade, not by the mere exertion of the ordinary right to contract and to trade, but by methods devised in order to monopolize the trade by driving competitors out of business, which were ruthlessly carried out upon the assumption that to work upon the fears or play upon the cupidity of competitors would make success possible . . .

Justice Harlan once again stated a strong dissent against the Rule of Reason, but the *American Tobacco* case served to reinforce the rule and the importance of behavior as well as structure in section 2 cases.

The American Tobacco Company was broken up into sixteen firms in a manner similar to the Standard Oil dissolution. The major remnant firms were a new American Tobacco Company, Liggett and Myers, P. Lorillard, and R. J. Reynolds. It took approximately a decade before competition developed between the major new companies, and then only a few more years for the new oligopolists to learn about the advantages of cooperation over competition. In the 1930s the government filed another major case against the tobacco oligopoly that resulted in another major legal precedent [3].

Cases Between the 1911 American Tobacco Case and 1920

After the Standard Oil and American Tobacco decisions, the government scored a number of victories at the lower court level that deserve brief mention. In June 1911 the Circuit Court of Delaware ruled that Du Pont had monopolized the explosives industry [*United States v. E. I. du Pont de Nemours & Co.* 188 Fed. 127 (1911)]. The facts in the *Du Pont* case were somewhat similar to those in the *Standard Oil* and *American Tobacco* cases, but Du Pont's behavior was not so blatantly aggressive as either Standard Oil's or American Tobacco's behavior. Du Pont had acquired sixty-four companies between 1902 and 1907 and gained control of between 64 and 100 percent of the various explosives markets. The economic impact of the case on the gunpowder market was minor, but the case was instrumental in Du Pont's decision to become a highly diversified chemical company.

In 1914 International Harvester was found to have monopolized the market for harvesting machinery [*United States v. International Harvester Co.* 214 Fed. 987 (1914)]. Despite the fact that International Harvester had behaved fairly and in a nonaggressive manner toward its competitors, in a 2-1 ruling the District Court of Minnesota declared that the consolidation of the five major manufacturers of harvesting equipment violated the Sherman Act. In a strong dissent, Judge Sanborn argued that International Harvester had not violated section 2 according to the Rule of Reason, because "in general their treatment of their smaller competitors has been fair and just." Judge Sanborn's position was soon to gain support from the Supreme Court.

In 1915 Eastman Kodak was found to have violated the Sherman Act by acquiring twenty competitors over a fifteen-year period [*United States v. Eastman Kodak Co.* 226 Fed. 62 (1915)]. Once again the facts closely paralleled the *Standard Oil* and *American Tobacco* cases.

Perhaps the most significant sign of things to come occurred in 1916 when the District Court of Maryland refused to accept the government's charge of monopolization against the American Can Company [*United States v. American Can Co.* 230 Fed. 859 (1916)]. American Can was organized in 1901 through the merger of ninety-five plants that manufactured 90 percent of the cans in the United States. Its market share declined between 1901 and 1916, however, and Judge Rose decided that dissolution would serve no positive purpose. Judge Rose did not completely dismiss the case, but instead warned American Can against any future aggressive actions.

Finally, it should be noted that in the *Corn Products* case, Judge Hand ruled that the Corn Products Refining Company had monopolized the glucose industry [*United States v. Corn Products Refining Co.* 234 Fed. 964 (1916)]. Judge Hand refused to accept the defense argument that only through monopoly could the industry avoid ruinous competition.

These lower court decisions, in particular the *American Can* decision and Judge Sanborn's dissent in the *International Harvester* case, set the stage for the next major Supreme Court ruling, one that greatly affected subsequent antitrust policy, the 1920 *United States Steel* decision.

United States v. United States Steel Corporation 251 U.S. 417 (1920) Prior to the formation of the United States Steel Corporation, the steel industry had been characterized by periods of aggressive competition in the 1890s. In fact, as the corporation began to take shape in 1900, steel prices were declining. U.S. Steel was formed in 1901 through the consolidation of twelve major steel companies. At the time, U.S. Steel accounted for over 65 percent of the industry's output. Despite the fact that U.S. Steel almost certainly had the power to force compliance with its pricing policies or eliminate its competitors, it chose a different path. Instead of aggressively attempting to eliminate its competitors, it chose to cooperate with them.

U.S. Steel cooperated with its competitors through a variety of methods, including pools, associations, trade meetings, and most famously (or infamously) through the "Gary Dinners," at which Judge Elbert Gary, President of U.S. Steel, invited competitors to dinner for the more or less express purpose of stabilizing and fixing prices. Because it decided to set prices at a level that attracted entry and because it refrained from predatory practices, U.S. Steel's market share declined almost continuously after its formation, and by the time the case was filed its market share had declined to approximately 50 percent. In hindsight, there is little doubt that U.S. Steel violated section 1 of the Sherman Act by fixing prices with its competitors, but the 1911 case dealt only with section 2 and charged that U.S. Steel had attempted to monopolize the steel industry.

By a 4–3 ruling, the Supreme Court acquitted U.S. Steel and, in so doing, considerably weakened section 2 for years to come. The four-justice majority believed that U.S. Steel could not control steel prices. In the majority's opinion, U.S. Steel had *no* monopoly power and could not have violated the Sherman Act. In what may seem like a strange twist of logic, the majority reasoned that since U.S. Steel had to conspire with its competitors to fix prices, it did not have monopoly power! This line of reasoning totally ignored the fact that *if* it had chosen to discipline its competitors, it almost certainly could have maintained and even increased its market share.

The majority reasoned as follows:

> The organizers [of U.S. Steel] . . . underestimated the opposing conditions and at the very beginning the Corporation instead of relying upon its own power sought and obtained the assistance and the cooperation of its competitors (the independent companies). In other words the view was expressed that the testimony did "not show that the corporation in and of itself ever possessed or exerted sufficient power when acting alone to control prices of the products of the industry." Its power was efficient only when in cooperation with its competitors, and hence it concerted with them in the expedients of pools, associations, trade meetings, and finally in a system of dinners inaugurated in 1907 by the president of the company, E. H. Gary, and called "the Gary Dinners." . . .
>
> The Corporation, it is said, did not at any time abuse the power or ascendency it possessed. It resorted to none of the brutalities or tyrannies that the cases illustrate of other combinations. Indeed it is said in many ways and illustrated that "instead of relying upon its own power to fix and maintain prices, the corporation, at its very beginning sought and obtained the assistance of others." It combined its power with that of its competitors. It did not have power in and of itself, and the control it exerted was only in and by association with its competitors. Its offense, therefore, such as it was, was not different from theirs and was distinguished from theirs "only in the leadership it assumed in promulgating and perfecting the policy." . . .
>
> Monopoly, therefore, was not achieved, and competitors had to be persuaded by pools, associations, trade meetings, and through the social form of dinners, all of them, it may be, violations of the law, but transient in their purpose and effect. . . .
>
> [U.S. Steel] is undoubtedly of impressive size and it takes an effort of resolution not to be affected by it or to exaggerate its influence. But we must adhere to the law and the law does not make mere size an offense or the

existence of unexerted power an offense. It, we repeat, requires overt acts and trusts its prohibition of them and its power to repress or punish them. It does not compel competion nor require all that is possible.

Justice Day spoke for the minority in his blistering dissent:

> This record shows that the power obtained by the corporation brought under its control large competing companies which were of themselves illegal combinations, and succeeded to their power; that some of the organizers of the Steel Corporation were parties to the preceding combinations, participated in their illegality, and by uniting them under a common direction intended to augment and perpetuate their power. It is the irresistible conclusion from these premises that great profits to be derived from unified control were the object of these organizations.
>
> The conclusion must be rejected that the combination was an inevitable evolution of industrial tendencies compelling union of endeavor. . . .
>
> I agree that the act offers no objection to the mere size of a corporation, nor to the continued exertion of its lawful power, when that size and power have been obtained by lawful means and developed by natural growth, although its resources, capital and strength may give to such corporation a dominating place in the business and industry with which it is concerned. . . . But I understand the reiterated decisions of this court construing the Sherman Act to hold that this power may not legally be derived from conspiracies, combinations, or contracts in restraint of trade. To permit this would be to practically annul the Sherman Law by judicial decree. . . .
>
> That [U.S. Steel] thus fortified and equipped could if it saw fit dominate the trade and control competition would seem to be a business proposition too plain to require extended argument to support it. . . . That the exercise of the power may be withheld, or exerted with forbearing benevolence, does not place such combinations beyond the authority of the statute which was intended to prohibit their formation, and when formed to deprive them of the power unlawfully attained.
>
> It is said that a complete monopolization of the steel business was never attained by the offending combinations. To insist upon such a result would be beyond the requirements of the statute and in most cases practicably impossible. . . .
>
> In my judgment the principles laid down [in the *American Tobacco* case] if followed now would make a very material difference in the steel industry. Instead of one dominating corporation, with scattered competitors, there would be competitive conditions throughout the whole trade which would carry into effect the policy of the law.

A shift of one vote would have reversed the outcome of the *U.S. Steel* decision and perhaps significantly changed the history of the Sherman Act, but the majority view became precedent: Dominant firms that refrained from predatory actions were more or less shielded from section 2 between 1920 and 1945. For a quarter of a century, "good trusts" were safe from antitrust attack. Furthermore, it became obvious that large mergers that achieved less than a 50 percent market share were virtually immune from section 2 attack. Only very aggressive firms with very large market shares had to worry about section 2 in the 1920s and throughout most of the 1930s. This policy changed abruptly in 1945 with the handing down of the *Alcoa* decision.

III   THE ALCOA ERA

***United States v. Aluminum Company of America* 148 F.2d 416 (1945)**   After the 1920 *U.S. Steel* decision, section 2 enforcement went into hibernation. In 1937, however, the Roosevelt administration charged the Aluminum Company of America (Alcoa) with monopolizing the aluminum ingot market. The district court, relying heavily on the *U.S. Steel* precedent, dismissed the case, and the Justice Department appealed. The Supreme Court could not obtain a quorum of six justices to the hear the case because four justices had previously been involved in the litigation of the case. As a result, the New York Court of Appeals served as the highest appeals court, and under the leadership of Judge Hand overturned the district court ruling. Judge Hand's Alcoa ruling established a precedent for section 2 cases that lasted for twenty-five years.

The correct market definition was the first major issue addressed by the courts. The district court had defined Alcoa's market share as 33 percent by including secondary ingots (ingots that are produced from scrap aluminum) in the same market definition as primary ingots. Furthermore, the district court had eliminated from the relevant market all ingots that Alcoa produced and then used in its own internal fabrication operations. The New York Court of Appeals, however, ruled that since Alcoa produced virtually all primary aluminum, it indirectly controlled the secondary scrap market. Judge Hand, therefore, eliminated scrap from the relevant market definition. The court of appeals also included ingots that Alcoa fabricated itself as part of its market share, because "all intermediate, or end, products which Alcoa fabricate[d] and [sold], *pro tanto* reduce[d] the demand for ingots [available to independent ingot suppliers]." After making these market definition changes, Alcoa's market share increased from 33 percent to 90 percent! Furthermore, since the remaining 10 percent was supplied by foreign producers, Alcoa supplied 100 percent of domestic primary ingot production.

The change in the relevant market definition was a major reason why Judge Hand overturned the district court. This is indicated by the following extract from his decision, which has become a de facto market share guideline in section 2 cases:

> The percentage we have already mentioned — over ninety — results only if we both include all "Alcoa's" production and exclude "secondary." That percentage is enough to constitute a monopoly: it is doubtful whether sixty or sixty-five percent would be enough: and certainly thirty-three percent is not.

Once Judge Hand established that Alcoa had a 90 percent market share, he next turned to the issue of Alcoa's intent. In keeping with judicial procedure, Judge Hand went to great lengths to make his ruling consistent with Chief Justice White's *Standard Oil* decision and the Rule of Reason. There was, however, little evidence in the case of aggressive practices such as existed in the *Standard Oil* or *American Tobacco* cases. In fact, Alcoa's market power originated from a cost advantage associated with patents rather than predatory behavior. Its continued market domination resulted from (1) high barriers to entry (especially economies of scale in the conversion of bauxite ore into aluminum oxide or alumina) and vertical integration into all four stages of production (bauxite ore, alumina, aluminum ingots, and fabrication) and (2) a moderate pricing policy, which kept profits at moderate levels and made entry relatively unattractive.

Judge Hand's decision greatly reduced the government's burden to show intent in section 2 cases, as indicated by the following major sections of his decision:

> Having proved that "Alcoa" had a monopoly of the domestic ingot market, the [government] had gone far enough; if it was an excuse, that "Alcoa' had not abused its power, it lay upon "Alcoa" to prove that it had not. But the whole issue is irrelevant anyway, for it is no excuse for "monopolizing" a market that the monopoly has not been used to extract from the consumer more than a "fair" profit. The Act has wider purposes. . . . Many people believe that possession of unchallenged economic power deadens initiative, discourages thrift and depresses energy; that immunity from competition is a narcotic, and rivalry is a stimulant, to industrial progress; that the spur of constant stress is necessary to counteract an inevitable disposition to let well enough alone. . . . Congress . . . did not condone "good trusts" and condemn "bad" ones; it forbade all. Moreover, in so doing it was not necessarily actuated by economic motives alone. It is possible, because of its indirect social or moral effect, to prefer a system of small producers, each dependent for his success upon his own skill and character, to one in which the great mass of those engaged must accept the direction of a few. . . .
> [When Alcoa] began to sell at all — it must sell at some price and the

only price at which it could sell is a price which it itself fixed. Thereafter the power and its exercise must needs coalesce. Indeed it would be absurd to condemn [price-fixing] contracts unconditionally, and not to extend the condemnation to monopolies; for the contracts are only steps toward that entire control which monopoly confers: they are really partial monopolies.

Judge Hand then provided one possible defense for a firm with a 90 percent market share:

It does not follow that because "Alcoa" had such a monopoly, that it "monopolized" the ingot market: it may not have achieved monopoly; monopoly may have been thrust upon it. . . . A market may for example, be so limited that it is impossible to produce at all and meet the cost of production except by a plant large enough to supply the whole demand. Or there may be changes in taste or in cost which drive out all but one purveyor. A single producer may be the survivor out of a group of active competitors, merely by virtue of his superior skill, foresight and industry. . . . The successful competitor having been urged to compete, must not be turned upon when he wins. . . .

[However,] not a pound of ingot ha[s] been produced by anyone else in the United States. . . . [T]his continued control did not fall undesigned into "Alcoa's" lap; obviously it could not have done so. It could only have resulted from a persistent determination to maintain the control, with which it found itself vested in 1912. . . . It was not inevitable that it should always anticipate increases in the demand for ingot and be prepared to supply them. Nothing compelled it to keep doubling and redoubling its capacity before others entered the field. It insists that it never excluded competitors; but we can think of no more effective exclusion than progressively to embrace each new opportunity as it opened, and to face every newcomer with new capacity already geared into a great organization; having the advantage of experience, trade connections and the elite of personnel. Only in case we interpret "exclusion" as limited to manoeuvres not honestly industrial, but actuated solely by a desire to prevent competition, can such a course, indefatigably pursued, be deemed not "exclusionary." So to limit it would in our judgment emasculate the Act; would permit just such con-solidations as it was designed to prevent. . . .

. . . To read the passage as demanding any "specific" intent, makes nonsense of it for no monopolist monopolizes unconscious of what he is doing. So here, "Alcoa" meant to keep, and did keep, that complete and exclusive hold upon the ingot market with which it started.

The government contended that Alcoa had followed a series of practices that were exclusionary, including the preemption of bauxite deposits and water power from competitors, the elimination of several potential competitors, and a price-squeeze policy against fabricators of sheet and cable aluminum, which raised the price of aluminum ingot and simultaneously reduced the price of fabricated aluminum sheet and cable. Judge Hand concluded, however, that except for a brief episode of price-squeezing in 1932, the evidence was insufficient to condemn Alcoa for any exclusionary practices. Judge Hand believed that Alcoa was basically a "good trust," in the U.S. Steel tradition; however, he still ruled that Alcoa had violated section 2. The *Alcoa* decision seemed to reverse the *U.S. Steel* precedent and set a new precedent: A monopolist with an overwhelming market share violated section 2 *unless* market power had been thrust upon it and was virtually unavoidable. The *Alcoa* decision represented a change from the previous behavioral approach toward section 2 toward a more structural approach. According to Judge Hand, a monopolist might violate the antitrust laws even if it had behaved nonaggressively toward its competitors.

There was no divestiture in the *Alcoa* case, but the government sold its war plants at low prices to Reynolds and Kaiser (two existing fabricators). As a result, Alcoa's market share declined to 50 percent, and the industry was transformed from a monopoly into an oligopoly. Additional entry in the 1950s further reduced Alcoa's market share [4].

United States v. Griffith Amusement Co. 334 U.S. 100 (1948)   In 1948, in the *Griffith* case, the Supreme Court appeared to take the structural position one step farther than in the *Alcoa* case. Griffith owned movie theaters in eighty-five towns, fifty-three of which had no competing theater. The government objected to Griffith's practice of negotiating one package for all of its theaters because this practice prevented "their competitors from obtaining enough first- or second-run films from distributors to operate successfully." The district court dismissed the government's complaint because of a lack of intent on Griffith's part.

The Supreme Court overturned the district court, with Justice Douglas delivering the opinion, which reads in part:

> It is, however, not always necessary to find a specific intent to restrain trade or to build a monopoly in order to find that the anti-trust laws has been violated. It is sufficient that a restraint of trade or monopoly results as the consequence of a defendant's conduct or business arrangements. To require a greater showing would cripple the Act. As stated in *United States v. Aluminum Co. of American, "no monopolist monopolizes unconscious of what he is doing."* Specific intent in the sense in which the common law used the term is necessary only where the acts fall short of the results condemned by the Act.

The *Griffith* decision seemed to imply that a monopoly was illegal regardless of intent. This decision was probably the high-water mark for a structural approach toward section 2.

United States v. United Shoe Machinery Corporation **110 F. Supp. 295 (1953), Affirmed 347 U.S. 521 (1954)**   Two years after the *Alcoa* decision, the government charged the United Shoe Machinery Corporation with monopolizing the shoe machinery industry. In 1917 United Shoe had been acquitted of the same charge by the Supreme Court. Using the Rule of Reason precedent, the 1917 Court ruled that United Shoe's 90 percent market share was "the result and cause of efficiency that was beneficial to the shoe manufacturers" [5].

United Shoe was a classic "good trust." Profits were normal; prices were uniform; its machines were reliable and efficient; service was provided free; and the cost of machinery was kept down to only 2 percent of the average wholesale price of shoes.

Despite United Shoe's good behavior, the Justice Department charged that its power resulted from an illegal long-term leasing policy. United Shoe refused to sell its machines; instead, it leased all of its machines for a minimum period of ten years. Lessees could return a machine prior to the expiration of a lease, but only if they paid a significant financial penalty. The ten-year leases created several problems for potential entrants. The leases eliminated competition from a second-hand market (such as exists in automobiles or business machines), increased the capital requirements for entry, and greatly limited the market available to potential entrants each year (to approximately one-tenth of the total shoe machinery market).

The Supreme Court affirmed the decision of the district court in favor of the Justice Department. In so doing it once again endorsed the *Alcoa* and *Griffith* decisions. The major points in District Court Judge Wyzanski's decision were as follows:

> [T]aken as a whole, the evidence [in this case] satisfies the tests laid down in both *Griffith* and *Aluminum*. The facts show that (1) defendant has, and exercises, such overwhelming strength in the shoe machinery market that it controls that market, (2) this strength excludes some potential, and limits some actual, competition, and (3) this strength is not attributable solely to defendant's ability, economies of scale, research, natural advantages, and adaptation to inevitable economic laws.
>
> In one sense, the leasing system and the miscellaneous activities just referred to . . . were natural and normal, for they were, in Judge Hand's words, "honestly industrial." . . . Yet, they were not practices which can be properly described as the inevitable consequences of ability, natural forces, or law. . . . They are contracts, arrangements, and policies which, instead of encouraging competition based on pure merit, further the dominance of a particular firm. In this sense, they are unnatural barriers; they unnecessarily exclude actual and potential competition; they restrict a free market. While the law allows many enterprises to use such practices, the Sherman Act is now construed by superior courts to forbid the continuance

of effective market control based in part upon such practices. Those courts hold that market control is inherently evil and constitutes a violation of Section 2 unless economically inevitable, or specifically authorized and regulated by law. . . .

. . . United's power does not rest on predatory practices. Probably few monopolies could produce a record so free from any taint of that kind of wrong-doing. The violation with which United is now charged depends not on moral considerations, but on solely economic considerations. United is denied the right to exercise effective control of the market by business policies that are not the inevitable consequences of its capacities or its natural advantages. That those policies are not immoral is irrelevant. . . .

Defendant intended to engage in the leasing practices and pricing policies which maintained its market power. That is all the intent which the law requires when both the complaint and the judgment rest on a charge of "monopolizing," not merely "attempting to monopolize." Defendant having willed the means, has willed the end.

The court at first refused to order major divestiture; however, the maximum lease term was shortened to five years, and the penalties for returning a machine after one year were almost eliminated. Furthermore, all machines had to be offered for sale; United Shoe had to license all of its patents on demand; it had to charge for all services; and the court required a review of the efficiency of the decree within ten years. Finally, some minor divestiture was ordered in certain auxiliary areas such as nails and tacks.

Given these changes in United Shoe's business practices and the court's requirement to review the decree within ten years, it is not surprising that United Shoe's market share declined significantly during the next decade. The entry of fifty-six new competitors helped reduce its share to approximately 60 percent [6]. Despite this decline in its market share, in 1968 the Supreme Court declared that workable competition had not been achieved, and it ordered United Shoe to divest itself of sufficient assets to reduce its market share to 33 percent [7].

United States v. E. I. du Pont de Nemours & Co. **351 U.S. 377 (1956)**   After the *Alcoa, Griffith,* and *United Shoe* decisions, the government appeared to have the advantage in section 2 cases. In 1956, however, the Supreme Court acquitted Du Pont of a charge that it had monopolized the cellophane industry. The major issue revolved around the definition of the relevant market. Du Pont admitted to controlling 75 percent of the cellophane market and receiving royalties on the remaining 25 percent. Du Pont contended, however, that cellophane competed so closely with all other flexible wrapping materials that all such materials should be included in the correct market definition. According to Du Pont's market definition, cellophane was in the same market as waxed paper, glassine, parchment paper, sulfite paper, aluminum foil, and cellulose acetate, and its market share was less than 20 percent.

The district court ruled in favor of Du Pont. The Supreme Court, by a 4–3 vote, affirmed the decision. The majority reasoned as follows:

> If cellophane is the "market" that du Pont is found to dominate, it may be assumed it does have monopoly power over that "market." Monopoly power is the power to control prices or exclude competition. It seems apparent that du Pont's power to set the price of cellophane has been limited only by the competition afforded by other flexible wrapping materials. Moreover, it may be practically impossible for anyone to commence manufacturing cellophane without full access to du Pont's technique. However, du Pont has no power to prevent competition from other wrapping materials. . . .
>
> The Government makes no challenge to Finding 283 that cellophane furnishes less than 7% of wrappings for bakery products, 25% for candy, 32% for snacks, 35% for meats and poultry, 27% for crackers and bisquits, 47% for fresh produce, and 34% for frozen foods. Seventy-five to eighty percent of cigarettes are wrapped in cellophane. Thus, cellophane shares the packaging market with others. The over-all result is that cellophane accounts for 17.9% of flexible wrapping materials, measured by the wrapping surface. . . .
>
> A glance at "Modern Packaging," a trade journal, will give, by its various advertisements, examples of the competition among manufacturers for the flexible packaging market. The trial judge visited the 1952 Annual Packaging Show at Atlantic City, with the consent of counsel. He observed exhibits offered by "machinery manufacturers, converters and manufacturers of flexible packaging materials." He states that these personal observations confirmed his estimate of the competition between cellophane and other packaging materials. . . .
>
> On the findings of the District Court, its judgment is *affirmed*.

Chief Justice Warren wrote the disenting opinion, which offers a good comparison of the two possible economic interpretations in this case. Chief Justice Warren stated

> We cannot agree that cellophane is "the selfsame product" as glassine, greaseproof and vegetable parchment papers, waxed paper, sulphite papers, aluminum foil, cellulose acetate, and Pliofilm and other films. . . .
>
> We cannot believe that buyers, practical businessmen, would have bought cellophane in increasing amounts over a quarter of a century if close substitutes were available at from one-seventh to one-half cellophane's price. That they did so is testimony to cellophane's distinctiveness. . . .

. . . Producers of glassine and waxed paper . . . displayed apparent indifference to du Pont's repeated and substantial price cuts. [Defense Exhibit] 994 shows that from 1924 to 1932 du Pont dropped the price of plain cellophane 84%, while the price of glassine remained constant. And during the period 1933–1946 the prices for glassine and waxed paper actually increased in the face of a further 21% decline in the price of cellophane. If "shifts of business" due to "price sensitivity" had been substantial, glassine and waxed paper producers who wanted to stay in business would have been compelled by market forces to meet du Pont's price challenge. . . .

From the first, du Pont recognized that it need not concern itself with competition from other packaging materials. For example, when du Pont was contemplating entry into cellophane production, its Development Department reported that glassine "is so inferior that it belongs in an entirely different class and has hardly to be considered as a competitor of cellophane." . . .

[T]he Court's opinion approves but does not follow, the formula of "reasonable interchangeability," as applied by the majority, appears indistinguishable from the theory of "interindustry competition." The danger in it is that, as demonstrated in this case, it is "perfectly compatible with a fully monopolized economy."

. . . The foregoing analysis of the record shows conclusively that cellophane is the relevant market. Since du Pont has the lion's share of that market, it must have monopoly power, as the majority concede. This being so, we think it clear that, in the circumstances of this case, du Pont is guilty of "monopolization."

Despite the Justice Department's defeat, the *Du Pont* case resulted in significant structural change in the cellophane industry. During the litigation period of the suit, Du Pont "invited" competitors into the cellophane industry. In the words of Chief Justice Warren, this was done "to reduce the hazard of being judged to have a monopoly of the U.S. cellophane business."

On November 4, 1949, Du Pont signed an agreement to help establish Olin Industries as a new competitor in cellophane. For a fee, Du Pont agreed to select a location for Olin's plant, design the plant, construct the plant, purchase materials and hire workers, and license all of its cellophane patents to Olin. In short, Du Pont built a new facility to be operated by a competitor [8]!

The *Du Pont* decision was an exception to a basically strict interpretation of section 2 that followed the *Alcoa* decision. In the *Du Pont* case, the Justice Department made little mention of Du Pont's behavior and relied entirely on its dominant market share. This probably was a significant tactical error because Du Pont's behavior, especially its restrictive patent behavior, could have been challenged in the 1947 suit.

***United States v. Grinnell Corporation* 384 U.S. 563 (1966)**   The last major Supreme Court decision during the Alcoa Era provides a sharp and fascinating contrast to the *Du Pont* decision. In the *Du Pont* case, the Supreme Court selected a broad market definition, which resulted in Du Pont's acquittal. In the *Grinnell* case, the Supreme Court selected the narrowest possible market definition and ruled in favor of the government.

The Justice Department's suit, filed in 1961, charged that Grinnell had monopolized the national market for accredited central station protection services. The suit centered around Grinnell's acquisition through merger of three companies: the American District Telegraph Company (ADT), the Automatic Fire Alarm Company (AFA), and the Holmes Electric Protection Company. The three firms controlled approximately 90 percent of the national accredited central station protection market.

Once again, the case revolved around the definition of the market; however, unlike the *Du Pont* case, the Justice Department also relied on evidence of Grinnell's aggressive marketing behavior. Using a narrow market definition, Grinnell had a dominant market share under the Alcoa doctrine; however, accredited central station protection services competed with other protection services, such as watchmen, audible alarms, proprietary security systems, watchdogs, and protection services connected directly to police and fire departments. If a broad definition such as all protection services and devices was adopted, Grinnell had a small market share.

In a 6–3 ruling, the Supreme Court adopted the narrowest possible market definition, accredited central station protection services, and found in favor of the government. The majority reasoned as follows (note the emphasis on behavior as well as structure):

> Grinnell manufactures plumbing supplies and fire sprinkler systems. It also owns 76% of the stock of ADT, 89% of the stock of AFA, and 100% of the stock of Holmes. . . .
>
> ADT over the years reduced its minimum basic rates to meet competition and renewed contracts at substantially increased rates in cities where it had a monopoly of accredited central station service. ADT threatened retaliation against firms that contemplated opening a new central station, ADT officials frequently stressed that such action would deter their competitors from opening a new station in that area. . . .
>
> . . . In the present case, 87% of the accredited central station service business leaves no doubt that . . . these defendants have monopoly power — power which, as our discussion of the record indicates, they did not hesitate to wield — if that business is the relevant market. The only remaining question therefore is, what is the relevant market?
>
> [Defendants] urge that *du Pont* requires that protective services other than those of the central station variety be included in the market definition.

But there is here a single use, i.e., the protection through a central station that receives signals. It is that service, accredited, that is unique and that competes with all the other forms of property protection. . . .

There are, to be sure, substitutes for the accredited central station service so as to meet the interchangeability test of the du Pont case. Nonautomatic and automatic local alarm systems appear on the record to have marked differences, not the low degree of differentiation required of substitute services as well as substitute articles.

Watchmen service is far more costly and less reliable. Systems that set off an audible alarm at the site of a fire or burglary are cheaper but often less reliable. . . . These alternate services and devices differ, we are told, in utility, efficiency, reliability, responsiveness, and continuity, and the record sustains that position. . . .

Defendants earnestly urge that despite these differences, they face competition from these other modes of protection. . . . What defendants overlook is that the high degree of differentiation between central station protection and the other forms means that for many customers, only central station protection will do. . . .

We also agree with the District Court that the geographic market for the accredited central station service is national. The activities of an individual station are in a sense local as it serves, ordinarily, only that area which is within a radius of 25 miles. But the record amply supports the conclusion that the business of providing such a service is operated on a national level. . . . The appellant ADT has a national schedule of prices, rates, and terms, though the rates may be varied to meet local conditions. . . .

We have said enough about the great hold that the defendants have on this market. The percentage is so high as to justify the finding of monopoly. And, as the facts already related indicate, this monopoly was achieved in large part by unlawful and exclusionary practices.

In their dissents Justices Fortas, Stewart, and Harlan suggested that the majority's market definition made little economic sense. Justice Fortas wrote

In this case, the relevant geographical and product markets have not been defined on the basis of the economic facts of the industry concerned. They have been tailored precisely to fit defendants' business. . . .

The geographical market is defined as nationwide. But the need and the service are intensely local. . . . [T]he central stations can provide service only within a 25-mile radius. Where the tenants of the premises turn to central stations for this service, they must make their contracts locally with the central station and purchase their services from it on the basis of local conditions.

. . .The court relies solely upon its finding that the services offered by accredited central stations are of better quality, and upon its conclusion that the insurance companies tend to give "noticeably larger" discounts to policyholders who use accredited central station protection services. This Court now approves this strange red-haired, bearded, one-eyed man-with-a-limp classification. . . .

Moreover, we are told that the "relevant market" must assume this strange and curious configuration despite evidence in the record and a finding of the trial court that "fringe competition" from such locally available alternatives as watchmen, local alarm systems, proprietary systems, and unaccredited central stations has, in at least 20 cities, forced the defendants to operate at a "loss" even though defendants have a total monopoly in these cities of the "market" — namely, the "accredited central station protection services." . . .

I believe this approach has no justification in economics, reason or law. . . .

I do not intend by any of the foregoing to suggest that, on this record, the relief granted by the trial court and the substantially more drastic relief ordered by this Court would necessarily be unjustified. It is entirely possible that monopoly or attempt to monopolize may be found and perhaps found with greater force — in local situations. Relief on a pervasive, system-wide, national basis might follow, as decreed by the trial court, as well as divestiture in appropriate local situations, as directed by this Court. It is impossible, I submit, to make judgments on the findings before us because of the distortion due to an incorrect and unreal definition of the "relevant market." . . . Since I am of the opinion that defendants and the courts are entitled to a reappraisal of the liability consequences as well as the appropriate provisions of the decree on the basis of a sound definition of the market, I would reverse and remand for these purposes.

It is difficult to explain how cellophane could be considered the selfsame product as waxed paper, while unaccredited central station protection could be considered an entirely different service from accredited central station protection. Taken together, the *Du Pont* and *Grinnell* cases suggest that courts can interpret similar economic facts and arrive at very different legal conclusions, but the two cases differed in one major respect. Unlike the *Du Pont* case, in the *Grinnell* case, the Justice Department relied on evidence of aggressive behavior as well as a large market share. The *Grinnell* decision, therefore, was completely consistent with Chief Justice White's Rule of Reason, which required aggressive behavior as well as monopoly power to find a firm guilty of violating section 2.

Grinnell was required to divest itself of ADT, AFA, and Holmes. Further divestiture by ADT, the largest company, was also required. After divestiture, there was a large increase in the rate of entry into the central station protection industry. Some of this undoubtedly occurred because demand was increasing rapidly; however, some entry almost certainly occurred as a result of the divestiture of the three firms by Grinnell [9].

IV   RECENT TRENDS IN SECTION 2 CASES: A RETURN TO THE RULE OF REASON

The Alcoa Era came to an end sometime in the mid-1970s. The Justice Department filed major suits against International Business Machines (IBM) in 1969 and against American Telephone and Telegraph (AT&T) in 1974; however, a series of decisions by courts of appeals favoring aggressive actions by dominant firms seems to have put an end, at least for the time being, to the structural approach of the *Alcoa, Griffith,* and *United Shoe* decisions. Two of these private cases are worth reviewing in some detail because they suggest a new direction, for better or worse, in antitrust law interpretation.

***Telex Corporation v. IBM Corporation* 510 F.2d 894 (1975)**   For almost thirty years IBM has been the dominant force in the general-purpose computer industry. Since a great deal of computer equipment is leased and not sold, it is possible to argue over how to measure market shares in the general-purpose computer industry correctly. One reasonable method is to base a firm's market share on the percentage of the rental value of the *installed base* of all computer equipment. On this basis, IBM controlled somewhere around 70 percent of the market during the period 1964–1972.

The computer industry is a complicated industry. A system consists of a central processing unit (CPU), which acts like a brain, and a great deal of peripheral equipment, which plugs into the CPU. Most computer users never see the large CPU, but almost everyone who has worked on a computer has seen a good deal of peripheral equipment, which includes such items as terminals, line printers, card readers, input and output tapes, disk drives, and tape drives. IBM and a few other firms, such a Burroughs and Honeywell, produce full systems, and many other smaller firms, such as Telex, produce only peripheral equipment.

The market for plug-compatible peripheral equipment had grown very rapidly in the late 1960s. In 1966 there were only three manufacturers of plug-compatible peripheral equipment, whereas by 1972 there were approximately 100 manufacturers. Of these 100, Telex and eleven other firms were primarily manufacturers of IBM-plug-compatible equipment. In the late 1960s, Telex and these other peripheral manufacturers were offering IBM-plug-compatible equipment at prices well below IBM's prices for comparable products. As a result, IBM lost a significant share of the market for IBM peripheral equipment.

The erosion in IBM's share of the IBM peripheral equipment market continued well into 1970, at which time IBM decided to respond to these inroads through the following actions:

1. In September and December 1970 IBM selectively and dramatically cut the price of certain peripheral equipment that competed directly with Telex's equipment.

2. IBM redesigned certain equipment so that it could be connected to the CPU only through an integrated file adapter, rather than through the traditional external disk control unit. Telex argued that this change artificially made the use of Telex equipment less attractive to IBM CPU users.

3. In May 1971 IBM announced a fixed-term leasing plan, which provided for an 8 percent price reduction for users signing a one-year lease on peripheral equipment and a 16 percent price reduction for signers of a two-year lease.

4. At the same time that IBM announced large price reductions on peripheral equipment, it announced large price *increases* on its CPUs, allegedly to recoup lost revenues.

As a result of these actions, Telex was forced to cut its prices drastically. Despite IBM's price cuts, Telex was able to increase its volume of business between 1970 and 1972, but its profits declined significantly.

The district court defined the market narrowly as peripheral equipment plug compatible to IBM's CPUs and ruled in favor of Telex on most issues. Basing its decision primarily on the *Alcoa, United Shoe,* and *Grinnell* precedents, it awarded Telex $259.5 million in damages plus $12 million in attorney's fees.

The Tenth Circuit Court of Appeals overturned the district court decision. First, the court of appeals redefined the market to include *all* plug-compatible equipment. Second, the court argued that IBM's actions were merely normal methods of competition. The following excerpts indicate the court of appeals major lines of reasoning:

> It seems clear that reasonable interchangeability is proven in the case at bar and hence the market should include not only peripheral products plug compatible with IBM CPUs, but all peripheral products, those compatible with non-IBM systems. This is wholly justifiable because the record shows that these products, although not fungible, are fully interchangeable and may be interchanged with minimal financial outlay, and so cross-elasticity exists within the meaning of the *Du Pont* decision. . . .

2. The Acts of IBM

> . . . IBM announced a new marketing plan in May 1971. This was the leasing of peripheral units, not central processing units, for a fixed term of years rather than on its old lease which permitted the user to cancel on thirty days' notice. . . .

> > "In view of the fact that most of IBM's system manufacturer, leasing company and peripheral equipment manufacturer competitors were offering long term leases by the Spring of 1971 (Finding F100), IBM expected to and was likely to, continue to lose substantial systems and peripheral business unless some plan was adopted." . . .

. . . The terms of [IBM's] leases are shorter than leases which had been offered by IBM's competitors, including plaintiffs, for some time prior to IBM's adoption of the fixed term and extended term plan. In a different context, the court in *United States v. United Shoe Machinery Corp.* . . . expressly sanctioned the use of five year term leases despite its conclusion that defendant had monopolized the market for shoe machinery. . . .

. . . The record shows that the central units on which prices were raised were the result of considerable development costs, had improvements incorporated in them, and contained a larger number of parts newly designed. There is no indication that the increase was not reasonable and the trial court did not find it to be otherwise. . . .

. . . The "acts" found by the trial court to be illegal were ordinary marketing methods available to all in the market. As to pricing, the trial court found it was used by IBM only to a limited extent, that is, within the "reasonable" range. The resulting prices were reasonable in that they yielded a reasonable profit. . . . The cases relied upon by the trial court all refer to the "use of monopoly power," and this is all the law condemns. Again under our assumption IBM gained its market position by technical advances and quality products. The record shows, during the period under consideration, that the parties and others in the market produced more advanced products better suited to the needs of the customers at lower prices. . . .

[W]e do not accept the requirement that the only permitted exceptions, or that the "trust upon" shorthand description means that the events or acts must be entirely involuntary. To do so would permit the defendant corporation to do nothing whatever by way of change in marketing. There must be some room to move for a defendant who sees his market share acquired by research and technical innovations being eroded by those who market copies of its products. . . .

. . . The record demonstrates that these acts of IBM are again part of the competitive scene in this volatile business inhabited by aggressive, skillful businessmen seeking to market a product cheaper and better than that of their competitors.

Not only did the court of appeals overturn the district court ruling against IBM, but it affirmed an award from Telex *to IBM* of $18.5 million for Telex's illegal use of IBM technology! The court of appeals decision appeared to turn sharply away from a structural view of section 2. In fact, by including terms such as *reasonable profit* and *acts in the reasonable range,* this decision is more in line with the 1920 *U.S. Steel* decision than with the *Alcoa* or *United Shoe* decisions. There is little doubt that IBM's behavior was more aggressive than Alcoa's, yet the court of appeals chose to permit IBM's actions.

At first, Telex planned to appeal the circuit court decision to the Supreme Court, but because Telex could not afford to pay $18.5 million in the event that it lost the appeal, in October 1975 it agreed to drop all charges. In return, IBM dropped its $18.5 million claim against Telex.

The Telex case was a clear retreat away from the structuralist position, and this retreat continued in 1979 in another private case, *Berkey Photo v. Eastman Kodak*.

Berkey Photo Inc. v. Eastman Kodak Co. 603 F.2d 263 (1979) There was never any question in the *Berkey Photo* case that Kodak had a monopoly market share in certain sectors of the photographic equipment industry, especially film. Berkey contended that Kodak was able to use its power in certain sectors to extend its power in other sectors of the industry. The case was extremely complicated because it dealt with Kodak's behavior in five markets: (1) amateur still cameras, (2) photographic film, (3) photofinishing services, (4) photofinishing equipment, and (5) color-print paper.

The Camera Market In the camera market Kodak had been the dominant firm since 1895, and in 1964 Kodak still cameras accounted for 90 percent of industry revenues. Berkey had entered the camera market in 1966 by acquiring the Keystone Camera Company. Berkey's market share between 1970 and 1977 was 8.2 percent of sales. In 1978, however, it sold its camera division and left the industry. Berkey then sued Kodak for, among other things, monopolization of the camera market.

Berkey's charges centered on the following Kodak practices:

1. Since Kodak was a monopolist in the film market, independent camera manufacturers could not produce a new camera unless the camera could use Kodak film. According to Berkey, "Kodak persistently refused to make film available for most formats other than those in which it made cameras. Since cameras are worthless without film, this policy effectively prevented other manufacturers from introducing cameras in new formats."

2. Kodak's simultaneous introduction of a new camera (the 110 pocket camera) with a new, improved film (Kodacolor II), which was only available in the 110 format, enabled Kodak to gain a greater share of the camera market than if it had simply introduced the 110 camera with its existing Kodacolor X film. Since Kodak had a film monopoly, the only way to use the new, improved Kodacolor II film when it was introduced was to purchase a Kodak 110 camera. Berkey contended, therefore, that the introduction of a film–camera system was anticompetitive.

3. Kodacolor II was only available in the 110 format for eighteen months after its introduction. This further extended Kodak's monopoly in the camera market because "any consumer wishing to use Kodak's 'remarkable new film' had to buy a 110 camera."

Berkey argued that Kodak should have predisclosed its introduction of both the 110 camera and Kodacolor II film to *all* camera manufacturers and to *all* film processors. By predisclosing its new system, Berkey contended that Kodak would have enabled other camera manufacturers to produce 110 cameras capable of using Kodacolor II. Furthermore, predisclosure would have enabled film processors to adopt the new technology necessary to process Kodacolor II film.

At the district court level, a jury found Kodak guilty of monopolizing the still camera market because it introduced the 110 camera and Kodacolor II as a system without predisclosure to competitors. Judge Frankel awarded Berkey $45.75 million in treble damages. The Second Circuit Court of Appeals, however, completely reversed this portion of the district court decision. Judge Kaufman wrote the following:

> If a finding of monopoly power were all that were necessary to complete a violation of Section 2, our task in this case would be considerably lightened. Kodak's control of the film and color paper markets clearly reached the level of a monopoly. And, while the issue is a much closer one, it appears that the evidence was sufficient for the jury to find that Kodak possessed such power in the camera market as well. But our inquiry into Kodak's liability cannot end there. . . .
>
> [W]hile proclaiming vigorously that monopoly power is the evil at which Section 2 is aimed, courts have declined to take what would have appeared to be the next logical step — declaring monopolies unlawful *per se* unless specifically authorized by law. To understand the reason for this, one must comprehend the fundamental tension — one might almost say the paradox — that is near the heart of Section 2. This tension creates much of the confusion surrounding Section 2. It makes the cryptic *Alcoa* opinion a litigant's wishing well, into which, it sometimes seems, one may peer and find nearly anything he wishes.
>
> The conundrum was indicated in characteristically striking prose by Judge Hand, who was not able to resolve it. Having stated that Congress "did not condone 'good trusts' and condemn 'bad' ones; it forbad all," . . . he declared with equal force, "The successful competitor, having been urged to compete, must not be turned upon when he wins." Hand, therefore, told us that it would be inherently unfair to condemn success when the Sherman Act itself mandates competition. Such a wooden rule, it was feared might also deprive the leading firm in an industry of the incentive to exert its best efforts. Further success would yield not rewards but legal castigation. The antitrust laws would thus compel the very sloth they were intended to prevent. . . .
>
> We turn now to the events surrounding Kodak's introduction of the 110 photographic system in 1972. . . .
>
> Shortly after initial production runs [of Kodacolor II film] began in October of 1971, Kodak recognized that "several product deficiencies"

would exist in the film . . . at the time of introduction. Indeed, just eight days before the joint announcement of the new camera, film, and photofinishing process, a technical committee listed eleven "presently identified" problems that could affect "the customer's ultimate quality." . . .

Despite these difficiencies, Kodak proceeded with its plans for introduction of the 110 system, of which Kodacolor II had become an integral part. On March 16, 1972, amid great fanfare, the system was announced. . . .

As Kodak had hoped, the 110 system proved to be a dramatic success. In 1972 — the system's first year — the company sold 2,984,000 Pocket Instamatics, more than 50% of its sales in the amateur conventional still camera market. . . . Its share of 110 sales did not fall below 50% until 1976. Meanwhile, by 1973 the 110 had taken over most of the amateur market from the 126, and three years later it accounted for nearly four-fifths of all sales.

Berkey's Keystone division was a late entrant in the 110 sweepstakes, joining the competition only in late 1973. Moreover, because of hasty design, the original models suffered from latent defects, and sales that year were a paltry 42,000. With interest in the 126 dwindling, Keystone thus suffered a net decline of 118,000 unit sales in 1973. The following year, however, it recovered strongly, in large part because improvements in its pocket cameras helped it sell 406,000 units, 7% of all 110s sold that year. . . .

There is little doubt that the evidence supports the jury's finding that Kodak had monopoly power in cameras. . . .

Judge Frankel did not decide that Kodak should have disclosed the details of the 110 to other camera manufacturers prior to introduction. Instead, he left the matter to the jury, instructing them as follows.

> [I]f you find that Kodak had monopoly power in cameras or in film, and if you find that this power was so great as to make it impossible for a competitor to compete with Kodak in the camera market unless it could offer products similar to Kodak's, you may decide whether in the light of other conduct you determine to be anti-competitive, Kodak's failure to predisclose was on balance an exclusionary course of conduct.

We hold that this instruction was [in] error and that, as a matter of law, Kodak did not have a duty to predisclose information about the 110 system to competing camera manufacturers. . . .

. . . If a firm that has engaged in the risks and expenses of research and development were required in all circumstances to share with its rivals the benefits of those endeavors, this incentive would very likely be vitiated.

Withholding from others advance knowledge of one's new products, therefore, ordinarily constitutes valid competitive conduct. . . .

. . . Berkey postulates that Kodak had a duty to disclose limited types of information to certain competitors under specific circumstances. But it is difficult to comprehend how a major corporation, accustomed though it is to making business decisions with antitrust considerations in mind, could possess the omniscience to anticipate all the instances in which a jury might one day in the future retrospectively conclude that predisclosure was warranted. . . .

. . . The first firm, even a monopolist, to design a new camera format has a right to the lead time that follows its success.

After ruling in favor of Kodak on the predisclosure issue, Judge Kaufman then addressed the issue of Kodak's introduction of the camera–film system:

Certainly the mere introduction of Kodacolor II along with the Pocket Instamatics did not coerce camera purchasers. Unless consumers desired to use the 110 camera for its own attractive qualities, they were not compelled to purchase Kodacolor II — especially since Kodak did not remove any other films from the market when it introduced the new one. . . .

. . . We shall assume *arguendo* that Kodak violated Section 2 of the Sherman Act if its decision to restrict Kodacolor II to the 110 format was not justified by the nature of the film but was motivated by a desire to impede competition in the manufacture of cameras capable of using the new film. . . .

But to prevail, Berkey must prove more, for injury is an element of a private treble damages action. Berkey must, therefore, demonstrate that some consumers who would have bought a Berkey camera were dissuaded from doing so because Kodacolor II was available only in the 110 format. This it has failed to establish. The record is totally devoid of evidence that Kodak or its retailers actually attempted to persuade customers to purchase the Pocket Instamatic because it was the only camera that could use Kodacolor II, or that, in fact, any consumers did choose the 110 in order to utilize the finer-grained film. . . .

. . . We conclude, therefore, that the jury could not find that Berkey suffered more than *de minimis* injury, if any, because Kodacolor II was limited to the 110 format. . . .

We, therefore, reverse so much of the judgment as awarded Berkey damages based on the introduction of the 110 camera.

The Photofinishing and Photofinishing Products Markets   In the photofinishing market Berkey charged that Kodak, by failing to predisclose the new high-temperature C-41 finishing process necessary for processing Kodacolor II, made it impossible for Berkey to process Kodacolor II. As a result, Berkey contended it lost considerable business through the end of 1973 on photofinishing of Kodacolor II.

The district court ruled in favor of Berkey and awarded $167,000 in damages. Furthermore, District Judge Frankel ordered that Kodak had to treat all photofinishers, including Kodak Color Print and Processing Laboratories (CP&P), alike. Judge Frankel ordered that for a $200 fee technological advances made available by Kodak to Kodak CP&P had to be promptly made available to all competitors.

The court of appeals remanded the damage award back to the district court for a new trial. Judge Kaufman stated

> Kodak's ability to gain a rapidly diminishing competitive advantage [in the film processing market] with the introduction of the 110 system may have been attributable to its innovation of a new system of photography, and not to its monopoly power. On the other hand, we cannot dismiss the possibility that Kodak's monopoly power in other markets was at least a partial root of its ability to gain an advantage over its photofinishing competitors and to sell them overpriced equipment. For example, it may be that, had Kodak possessed only a small portion of the film market, other manufacturers would have found it more feasible to bring out their C-22 films in the 110 size. CP&P would then have had no competitive advantage for a large percentage of 110 photofinishing. Moreover, absent a Kodak film monopoly, the independent photofinishers might not have felt an urgent need to buy expensive equipment for the C-41 process. . . .
>
> . . . The parties quite naturally gave relatively little attention to this aspect of the case, in light of the comparatively small sums involved. If the parties wish to pursue these claims to a final determination, therefore, a new trial will be necessary.

Judge Kaufman also eliminated the requirement that Kodak treat all photofinishers identically. He ruled that since Kodak had not monopolized or attempted to monopolize the photofinishing market, the court had no power to restructure that industry.

The Film Market   In the film market, Berkey charged that because Kodak had monopoly power, Berkey was forced to buy film from Kodak at monopoly prices. Berkey, therefore, was injured by Kodak's monopoly power. Furthermore, Berkey argued that Kodak's monopoly in film had been bolstered by two actions: (1) the introduction of the 110 system, and (2) the refusal of Kodak CP&P to process any non-Kodak film. The district court agreed with Berkey and awarded $34.5 million in treble damages because Kodak's monopoly power had resulted in overcharges for film.

The court of appeals, however, remanded this issue to the district court for a new trial. Despite admitting that Kodak clearly had monopoly power over film, Judge Kaufman wrote that

> [U]nless the monopoly has bolstered its power by wrongful actions, it will not be required to pay damages merely because its prices may later be found excessive. Setting a high price may be a use of monopoly power, but it is not in itself anticompetitive. Indeed, although a monopolist may be expected to charge a somewhat higher price than would prevail in a

competitive market, there is probably no better way for it to guarantee that its dominance will be challenged than by greedily extracting the highest price it can. . . . If a firm has taken no action to destroy competition it may be unfair to deprive it of the ordinary opportunity to set prices at a profit-maximizing level. . . .

It is clear from our holdings that we believe both the film and color paper claims must be remanded for retrial. . . . Berkey has a right to establish at a new trial that anticompetitive conduct, both before and after 1969, enhanced the price it paid for Kodak film. . . .

In another section of the decision, the court of appeals affirmed that Kodak had violated *section 1* of the Sherman Act by conspiring with Sylvania and General Electric in the introduction of both the Magicube and Flip-flash systems. This section, however, did not deal with the section 2 issue of monopolization. Furthermore, the treble damages awarded to Berkey amounted to less than $1 million.

In summary, on the most important issues, the court of appeals favored Kodak. The court did remand several of Berkey's complaints for a new trial, but it also appeared to widen the discretion permitted a firm with monopoly power. The court of appeals recognized Kodak's monopoly power; however, it refused to take a structural approach to the case. More important, Judge Kaufman refused to order any remedy such as forced predisclosure of technological advances.

Berkey appealed the decision to the Supreme Court, but on February 2, 1980, the Supreme Court refused to review the decision. Only three justices wished to hear the case — one short of the necessary four. As a result, the case was sent back to the district court.

On September 24, 1981, Berkey and Kodak reached an out-of-court settlement whereby Kodak agreed to pay Berkey $6.75 million in damages. Kodak agreed to pay damages on the flashcube conspiracy charges only. In return, Berkey agreed to drop all other charges.

V   OTHER DEVELOPMENTS SINCE 1970

In addition to the *Telex* and *Berkey Photo* decisions, several other significant actions during the 1970s and early 1980s deserve mention.

***Federal Trade Commission v. Xerox* 86 F.T.C. 364 (1975)**   In 1973 the Federal Trade Commission (FTC) charged Xerox with monopolizing the copier industry. At the time, Xerox maintained approximately an 86 percent market share of the copier industry and a 95 percent share of the plain-paper copier industry.

The FTC charged Xerox with a variety of monopolization practices, many of which were reminiscent of the *United Shoe* case. The FTC charged Xerox with following a leasing-only policy, using package leasing plans and quantity discount plans that unfairly discriminated between customers, announcing the introduction of new models before they were available for lease or sale, requiring in its leases that Xerox would be the exclusive servicing company for all machines, falsely disparaging competitive supplies, and tying supplies to machine leases.

The FTC also complained about certain Xerox patent practices, including an attempt to monopolize patents relating to office copiers, using its patents to obtain access to its competitors' patents, and entering into cross-licensing agreements, which restricted competition.

On July 29, 1975, Xerox and the FTC signed a consent decree. Xerox agreed to license its more than 1,700 existing patents and all future patents on the following basis. First, Xerox agreed to license up to three patents royalty free on each copier product. The next three patents licensed for any *one* royalty-bearing product would be licensed at a royalty rate not to exceed ½ percent of net revenues, and any additional licenses on any *one* royalty-bearing product would be free. As a result of this agreement, Xerox could obtain a maximum royalty of 1½ percent on any of its competitors' products.

Xerox also agreed to supply its know-how to all licensees *except* IBM, to refrain for ten years from acquiring from any person or corporation any patents dealing with copier technology, to eliminate its pricing plans based on quantity leasing or purchasing plans, to refrain from announcing or taking orders on any copying machine prior to three months before Xerox expected to introduce the machine, and to announce a sale price, in addition to a rental rate, for each of its copiers.

Despite the fact that many economists were skeptical of the decree, Xerox's market share declined rapidly after 1975. By 1979 its share in the copier industry was down to 54 percent and still declining. Furthermore, Xerox's profit rate decreased significantly from an average of over 22 percent on equity in 1969–1974 to an average of just over 18 percent in 1975–1979. Although it is impossible to attribute all, or even most, of the decline in its market share and profits to the 1973 case and 1975 decree, it is certainly likely that the case had some impact [10].

Federal Trade Commission v. Kellogg F.T.C. Docket 8883 (1981)

In 1972 the FTC attempted an original approach to the problem of market power. The commission charged the major cereal producers with a shared monopoly. Initially the FTC filed a suit against the four leading cereal producers, Kellogg, General Mills, General Foods (Post brand), and Quaker Oats. Quaker Oats was later dropped as a defendant. The remaining three companies controlled over 80 percent of the market; however, no one firm controlled more than 45 percent. Even the leading producer, Kellogg, could not be charged with monopolization.

The FTC charged that the three firms had "tacitly colluded and cooperated to maintain and exercise monopoly power." Specifically, the complaint charged that all three had reached an understanding to avoid price competition and instead channel their energies into practices that raised entry barriers. These practices included excessive advertising, brand proliferation, the control of shelf space, and the elimination of some private-label brands.

A number of major remedies were requested by the FTC. Kellogg was to be divested by spinning off three viable firms; General Mills and General Foods were each to spin off one viable firm. These three firms were also to be required to license all of their cereal brands, such as Cheerios and Sugar Smacks, royalty free for twenty years. Finally, there was a request to ban shelf-space allocation programs that covered more than a firm's own brands.

The FTC relied heavily on two pieces of economic evidence: the high profitability of the cereal industry and, despite high profits, the complete lack of entry for decades.

On September 1, 1981, Administrative Law Judge Berman recommended that the complaint be dismissed. Judge Berman wrote in part

> Complaint counsel advance two grounds for asserting that respondents have violated Section 5 of the Federal Trade Commission Act: (1) Conspiracy; and (2) Acts and practices of respondents and economic performance of respondents and the RTE [ready-to-eat] cereal industry, under a shared monopoly industry structure. . . .
>
> . . . A pricing pattern consistent with coordination was established with respect to only three sets of products — Kellogg's Corn Flakes and General Foods' Post Toasties; Kellogg's and General Foods' Raisin Bran; and Kellogg's Sugar Frosted Flakes and General Foods' Sugar Coated Corn Flakes. Other than for these three sets of similar products, there is no evidence of price uniformity, maintenance of pricing levels, or pricing responses consistent with a pricing agreement or arrangement among respondents or with price leadership and followership. . . . Kellogg set prices for RTE cereals on the basis of a guideline for gross margins and a target net profit figure. It did not establish prices in order to maintain a profitable price structure for its RTE cereal competitors. . . .
>
> Complaint counsel assert that respondents had a tacit agreement to avoid competition for shelf space in retail stores; that Kellogg formulated and implemented a shelf space allocation plan and General Mills and General Foods acquiesced in that plan. The assertion has no record basis. . . .
>
> Retailers adopted Kellogg's recommendations because such recommendations served their own profitability and efficiency interests and were considered the most reasonable way of stocking RTE cereals.
>
> Faced with Kellogg's shelving program which advocated space according to sales and grouping by manufacturers, which principles were logical and advantageous to retailers, as well as ones to which retailers

were accustomed, it is not surprising that General Mills and General Foods advocated the same guidelines when they competed for shelf space. . . .

Complaint counsel assert that the RTE cereal industry is marked by high barriers to entry of new firms and that there are no barriers to entry unrelated to respondents' conduct. The conduct so targeted by complaint counsel is brand proliferation which is asserted to provide the complete answer to lack of entry. . . .

Brand proliferation is nothing more than the introduction of new brands which is a legitimate means of competition. Respondents' brand proliferation is vigorously competitive and, as conceded by complaint counsel, is not predatory and not in itself unlawful. Respondents engaged in intense, unrestrained and uncoordinated competition in the introduction of new products. There is no evidence of a conspiracy or intent to deter entry by means of new product introductions. . . .

Basic to complaint counsel's shared monopoly theory is the allegation that respondents have maintained a pattern of conduct that had enabled them to charge supracompetitive prices and to reap monopoly level profits; and that this demonstrates that they are sharing monopoly power. . . .

A higher than average return is still considered competitive or normal if the amount above the average is compensation for above average risk. A normal rate of return for a business with above average risk would be greater than for less risky businesses. RTE cereal is a relatively high risk industry. . . .

Thus complaint counsel's factual assertion basic to its shared monopoly theory, that respondents and others in the RTE cereal industry realized supracompetitive profits, fails for lack of proof. . . .

Complaint counsel assert that advertising cost levels in the RTE cereal industry are excessive and wasteful. While the advertising-to-sales ratio for the RTE cereal industry is almost at the top of all manufacturing industries, RTE cereal industry advertising cannot be found to be excessive.

Advertising performs a necessary and legitimate function of advising prospective customers of the attributes of products offered for sale. The large number of nonhomogeneous RTE cereal products, each with its requirements for separate advertising, dictates a relatively high A/S ratio. The requirement is further impacted by the high incidence of new product introduction which necessitates high levels of advertising. . . .

. . . Our concept of a free competitive system does not envision imposition by government of permissible levels of advertising. . . .

Consciously parallel conduct is circumstantial evidence that competitors have acted pursuant to a tacit agreement. Standing alone, however, parallel business behavior does not constitute violation of the antitrust laws. . . .

IT IS ORDERED that the complaint in this proceeding be, and it hereby is, dismissed as to all respondents.

In January 1982 the FTC agreed to let Judge Berman's decision stand. The FTC experiment with a shared-monopoly theory had died a slow death over almost a decade, leaving virtually no possibility of a revival of this theory in the near future.

United States v. American Telephone and Telegraph Company
Consent Decree (1982)   In 1974 the Justice Department filed a suit against the American Telephone and Telegraph Company (AT&T), the largest private corporation in the world. In 1981 AT&T had assets exceeding $130 billion and a market share of 83 percent of all telephones in the United States.

AT&T was a holding company that controlled twenty-three local telephone companies, Bell Long Lines Division, Western Electric, and Bell Labs. Its control of the telecommunications industry was built on a combination of government regulation, vertical integration, and aggressive competitive practices. In 1956 AT&T had settled an earlier Justice Department antitrust case by consenting to operate only in regulated markets; yet after 1956 it continued to follow competitive policies that made it virtually impossible for independents to enter the industry at almost any level.

The 1974 complaint charged that AT&T had monopolized the industry by adopting two major policies. First, AT&T had foreclosed independent equipment manufacturers by purchasing its equipment requirements from its own equipment manufacturing arm, Western Electric. Second, it had prevented competition by obstructing independent equipment and independent long-distance carriers from interconnecting with the national AT&T system.

Originally, the government complaint suggested that AT&T be permitted to keep the twenty-three regulated local operating companies and be divested of Western Electric, Long Lines, and Bell Labs. On January 8, 1982, however, the Justice Department and AT&T signed a consent decree with just the opposite result. AT&T was permitted to keep Western Electric, Long Lines, and Bell Labs; but it agreed to divest all of its twenty-three local operating companies. Furthermore, AT&T was given permission to enter nonregulated markets.

When the decree was carried out, it resulted in the largest divestiture in antitrust history, over $87 billion in assets. There is little doubt that new competition will develop as a result of the decree; however, there are some questions concerning the decree's wisdom. First, the decree leaves AT&T partially regulated (Long Lines Division) and partially unregulated (Western Electric, Bell Labs), which could result in problems if AT&T is able to use its secure regulated profits to subsidize its operations in unregulated areas such as equipment. This potential problem could have been prevented if three separate companies had been created, one each out of Western Electric, Long Lines, and

Bell Labs, or two companies had been created, one a combination of Western Electric and Bell Labs and the other simply Long Lines.

There has also been some speculation that the decree will result in higher rates for basic monthly telephone service. The concern stems from the fact that the independent local companies will not be able to subsidize basic telephone rates with profits earned from long-distance services. It is certainly likely that basic-service rates will increase, but it is impossible to predict by how much, because the local companies will be able to charge long-distance companies (such as AT&T's Long Lines Division, MCI, and Sprint) for interconnection privileges. The charges for interconnection privileges may enable the local companies to keep basic-service rate increases within reasonable limits.

In any event, the decree will certainly result in increased competition in the equipment and long-distance markets since the local companies will no longer have an incentive to deal exclusively with AT&T in either market. As a result, it is likely that significant entry will occur in both of these markets.

Despite being divested of $87 billion in assets, AT&T also gained by the decree. It was able to divest itself of the "dinosaur" elements of its operation while keeping the modern, technologically advanced elements. Furthermore, the decree opened up vast new opportunities for AT&T, particularly in the computer and data processing markets, where it will be able to compete with other giant corporations, particularly IBM. In fact, this element of the AT&T decree probably explains why the Justice Department chose to announce, on the same day that it signed the AT&T decree, that it was dismissing its one other major pending section 2 case, the *IBM* case.

United States v. IBM Dismissed (1982)   Having already examined the *Telex v. IBM* case, we need not analyze the 1969 Justice Department case in great detail. Although the market definition was different in the Justice Department's case, most of the charges were similar in tone, if not necessarily in content.

On the last day of the Johnson administration, the government charged IBM with attempting to monopolize the general-purpose electronic digital computer market. The Justice Department measured IBM's market share at approximately 75 percent, based on the lease value of the installed base of electronic data processing (EDP) equipment. IBM contended that its market share was only 33 percent of the correct relevant market, which it defined as *all* data procesing equipment, including computers, programmable hand-held calculators, message-switching equipment, and just about any other piece of electronic information equipment imaginable.

Specifically, the government charged IBM with a series of aggressive actions. The complaint alleged that IBM bundled systems together by charging a single price for the central processor, related software, and maintenance, rather than charging different prices for each individual piece of equipment. Such a bundling policy made it possible for IBM to discriminate effectively between different users, because the price a user paid for an individual piece of equipment was unknown. IBM was also accused of introducing new computer lines (particularly the 360 line) in ways that were aimed at destroying the sales of machines recently introduced by competitors. In particular, the government complained about IBM's practice of announcing the introduction of a new line of computers well in advance of its actual introduction. Furthermore, there were instances when IBM announced that a machine would be forthcoming even though no such machine existed or was planned.

On January 8, 1982, on the same day it announced the AT&T consent decree, the Justice Department announced that it was dismissing the IBM case. The timing was far from coincidental. The AT&T decree ensured that IBM would be faced with a major new competitor within a few years. President Reagan's assistant attorney general in charge of antitrust, William Baxter, decided that IBM had not committed any major violations of the antitrust laws and, therefore, the case was "without merit." Baxter also believed that there was very little chance of a government victory. Given the *Telex* and *Berkey Photo* decisions, he may have been right. In any event, the dismissing of the *IBM* case was a further step away from the *Alcoa* precedent and the structuralist position.

VI   SUMMARY

The interpretation of section 2 in the courts has gone through a complete cycle: from a behavioral interpretation to a structural interpretation, and then back again to a behavioral interpretation. Although the courts appear to be taking a position that is reminiscent of earlier cases such as *United Shoe* (1917) and *U.S. Steel* (1920), it is impossible to predict that this interpretation is permanent. In fact, an historical perspective would suggest that the courts' position will change again one day.

Someday, the courts' might revert all the way to the *Alcoa* precedent. As things stand today, however, even dominant firms such as IBM and Kodak can follow fairly aggressive policies with little fear of the antitrust laws. Only time will tell whether or not this is a wise economic policy.

NOTES

1. J. S. McGee, "Predatory Price Cutting: The Standard Oil (N.J.) Case," *Journal of Law and Economics,* October 1958, pages 137–169.

2. W. S. Measday, "The Petroleum Industry" in W. Adams (ed.), *The Structure of American Industry,* 6th edition (New York: Macmillan, 1982), pages 36–72.

3. *United States v. American Tobacco Co.* 147 F.2d 93 (1946).

4. D. F. Greer, *Business, Government, and Society* (New York: Macmillan, 1983), pages 153–154.

5. *United States v. United Shoe Machinery Co. of New Jersey* 247 U.S. 32 (1918).

6. D. E. Waldman, *Antitrust Action and Market Structure* (Lexington, Mass.: Heath, 1978), pages 40–49.

7. *United States v. United Shoe Machinery Corporation,* 391 U.S. 244 (1968).

8. Waldman, *Antitrust Action and Market Structure,* pages 31–40.

9. Ibid., pages 49–57.

10. D. E. Waldman, "Economic Benefits in the IBM, AT&T, and Xerox Cases: Government Antitrust Policy in the 70s," *Antitrust Law and Economics Review,* No. 2, 1980, pages 75–92.

CHAPTER

FOUR

Mergers

I   INTRODUCTION

Mergers raise some of the most intriguing antitrust problems because virtually every merger has positive as well as negative effects on competition and efficiency. Currently, there is a great debate among economists over whether mergers generally promote greater efficiency or greater market power. It is, therefore, important to point out both the positive and negative effects of mergers and then decide whether the positive or negative effects dominate a particular merger.

There are three broad merger categories: horizontal, vertical, and conglomerate. *Horizontal mergers* involve firms that are *direct* competitors; the firms must compete in *both* the same product market *and* the same geographic market. *Vertical mergers* involve firms that produce at different stages of production in the same industry. If U.S. Steel purchased an iron ore mining company, it would be classified as a vertical merger. *Conglomerate mergers* involve companies that operate in *either* different product markets *or* in the same product market but with different geographic markets. Conglomerate mergers are usually subdivided into three types: (1) *product extension mergers* between companies that produce different but related products (for example, laundry detergent and liquid bleach), (2) *geographic extension mergers* between companies that produce the same product in different locations (for example, a Midwestern beer producer purchases a Northeastern beer producer), and (3) *pure conglomerate mergers* between firms operating in entirely different markets (for example, a telephone company purchases a rental car company).

II MOTIVES FOR MERGER

In a sense all mergers occur for the same reason: One group believes that the acquired company is worth more than the acquired company's owners believe it is worth. No merger will take place unless this condition is fulfilled. Because the owners and managers of a company often have a better sense of a company's true worth than a group of outsiders, many mergers are far from successful. There are several major reasons that are commonly advanced to explain mergers. Seven of these reasons are discussed below.

Market Power

Horizontal Mergers   The first merger wave, at the turn of the century, was primarily an attempt to gain market power. Horizontal mergers rather than vertical or conglomerate mergers have the greatest potential for increasing market power. When direct competitors merge, market power often increases, and, as a result, firms may be able to increase their prices and profits. If General Motors acquired Ford, it is very likely that prices and profits would increase in the automobile industry, even given competition from the Japanese and Europeans. Increased market power, therefore, is often an incentive for major horizontal mergers, and horizontal mergers should be examined carefully.

On the other hand, not all horizontal mergers result in increased market power. If two small firms merged to compete more effectively against a dominant firm, the merger might reduce the market power of the dominant firm and increase effective competition.

Vertical Mergers   There are also legal and economic theories that suggest vertical and conglomerate mergers, as well as horizontal mergers, can be motivated by a desire to increase a firm's market power. The major *legal* theory against vertical mergers is quite controversial among economists, but has become accepted in many courts. According to this theory, vertical mergers may result in *foreclosure*. Foreclosure refers to the possibility that a merger may prevent some firms from supplying inputs to one of the merger partners. If McDonald's purchased a large producer of restaurant equipment, McDonald's would probably purchase its equipment from its own subsidiary; therefore, the merger would probably foreclose other equipment suppliers from selling to McDonald's. In theory, such a merger might result in the demise of restaurant equipment suppliers that formerly had supplied McDonald's, and, as a result, market structure might deteriorate in the equipment industry. Furthermore, after the merger, McDonald's competitors might be forced to pay higher equipment prices, and this might ultimately result in higher fast food prices to consumers.

The preceding argument is totally dependent on the existence of market power in at least one of the markets, either the restaurant equipment market or the fast food market. If both markets were competitive, vertical integration and foreclosure could not possibly have any effect on efficiency since prices in *both* markets would equal marginal cost, regardless of the degree of vertical integration. Furthermore, if both firms had *complete* monopoly power in their respective markets *(bilateral monopoly)*, vertical integration would still have *no negative* effect on efficiency. In the case of *bilateral monopoly* without vertical integration, the equipment monopolist could charge the fast food monopolist the monopoly price for equipment. The fast food monopolist could then charge a monopoly price for fast food based on a high monopoly input price of equipment. Surprisingly, in the case of bilateral monopoly, vertical integration can only *improve* economic efficiency and at the same time *increase* joint profits. This result occurs because with vertical integration, the fast food monopolist will calculate the cost of equipment as the *lower* opportunity cost of production rather than the *higher* monopoly price of equipment. As a result, if the fast food monopolist owns the equipment monopolist, it will generally charge a *lower* price for fast food than if it purchased equipment from an independent equipment monopolist.

If one vertical stage of production is competitive while the other is controlled by a monopolist, economic *theory* still suggests that vertical integration *cannot* be used to extend monopoly power into the competitive sector. Suppose McDonald's is a fast food monopolist, but the equipment industry is competitive. McDonald's will purchase equipment at marginal cost and then charge a monopoly price for fast food. If McDonald's owned its own equipment company, it would calculate equipment cost as the marginal opportunity cost of producing equipment and then charge a monopoly price for fast food based on a marginal-cost evaluation of equipment prices. Since equipment prices would be calculated as marginal opportunity costs in both cases, the monopoly price for fast food would be identical with or without vertical integration. In this case, vertical integration cannot be used to extend the fast food monopoly into equipment.

Alternatively, suppose that fast food is sold in a competitive market, but equipment is sold by a monopolist. McDonald's is then required to pay a monopoly price for equipment, but sell fast food at a competitive price based on a monopoly price for one input, equipment. All other *competitive* fast food firms must do the same thing; therefore, they all charge the same price for fast food. Now suppose that the equipment monopolist purchases McDonald's and refuses to sell equipment to any other fast food firm. As a result, McDonald's now has a monopoly on fast food, but this puts us back in a case that is similar to the case of *bilateral monopoly,* and profit maximization will once again *require* that equipment prices be calculated on the basis of marginal opportunity costs. In a sense, the fast food monopolist will now *behave as if* the equipment market were competitive, and price will once again be the same as if a monopoly existed only at one stage of production.

The preceding analysis suggests that vertical integration can *never* be used to extend monopoly power from one stage of production into another. If this argument is correct, vertical integration can only result in lower prices, either by providing true technical economies or by reducing the potential economic costs of bilateral monopoly. This theory is accepted by a large number of economists, and naturally these economists argue that vertical mergers should *never* be prevented by antitrust action [1].

Before accepting the argument that vertical integration is *never* anticompetitive, however, it must be realized that the preceding argument is based on a world of *perfect competition* in *most* markets and *perfect* knowledge with *no* uncertainty throughout the economy. By relaxing these assumptions, some economists have theorized that vertical integration can have anticompetitive consequences. Specifically, these economists have suggested that vertical integration can raise the capital barrier to entry, result in price squeezes, and facilitate collusion.

Increased Entry Barriers   The same McDonald's example can be used to demonstrate how a vertical merger might increase the capital barrier. Suppose that as a result of a merger between McDonald's and the nation's leading restaurant equipment manufacturer, there were few independent producers of restaurant equipment left in the United States. Potential entrants into the fast food industry might then be forced to manufacture their own equipment, and as a result large-scale entry into the fast food industry would require greatly increased capital costs. If capital markets are imperfect, the increased capital requirements associated with entry into two markets (equipment and fast food) instead of one market (fast food) might erect a large capital barrier to entry.

Capital barriers to entry arise because there are market imperfections in American capital markets that make the cost of capital vary from borrower to borrower. There are several reasons why the cost of capital varies from borrower to borrower. First, the transaction costs per dollar are lower on a large loan than on a small loan because certain costs are fixed regardless of the size of the loan. The bank's costs of checking the applicant's record, processing the loan application, and servicing the loan are largely independent of the size of the loan. Since transaction costs per dollar are smaller on a large loan, the bank may charge a lower interest rate on large loans. This is economically justified since the cost savings are real.

Second, large companies are often less likely to default on a loan than small companies or individual borrowers; therefore, the risk associated with a loan to a large firm is often lower than the risk associated with a loan to a small company. Lower risk is also a legitimate reason for charging large companies lower interest rates than small companies or individual borrowers. At least one major study, however, concluded that even after considering risk differentials, small companies paid higher interest rates to secure loans [2].

Third, market imperfections almost certainly exist in the banking industry that further increase the advantages available to large borrowers. Empirical evidence has shown that interest rates tend to be higher the more concentrated the banking market [3]. Furthermore, national banking concentration is much lower than regional banking concentration. Since large firms usually have access to the entire nation's banking system, they can shop around for the best rates. Small or regional companies and individuals, however, must depend on local banks, which have some degree of market power and can, therefore, charge higher interest rates for loans. This advantage of size has nothing to do with costs or risk, it results directly from imperfections in the banking industry and cannot be justified on efficiency grounds.

If capital markets are imperfect, entry into two stages of production will be more difficult than entry into one stage, and vertical integration can result in an increased capital barrier to entry.

Price Squeeze   Another potential anticompetitive effect of vertical integration is the use of a price squeeze to reduce competition in the forward market. A price squeeze exists when a vertically integrated firm increases its input price while it lowers the price of its manufactured product. Suppose a firm produced aluminum ingots and also produced fabricated aluminum products. If the firm had monopoly power in ingots, it might simultaneously increase the price of ingots and decrease the price of fabricated products. Such a price squeeze would make it difficult for independent fabricators dependent on the monopolist's ingots to compete in the market for fabricated products because it would squeeze their margin between the price of ingots and the price of fabricated products.

In the preceding case, a price squeeze may discourage single-stage entry into fabrication and thereby increase the capital barrier to entry. By discouraging entry and expansion in the fabrication market, the ingot manufacturer might hope to gain a larger market share in the fabrication market. Of course, it is not clear why the ingot manufacturer's use of a price squeeze would be anticompetitive since even if the ingot manufacturer *monopolized* the entire fabrication market, it would still maximize profits by pricing as if the ingot market were competitive. However, the use of a price squeeze can be quite rational if the third possible anticompetitive consequence of vertical integration is considered — vertical integration might facilitate collusion.

Collusion   Suppose the aluminum market is initially composed of three *nonintegrated* ingot manufacturers and thirty *nonintegrated* fabricators. In other words, the ingot market is a tight oligopoly, and the fabrication market is much more competitively structured. The independence of the thirty fabricators might undermine any attempt by the ingot manufacturers to set prices because the fabricators might compete on the basis of price and attempt to extract price concessions from the ingot manufacturers. Furthermore, even if the fabricators maintain prices, the ingot suppliers might have an incentive to offer secret price cuts to gain a larger market share, particularly during periods of weak demand. Now suppose that each of the three ingot manufacturers acquires ten of the fabricators so that the industry is entirely integrated. Price agreements at the fabrication level should now be much easier to reach and maintain because the number of firms either directly or indirectly involved in an agreement has been reduced from thirty-three to just three. Most economists accept the argument that overt or tacit collusion is easier to maintain the smaller the number of firms involved [4]. By reducing the number of firms necessary to maintain a collusive agreement, vertical integration might increase the likelihood of effective collusion. An increased probability of effective collusion is probably the strongest economic argument against vertical mergers.

Conglomerate Mergers   Conglomerate mergers have also been identified with possible increases in market power. The attacks have been based primarily along four lines: the elimination of potential competition, reciprocal buying, subsidization, and forebearance.

The classic *potential competition* argument was advanced when Procter & Gamble, the nation's leading detergent producer, purchased Clorox, the nation's leading bleach producer. The government argued that Procter & Gamble's existence as a potential entrant into the liquid bleach market served as a check on the pricing behavior of existing bleach manufacturers because existing bleach producers were aware that high prices and profits might encourage Procter & Gamble to enter.

According to this argument, once Procter & Gamble purchased Clorox, this potential competition was eliminated, and the price of bleach would increase.

Reciprocity refers to the possibility that a large conglomerate can encourage its suppliers to purchase inputs from another of the conglomerate's divisions; in other words, a policy of "You tickle me, I'll tickle you." If a large food wholesaler purchased a major spice manufacturer it might request that its food suppliers purchase their spice requirements from its spice division. As a result, the market power of the acquired spice manufacturer might increase, and small independent spice manufacturers might be forced to withdraw from the market.

Subsidization is another commonly advanced argument against conglomerate mergers. According to this theory, conglomerates will attempt to gain an increased market share in one market by using profits earned in another market to subsidize short-run losses. It has been argued that when Philip Morris purchased Miller Beer, it chose to subsidize Miller's extensive advertising campaign with profits earned in other markets. This practice may be both rational and anticompetitive if it results in higher concentration and increased long-run prices and profits. In reality, however, there are probably few conglomerate mergers that result in major subsidization because unless entry barriers are high, the short-run losses associated with subsidization will usually be greater than the potential long-run profit increases.

Some economists have also theorized that conglomerate mergers will result in *economic forebearance* between the nation's leading firms, or a situation where no conglomerate firm will rock the boat in one market because it fears retaliation in another. Suppose General Motors owned McDonald's and Ford owned Burger King. Ford might discourage Burger King from competing aggressively against McDonald's because General Motors might retaliate in the automobile market. As a result, both firms might compete less aggressively in *both* markets.

Efficiency Gains

If one believed the arguments of acquiring firms, virtually every merger is motivated primarily by a desire to increase economic efficiency. Unfortunately, not all mergers result in efficiency gains, and these claims must be examined carefully. Economies of scale may result from any merger, but are most common in either horizontal or vertical mergers. A horizontal merger may enable the consolidated firm to reduce its production or marketing costs. The consolidation of AMC's and Renault's American operations in the automobile industry has undoubtedly resulted in real cost savings. Vertical mergers may also result in real economies by reducing the transaction costs associated with coordinating the different stages of production. Recent evidence suggests that many mergers, particularly horizontal mergers, result in some economies, but that the savings are usually small [5].

Financial Motives

One of the major motives for recent mergers, particularly conglomerate mergers, is speculation that the whole is worth more than the sum of its parts. When a large conglomerate is "on a roll" of good purchases, its stock value will rise and so will its price/earnings ratio. If this successful conglomerate purchases another profitable company with a *lower* price/earnings ratio and finances the purchase by exchanging its stock for the acquired firm's stock, all parties may gain financially in the short run. The owners of the acquired firm gain if the conglomerate pays a premium for their stock, that is, if the conglomerate pays more than the stock is worth on the open market. In addition, the owners of the conglomerate may gain because earnings per share may rise when the acquired firm's profits are added to the conglomerate's profits. All of this is quite complicated, but it boils down to a simple phenomenon: Because of stock market myopia, even in the absence of *any* real benefits from the merger, the stock market may behave as if the acquired firm will fare better under the conglomerate's ownership. Unfortunately, if the stock market stops believing in the conglomerate's magic, the conglomerate's stock value will tumble, and existing stockholders will "take a bath." By that time many of the original conglomerate stockholders will have sold their stock for large short-term capital gains. This motive was probably greatest during the merger wave of the late 1960s and probably plays a less important role today since the Midas touch associated with many conglomerates has disappeared.

The American tax code provides another financial motive for merger. Since paid-out corporate profits are taxed twice, first as corporate profits and then as individual income, there is an incentive for firms to retain profits and reinvest these retained profits in ways that lower their stockholders' personal income tax burden. If retained earnings are used to acquire companies and the acquisitions result in an increase in the conglomerate's stock value, then capital gains result. Capital gains are taxed at a lower rate than other types of personal income, so it is preferable from a tax standpoint to receive income in the form of capital gains rather than as distributed corporate profits. Tax laws, therefore, result in an additional incentive for merger.

Risk Reduction

It is often argued that mergers, particularly conglomerate mergers, reduce risk, and there is some truth to the old saying "Don't put all your eggs in one basket." Technically, a merger reduces risk so long as the acquiring firm's profits are not *perfectly correlated* with the acquired firm's profits. This technical condition is met in most mergers, but a merger will *not* reduce risk *significantly* if the acquired firm operates in an industry that is highly *interdependent* with the acquiring firm's other business activities. In the case of significant interdependence, when one part of the acquiring firm's business operation flounders, so will the acquired part.

Pure conglomerate mergers are the most likely type of mergers to reduce risk significantly. Few horizontal, vertical, product extension, or geographic extension mergers *significantly* reduce risk because these mergers usually involve markets that are interdependent with the firm's other operations. If two coal companies merged and then the market for coal became depressed, both firms would suffer, and the merger would have done little to reduce risk. Similarly, if a hotel firm purchased a rental car company and then because of a recession the demand for vacations declined, both the hotel and car rental businesses would suffer. Since pure conglomerate mergers make up a relatively small percentage of all mergers, most mergers probably reduce risk only slightly [6].

Empire Building

Another factor encouraging some mergers is a desire by an individual to build a financial empire. Strange as it may seem, many mergers are primarily the result of an individual's effort at self-aggrandizement. Perhaps the two best examples are the efforts of Harold Geneen at ITT and the late Charles Bluhdorn at Gulf & Western. To these individuals, growth, pure and simple, was often enough of a motive for a merger.

Failing Firm

When a firm is on the verge of bankruptcy, it will often attempt to find a buyer to bail it out. The Penn-Central railroad merger, which ended in disaster, was a classic example. The AMC-Renault combination represents a less extreme variation of the failing-firm merger; one hopes it will result in a better outcome and increased competition in the automobile market.

Aging Owners

In some cases one of the motives for merger is the age structure of a company's ownership. If a small company is owned and controlled by an individual without heirs, or without heirs who have a desire to operate the business, then the owner will sometimes search for a buyer. A merger permits the owner to retire on the anticipated *future* earnings of the firm since these future earnings are capitalized into the present value of the firm.

Upon reviewing these merger motives, one point stands out. Of these seven motives, only true efficiency gains provide a strong economic justification for mergers. Any merger that fails to provide significant efficiency gains should be viewed with at least some suspicion by economists and examined carefully for any possible negative effects on competition. As we explore specific mergers, it will become clear that every merger has its own unique set of effects on competition, and, therefore, it is dangerous to generalize about the effects of *all* mergers.

III PUBLIC POLICY: HORIZONTAL MERGERS

As noted above, horizontal mergers may be associated with significant negative economic impacts. Since horizontal mergers may significantly increase market power, they may result in any of the possible ills associated with market power (see Chapter 1), including allocative inefficiency, X inefficiencies, a slower rate of technological advance, and/or an increased probability of collusion.

Horizontal mergers, however, can also increase the level of effective competition if two firms combine to challenge a dominant firm or firms. Furthermore, horizontal mergers may result in real economies of scale, but one must be careful to distinguish *real* economies from *pecuniary* economies. Pecuniary economies result when increased market power gives a firm the ability to obtain inputs, including capital, at lower prices than its competitors. Such pecuniary economies result only in a change in the distribution of income between firms, but do *not* result in lower costs (opportunity costs) of production. Horizontal mergers may also act as a protection against large X inefficiencies. Since an inefficient and undervalued firm can be taken over by a competitor, the threat of a horizontal merger may keep managers on their toes in order to prevent an undervaluation of the firm's stock. This would tend to prevent the development of large X inefficiencies.

An optimal public policy should prevent horizontal mergers with anticompetitive impacts, but should permit those mergers that provide net social benefits. In practice, however, there was no effective public policy toward horizontal mergers until 1950, and by then many horizontal mergers with significant negative effects had already taken place.

Policy Prior to 1950

In Chapter 2 it was noted that section 1 of the Sherman Act, by preventing price-fixing and other restraints of trade, encouraged mergers. Ironically, therefore, the Sherman Act resulted in a large number of horizontal mergers at the turn of the century, and it was not until 1914 that Congress acted to tighten up the law with the passage of the Clayton Act.

Unfortunately, the Clayton Act outlawed only mergers by *stock* acquisition. It made no mention of *asset* acquisition mergers, where one firm purchased the physical plant and equipment of another firm. The courts could have interpreted Congress's intent as including asset, as well as stock, acquisitions, but on November 23, 1926, the Supreme Court gutted section 7 when it handed down three simultaneous rulings. The most famous of these was a simple two-page decision in the *Thatcher Manufacturing* case.

Thatcher Manufacturing Company v. Federal Trade Commission **272 U.S. 554 (1926)**   Thatcher was a major glass manufacturer that acquired the stock of three direct competitors, Lockport Glass, Essex Glass, and Travis Glass. After purchasing the stock, Thatcher purchased the assets of all three companies, so that as of January 13, 1921, the three firms had ceased to exist. On March 1, 1921, one month after Thatcher had dissolved the three acquisitions, the FTC staff filed a complaint charging Thatcher with violating the Clayton Act. The commission ordered Thatcher to divest itself of all assets that were formerly held by the three acquired firms.

The Supreme Court, however, overturned the commission and ruled

> When the Commission institutes a proceeding based upon the holding of stock contrary to Section 7 of the Clayton Act, its power is limited . . . to an order requiring the guilty person to cease and desist from such violation, effectually to divest itself of the stock, and to make no further use of it. The Act has no application to ownership of a competitor's property and business obtained prior to any action by the Commission, even though this was brought about through stock unlawfully held. . . . The Commission is without authority under such circumstances.

The ruling effectively meant that so long as a firm acquired the assets, rather than the stock, of a competing company, there was nothing the government could do under the Clayton Act. Later cases made it clear that even if a firm purposely purchased the assets, rather than the stock, of a competitor just to avoid the Clayton Act, the Supreme Court would not condemn the merger [see *Arrow-Hart & Hegeman Electric Co. v. Federal Trade Commission* 291 U.S. 584 (1934)].

In the 1930 *International Shoe* case (280 U.S. 291), the Supreme Court further limited the reach of section 7 in cases involving stock acquisitions. When two of the nation's largest shoe manufacturers, International Shoe Company and W. H. McElwain, merged, the district court condemned the merger. The Supreme Court, however, ruled that the merger did not lessen competition to a substantial degree because McElwain's shoes were considered by buyers to be of a higher quality than International's shoes, and, therefore, they did not compete with International's shoes. The majority's opinion was based on a highly questionable definition of effective competition. The majority reasoned that McElwain's shoes did not compete with International's shoes because, upon request, McElwain would stamp the dealer's name on its shoes, but International Shoe would not. After the *International Shoe* decision, for all practical purposes, section 7 was useless.

The Celler-Kefauver Act of 1950

In 1950 Congress acted to shore up the loophole in section 7 by passing the Celler-Kefauver Act. The act extended the ban on mergers to asset as well as stock acquisitions and also extended the reach of the law to vertical and conglomerate mergers, as well as to horizontal mergers. The first major test of the new law came in 1958 in the *Bethlehem Steel* decision.

United States v. Bethlehem Steel Corporation **168 F. Supp. 576 (1958)**   On December 11, 1956, Bethlehem Steel and Youngstown Steel entered into an agreement whereby Bethlehem obtained all of Youngstown's assets. The Justice Department filed a complaint. At the time of the merger, Bethlehem ranked as the nation's second-largest steelmaker, with a 15 percent national market share, and Youngstown ranked sixth, with a 5 percent market share. U.S. Steel was the nation's leading producer with approximately a 30 percent market share, and the industry was highly concentrated with a four-firm concentration ratio of 60 percent.

Bethlehem and Youngstown defended the merger on two grounds. First, they argued that Bethlehem and Youngstown competed in different geographic markets and that Bethlehem would *never* consider entry into Youngstown's market. Second, they argued that the beneficial aspects of the merger outweighed any possible negative effects because the merger would enable Bethlehem to compete more effectively against U.S. Steel. The district court disagreed with both defenses.

Judge Weinfeld wrote

> The Government's basic position is that for the iron and steel industry as a whole and for the various component lines of commerce included therein the appropriate geographic market is the nation as a whole. In addition it proposes several alternative sections, from the single states of Michigan and Ohio to several groupings of states, the largest of which coincides with the northeast quadrant of the United States. . . .

[D]efendants maintain that Bethlehem is an "effective competitor" only in the Eastern and Western Areas where its plants are located and that Youngstown is an "effective competitor" only in the Mid-Continent Area where its plants are located. . . .

Assuming arguendo that the defendants' standard for determining sections of the country is proper, although this is disputed by the Government, the facts do not support their tri-partite division of the country. In 1955 Bethlehem shipped into the Mid-Continent Area 2,034,783 tons of "common finished steel products," or 4.9% of total industry shipments. Youngstown in the same year shipped into that area 2,823,992 tons or 6.7% of total industry shipments. Youngstown's total capacity is within the Mid-Continent Area. Bethlehem's shipments of more than 2 million tons into the area demonstrates beyond challenge that in fact it is an "effective competitor" in that area. . . .

The picture is even more clear in the two states of Michigan and Ohio, which in 1955 received almost 50% of the total industry shipments of "common steel products" made to the Mid-Continent Area and over 30% of nationwide shipments of such products. The industry total of these shipments to Ohio and Michigan was 19,930,000 tons. Bethlehem alone accounted for 1,805,893 tons representing 9.1%, and Youngstown accounted for 1,142,617 tons representing 5.7% of total industry shipments. Thus Bethlehem's shipments of common finished steel products there exceeded those of Youngstown by almost 700,000 tons. The conclusion is compelled that in the two most important steel consuming states in the Mid-Continent Area, as well as in the nation as a whole, Bethlehem was a very substantial competitor. . . .

The defendants urge earnestly that in considering the impact on competition of the proposed merger the Court take into account what they point to as its beneficial aspects. Any lessening of competition resulting from the merger should be balanced, they say, against the benefits which would accrue from Bethlehem's plan to expand the Youngstown plants thus creating new steel capacity in an existing deficit area and enhancing the power of the merged company to give United States Steel more effective and vigorous competition than Bethlehem and Youngstown can now give separately. . . .

[T]he argument does not hold up as a matter of law. If the merger offends the statute in any relevant market then good motives and even demonstrable benefits are irrelevant and afford no defense.

A merger may have a different impact in different markets — but if the proscribed effect is visited on one or more relevant markets then it matters not what the claimed benefits may be elsewhere.

Bethlehem's contention that it would never enter the Midwest market *de novo* proved to be false. A few years later, Bethlehem constructed a large integrated steel complex in Burns Harbor, Indiana [7].

Furthermore, Youngstown modernized its Indian Harbor facility in the same area. If nothing else, the case suggests that one should treat a company's claim that it will never enter a new market with some skepticism. The *Bethlehem Steel* case was not appealed to the Supreme Court; however, a few years later the highest court upheld its major precedents in the *Brown Shoe* case.

Brown Shoe Company v. United States 370 U.S. 294 (1962)   The *Brown Shoe* case established major precedents for both horizontal and vertical mergers. First, the horizontal elements of the case are analyzed. The vertical elements are discussed in the next section.

In 1955 Brown Shoe purchased Kinney. Each firm was both a manufacturer and a retailer of shoes. Brown was the fourth-largest manufacturer with a 4 percent market share, and Kinney was the twelfth-largest manufacturer with a 0.5 percent share. In retailing, Kinney was the nation's largest chain retailer, operating over 350 family shoe stores, and it ranked eighth among all shoe retailers in sales. Brown was the nation's third-largest shoe retailer by sales volumes.

The shoe industry was highly competitive in both sectors. In manufacturing the top twenty-four firms controlled only 35 percent. In retailing, there were virtually no entry barriers, and thousands of independents competed successfully against the large chains. Despite the almost perfectly competitive nature of the shoe retailing industry, the Supreme Court handed down a strong decision against Brown Shoe. The Court based its decision on the fact that Brown and Kinney shoe stores competed against each other in many cities. The ruling was an obvious attempt to deter future horizontal mergers, even in competitive industries where the potential negative effects of such mergers would be minimal or nonexistent.

Chief Justice Warren wrote the opinion, which stated in part

> The dominant theme pervading congressional consideration of the 1950 amendments was a fear of what was considered to be a rising tide of economic concentration in the American economy. . . . Throughout the recorded discussion may be found examples of Congress' fear not only of accelerated concentration of economic power on economic grounds, but also of the threat to other values a trend toward concentration was thought to pose.

> The Horizontal Aspects of the Merger.
> We . . . agree that the District Court properly defined the relevant geographic markets in which to analyze this merger as those cities with a population exceeding 10,000 and their environs in which both Brown and Kinney retailed shoes through their own outlets. . . .

[I]n 32 separate cities, ranging in size and location from Topeka, Kansas, to Batavia, New York, and Hobbs, New Mexico, the combined share of Brown and Kinney sales of women's shoes (by unit volume) exceeded 20%. In 31 cities . . . the combined share of children's shoes exceeded 20%; in 6 cities their share exceeded 40%. In Dodge City, Kansas, their combined share of the market for women's shoes was over 57%; their share of the children's shoe market in that city was 49%. In the 7 cities in which Brown's and Kinney's combined shares of the market for women's shoes were greatest (ranging from 33% to 57%) each of the parties alone, prior to the merger, had captured substantial portions of those markets (ranging from 13% to 34%); the merger intensified this existing concentration. In 118 separate cities the combined shares of the market of Brown and Kinney in the sale of one of the relevant lines of commerce exceeded 5% in all three lines. . . .

If a merger achieving 5% control were now approved, we might be required to approve future merger efforts by Brown's competitors seeking similar market shares. The oligopoly Congress sought to avoid would then be furthered and it would be difficult to dissolve the combinations previously approved.

The *Brown Shoe* decision established the *incipiency* precedent with regard to horizontal mergers. The incipiency precedent suggested that horizontal mergers should be banned, even in competitive markets, to prevent future increases in concentration. Four years later, the Supreme Court not only reinforced this precedent, but seemed to extend it further in the *Von's Grocery* case.

United States v. Von's Grocery Company 384 U.S. 270 (1966)   On March 25, 1960, Von's Grocery acquired Shopping Bag Food Stores. The merger resulted in a combination between the third- and sixth-largest food retailers in the Los Angeles area. Von's held a 4.3 percent share, and Shopping Bag held a 3.2 percent share. Safeway was the leading firm in the area, and Von's argued that the merger would enable it to compete more effectively against Safeway. The Supreme Court, however, ruled 6–2 in favor of the government.

Justice Black stated the majority opinion:

Like the Sherman Act in 1890 and the Clayton Act in 1914, the basic purpose of the 1950 Celler-Kefauver Act was to prevent economic concentration in the American economy by keeping a large number of small competitors in business. In stating the purposes of their bill, both of its sponsors, . . . emphasized their fear, widely shared by other members of Congress, that this concentration was rapidly driving the small businessman out of the market. . . .

This merger cannot be defended on the ground that one of the companies was about to fail or that the two had to merge to save themselves from destruction by some larger and more powerful competitor. . . .

Appellees' primary argument is that the merger between Von's and Shopping Bag is not prohibited by section 7 because the Los Angeles grocery market was competitive before the merger, has been since, and may continue to be in the future. . . . It is enough for us that Congress feared that a market marked at the same time by both a continuous decline in the number of small businesses and a large number of mergers would slowly but inevitably gravitate from a market of many small competitors to one dominated by a few giants, and competition would thereby be destroyed. . . .

[W]e not only reverse the judgment below but direct the District Court to order divestiture without delay.

Justice Stewart delivered a dissent based on the highly competitive nature of the industry:

The Court makes no effort to appraise the competitive effects of this acquisition in terms of the contemporary economy of the retail food industry in the Los Angeles area. Instead, through a simple exercise in sums, it finds that the number of individual competitors in the market has decreased over the years, and, apparently on the theory that the degree of competition is invariably proportional to the number of competitors, it holds that this historic reduction in the number of competing units is enough under section 7 to invalidate a merger within the market, with no need to examine the economic concentration of the market, the level of competition in the market, or the potential adverse effect of the merger on that competition. . . .

Section 7 was never intended by Congress for use by the Court as a charter to roll back the supermarket revolution. Yet the Court's opinion is hardly more than a requiem for the so-called "Mom and Pop" grocery stores — the bakery and butcher shops, the vegetable and fish markets — that are now economically and technologically obsolete in many parts of the country. No action by this Court can resurrect the old single-line Los Angeles food stores that have been run over by the automobile or obliterated by the freeway. . . .

It is true that between 1948 and 1958, the combined shares of the top 20 firms in the market increased from 44% to 57%. The crucial fact here, however, is that seven of these top 20 firms in 1958 were not even in existence as chains in 1948. Because of the substantial turnover in the membership of the top 20 firms, the increase in market share of the top 20 as a group is hardly a reliable indicator of any tendency toward market concentration. . . .

Nothing in the present record indicates that there is more than an ephemeral possibility that the effect of this merger may be substantially to lessen competition. Section 7 clearly takes "reasonable probability" as its standard. That standard has not been met here, and I would therefore affirm the judgment of the District Court.

The *Von's Grocery* case set a very strict standard for horizontal merger cases. Even when economic circumstances seemed to call for a reduction in the number of firms in an industry, the *Von's Grocery* decision suggested that the Supreme Court would try to stem the tide. In both the *Brown Shoe* and *Von's Grocery* cases, the social goal of maintaining a large number of competitors was considered at least as important as the economic goal of efficiency.

United States v. Philadelphia National Bank 374 U.S. 321 (1964)

Between the 1962 *Brown Shoe* decision and the 1966 *Von's Grocery* decision, the Supreme Court handed down a major ruling in the *Philadelphia National Bank* (PNB) case. In the *PNB* case, the Supreme Court addressed several major questions. First, did the federal courts have antitrust jurisdiction over a highly regulated industry such as banking? Second, could a merger be declared illegal without a major analysis of the competitive effects of the merger simply because the consolidated firm would have a large market share? Finally, would the Supreme Court ever accept the defense that the benefits of a merger outweighed the costs? On all three issues, the Supreme Court took a stand favorable toward the government.

In November 1960, PNB attempted to acquire the Girard Trust Corn Exchange Bank (Girard). The two banks ranked second and third, respectively, among Philadelphia's forty-two commercial banks, and the merger would have created the largest bank in the Philadelphia area. Had the merger been approved, the four-firm concentration ratio in Philadelphia would have risen to 78 percent of deposits. Unlike the *Brown Shoe* and *Von's Grocery* cases, the *PNB* case involved a highly concentrated market. The banking industry, however, was regulated by the state of Pennsylvania, and the controller of the state had already approved the merger (a requirement of the Bank Merger Act of 1960). The Justice Department charged that the merger violated amended section 7, but the district court ruled that banks were not within the federal courts' antitrust jurisdiction and that the relevant geographic market was the New York–Philadelphia region; therefore, the merger would not significantly reduce competition.

The Supreme Court overturned the district court, with Justice Brennan delivering the opinion of the Court:

> The Appellees contended below that the Bank Merger Act, by directing the banking agencies to consider competitive factors before approving mergers, . . . immunizes approved mergers from challenge under the federal antitrust laws. . . . No express immunity is conferred by the Act. . . .

Both the House and Senate Committee Reports stated that the Act would not affect in any way the applicability of the antitrust laws to bank acquisitions. . . .

We [also] part company with the District Court on the determination of the appropriate "section of the country.". . .

We think that the four-county Philadelphia metropolitan area, which state law apparently recognizes as a meaningful banking community in allowing Philadelphia banks to branch within it, and which would seem roughly to delineate the area in which bank customers that are neither very large nor very small find it practical to do their banking business, is a more appropriate "section of the country" in which to appraise the instant merger than any larger or smaller or different area. . . .

Specifically, we think that a merger which produces a firm controlling an undue percentage share of the relevant market, and results in a significant increase in concentration of firms in that market, is so inherently likely to lessen competition substantially that it must be enjoined in the absence of evidence clearly showing that the merger is not likely to have such anti-competitive effects. . . .

Such a test lightens the burden of proving illegality only with respect to mergers whose size makes them inherently suspect in light of Congress' design in section 7 to prevent undue concentration. . . .

The merger of appellees will result in a single bank's controlling at least 30% of the commercial banking business in the four-county Philadelphia metropolitan area. Without attempting to specify the smallest market share which would still be considered to threaten undue concentration, we are clear that 30% presents that threat. Further, whereas presently the two largest banks in the area (First Pennsylvania and PNB) control between them approximately 44% of the area's commercial banking business, the two largest after the merger (PNB-Girard and First Pennsylvania) will control 59%. Plainly, we think, this increase of more than 33% in concentration must be regarded as significant.

We turn now to three affirmative justifications which appellees offer for the proposed merger. The first is that only through mergers can banks follow their customers to the suburbs and retain their business. . . . There is an alternative to the merger route: the opening of new branches in the areas to which the customers have moved — so called *de novo* branching. . . .

Second, it is suggested that the increased lending limit of the resulting bank will enable it to compete with the large out-of-state banks, particularly the New York banks, for very large loans. . . . If anticompetitive effects in one market could be justified by pro-competitive consequences in another, the logical upshot would be that every firm in an industry could, without violating section 7, embark on a series of mergers that would make it in the end as large as the industry leader. For if all the commercial banks in the Philadelphia area merged into one, it would be smaller than the largest bank in New York City. . . .

This brings us to appellees' final contention, that Philadelphia needs a bank larger than it now has in order to bring business to the area and stimulate its economic development. . . . We are clear, however, that a merger the effect of which "may be substantially to lessen competition" is not saved because, on some ultimate reckoning of social or economic debits and credits, it may be deemed beneficial.

The *PNB* decision suggested that, unless there were great mitigating circumstances, a horizontal merger between two large firms in a concentrated market would be considered a violation of section 7. The *PNB* decision, combined with the *Von's Grocery* decision, made horizontal mergers almost per se illegal under the Warren Court of the 1960s. A more conservative Supreme Court in the 1970s took a more lenient attitude toward horizontal mergers beginning in 1974.

United States v. General Dynamics Corporation **415 U.S. 486 (1974)**   The *General Dynamics* case revolved around the activities of one of General Dynamics' acquisitions, Material Service Corporation. Material Service was a large Midwestern producer of building materials, concrete, limestone, and coal. All of Material Service's coal production was from deep-shaft mines. In 1954 Material Service began purchasing the stock of United Electric Coal, and by 1959 it had acquired 34 percent of United Electric's stock, easily enabling Material Service to control United Electric. When General Dynamics acquired Material Service in 1959, it acquired the nation's fifth-largest coal producer.

The Justice Department's complaint contended that Material Service's acquisition of United Electric substantially reduced competition in two geographic markets: (1) the Eastern Interior Coal Province Sales Area, consisting of Illinois and Indiana, and parts of Kentucky, Tennessee, Iowa, Minnesota, Wisconsin, and Missouri, and (2) the state of Illinois. At the time of the merger, Material Service ranked as the second-largest producer in both submarkets with a 7.6 percent share in the eastern province, and a 15.1 percent share in Illinois. United Electric ranked sixth in the eastern province, with a 4.8 percent share, and it ranked fifth in Illinois with an 8.1 percent share. In both submarkets, therefore, the combined shares of Material Service and United Electric greatly exceeded the limits set down in the *Von's Grocery* decision.

The defense argued that despite these market share figures, the merger was justified on two grounds. First, United Electric had only a small quantity of reserves; without a buyer, United would cease to be a significant competitive factor in the near future. Second, because United Electric operated only strip mines, it competed in an entirely different market from Material Service, which operated only deep-shaft mines.

By 5–4, the Supreme Court found in favor of General Dynamics. Justice Stewart, who so often had dissented from the majority in past antitrust decisions, stated

> In prior decisions involving horizontal mergers between competitors, this Court has found prima facie violations of section 7 of the Clayton Act from aggregated statistics of the sort relied on by the United States in this case. . . .
>
> A . . . significant indicator of a company's power effectively to compete with other companies lies in the state of a company's uncommitted reserves of recoverable coal. A company with relatively large supplies of coal which are not already under contract to a consumer will have a more important influence upon competition in the contemporaneous negotiation of supply contracts than a firm with small reserves, even though the latter may presently produce a greater tonnage of coal. . . .
>
> While United ranked fifth among Illinois coal producers in terms of annual production, it was 10th in reserves held by coal producers in Illinois, Indiana, and western Kentucky. . . . Many of the reserves held by United had already been depleted at the time of trial forcing the closing of some of United's midwest mines. Even more significantly, the District Court found that of 52,033,304 tons of currently available reserves in Illinois, Indiana, and Kentucky controlled by United, only four million tons had not already been committed under long-term contracts. . . . In addition, the District Court found that "United Electric has neither the possibility of acquiring more [reserves] nor the ability to develop deep coal reserves," and thus was not in a position to increase its reserves to replace those already depleted or committed. . . .
>
> The Government asserts that the paucity of United Electric's coal reserves could not have the significance perceived by the District Court, since all companies engaged in extracting minerals at some point deplete their reserves and then acquire new reserves or the new technology required to extract more minerals from their existing holdings. United Electric, the Government suggests, could at any point either purchase new strip reserves or acquire the expertise to recover currently held deep reserves. . . .
>
> The Government failed to come forward with any evidence that such reserves are *presently* available. . . . In addition, there was considerable testimony at trial, apparently credited by the District Court, indicating that United Electric and others had tried to find additional strip reserves not already held for coal production, and had been largely unable to do so. . . .
>
> The mere possibility that United Electric, in common with all other companies with the inclination and the corporate treasury to do so, could some day expand into an essentially new line of business, [deep-shaft mining,] does not depreciate the validity of the conclusion that United Electric at the time of the trial did not have the power to compete on a

significant scale for the procurement of future long-term contracts, nor does it vest in the production statistics relied on by the Government more significance than ascribed to them by the District Court.

Justice Douglas, who usually spoke for the majority on antitrust matters during the 1960s, now wrote the dissenting opinion:

> Many of the commitments here which reduced United's available reserves occurred after the acquisition; 21 million tons for example were committed in 1968. Similarly, though the District Court found further mine-able strip reserves unavailable at the time of the trial, there is no finding that they were unavailable in 1959 or 1967. To the contrary, the record demonstrates that other coal producers did acquire new strip reserves during the 1960's. . . .
>
> While it is true that United is a strip-mining company which had not extracted deep reserves since 1954, this does not mean that United would not develop deep-mining expertise if deep reserves were all it had left or that it could not sell the reserves to some company which poses less of a threat to increased concentration in the coal market than does [Material Service]. . . . At the time of the merger it had access to at least 27 million tons of deep reserves and it had operated a deep mine only five years previously. While deep-coal mining may have been an essentially new line of business for many, it was for United merely a matter of regaining the expertise it once had to extract reserves it already owned for sale in a market where it already had a good name. . . .
>
> On the basis of a record so devoid of findings based on correct legal standards, the judgment may not be affirmed except on a deep-seated judicial bias against section 7 of the Clayton Act. . . . I dissent from the affirmance of the District Court's judgment.

The *General Dynamics* decision signaled that a more conservative Supreme Court would no longer automatically side with the government in all section 7 cases, and this lesson was not lost on other government agencies. By 1979 the FTC had also moved toward a more lenient attitude, as indicated by the commission's decision in the *Pillsbury* case.

In the Matter of the Pillsbury Company 93 F.T.C. 966 (1979)   In November 1976, Pillsbury acquired Fox Deluxe Foods; both firms produced frozen prepared pizza. Pillsbury held a 15.4 percent market share through an earlier acquisition, Totino's, and Fox held a 1.7 percent share. The two firms ranked third and eleventh, respectively, in terms of national market shares.

At the time of the merger, Fox had been experiencing a series of business setbacks. Most of these problems, however, were in its hotel and restaurant division, not in its pizza division. Nevertheless, one of

Pillsbury's defenses was a failing-firm defense. The commission rejected the failing-firm defense, but still permitted the merger.

Commissioner Pitofsky wrote the majority opinion:

Respondent contends that regardless of . . . market shares and other aspects of customary analysis of the anticompetitive effects of mergers, this acquisition should be found legal because Fox was a "failing company." The burden of proving such a defense falls, of course, "on those who seek refuge under it.". . . We agree with the [administrative law judge] that Pillsbury has failed to discharge its burden of proof. . . .

First, the company must be in such poor competitive condition that "the only alternatives presented are involuntary liquidation, insolvency, or outright sale.". . .

Second, there must have been a good faith effort to determine whether there were other purchasers available whose acquisition of the company would have resulted in less anticomptitive effects. . . .

These descriptions of the essential predicate paint a different picture from the one we have of Fox prior to the acquisition. . . .

We conclude that while Fox faced serious financial problems, it did not satisfy the stringent standards that apply to a "failing company" defense. . . .

Although Fox does not qualify as a "failing company" and is not entitled to any variation of the *"General Dynamics"* defense, we nevertheless find that the Pillsbury-Fox merger does not violate Section 7 because it is not likely to have significant anticompetitive effects.

Pillsbury ranked third in 1976 with 15.4%. Fox's share had decreased from 2.4% in 1975 to 1.7% in 1976. On a strict percentage basis, these market shares fall in the gray area at the edge of potential illegality in the Department of Justice guidelines for horizontal mergers, but a finding of a violation would not be entirely unprecedented. We note in addition, however, that while the four-firm concentration ratio for the national frozen pizza market was found by the [administrative law judge] to be 60.8%, barriers to entry, even for fairly small companies, were moderate to low.

Fox was not only small but it was in no sense a company with special competitive potential which might lead to a conclusion that modest market shares understated the future competitive significance of the acquired firm. . . .

Here, there is simply no reason to believe that Fox could have combined with other small frozen pizza manufacturers to challenge larger companies in the market. Also, given Fox's size and nature of its assets, there is no reason to believe that Fox, if acquired by a company outside the market, could have constituted a springboard to permit a new entrant to challenge the market leaders. Despite a trend toward concentration in this industry, it is clear that *de novo* entry is feasible and has actually occurred. Thus it would appear that an outsider could as easily achieve a significant market position through complete *de novo* entry as through the acquisition of Fox, and, as a result, the importance of preserving Fox as an eventual deconcentrator fades. . . .

Horizontal mergers have never been viewed as illegal *per se* under the antitrust laws even though a merger predictably will eliminate competition more completely than any price-fixing or other anticompetitive agreement. Long-term competitive considerations require preservation of ease of entry, and opportunity for businessmen to take entrepreneurial risks. . . . It is essential that the owners of very small businesses with slight competitive potential have some reasonable flexibility to sell out.

Despite the *General Dynamics* and *Pillsbury* decisions, horizontal mergers remain an area where the antitrust laws have some punch. It is doubtful that even the conservative Supreme Court of the early 1980s would permit a merger between two dominant firms in a concentrated market. On the other hand, it is extremely doubtful that the government could win a case similar to the *Von's Grocery* case today. There is no longer a Supreme Court majority that believes in the incipiency argument, and a merger between two small firms is much more likely to be permitted today than in the past. Recognizing this, and also believing in this policy, President Reagan's assistant attorney general in charge of antitrust, William Baxter, rewrote the merger guidelines in 1982 to reflect a more lenient attitude (see Section VI of this chapter), but even the Reagan administration has challenged a few horizontal mergers, such as the proposed merger of Jones & Laughlin Steel (a subsidiary of LTV) with Republic Steel and the attempted merger of Schlitz and Heileman in the beer industry.

On the other hand, the Reagan administration chose not to challenge Texaco's takeover of Getty Oil, the proposed merger of Standard Oil of California (Chevron) with Gulf Oil, or the joint venture between General Motors and Toyota to produce small cars in California. In fact, regardless of the administration in charge, the government has objected to only a small percentage of horizontal mergers over the past twenty-five years. Although the precedents against horizontal mergers have been fairly strong, enforcement has been much weaker.

IV VERTICAL MERGERS

Unlike horizontal mergers, vertical mergers have no direct effect on concentration in particular markets. Furthermore, by reducing transaction costs, vertical mergers almost always result in some real economies. Recently, economists have become much more aware of the significant cost reductions that may result from vertical mergers. Vertical mergers are less likely to have anticompetitive impacts than horizontal mergers; however, they can significantly increase entry barriers in more than one market and should be examined for any possible negative effects. From a legal standpoint, vertical merger cases have dealt primarily with one issue: foreclosure.

United States v. E. I. du Pont de Nemours & Co. 353 U.S. 586 (1957)

The first major vertical merger case involved two of America's corporate giants, General Motors (GM) and Du Pont. Back in 1917, before General Motors became the dominant automobile producer, Du Pont began to acquire GM stock, until by 1919 it controlled 23 percent of GM. Thirty years later, in 1949, the Justice Department filed a complaint under the Clayton Act charging that Du Pont's stock interest foreclosed other firms from the market for paints and fabrics used by GM. The Justice Department argued that the stock acquisition had significantly lessened competition in the market for automobile and appliance paints and fabrics.

Du Pont contended that the government's market definition was incorrect because automobile and appliance paints and fabrics made up a very small percentage of the total paint and fabric market. Furthermore, Du Pont argued that despite the stock link, GM often bought inputs from other companies. Finally, Du Pont raised the obvious issue of timing. Could the government file a section 7 case thirty years after the alleged violation? In 1957, forty years after the stock acquisition, the Supreme Court ruled that the link between Du Pont and GM violated the Clayton Act.

Justice Brennan delivered the 4–2 majority opinion:

> General Motors is the colossus of the giant automobile industry. It accounts annually for upwards of two-fifths of the total sales of automotive vehicles in the Nation. . . . In 1947 General Motors' total purchases of all products from du Pont were $26,628,274, of which $18,938,229 (71%) represented purchases from du Pont's Finishes Division. . . . Purchases by General Motors of du Pont fabrics in 1948 amounted to $3,700,000, making it the largest account of du Pont's Fabrics Division. Expressed in percentages, du Pont supplied 67% of General Motors' requirements for finishes in 1946 and 68% in 1947. In fabrics du Pont supplied 52.3% of requirements in 1946, and 38.5% in 1947. . . .
>
> "Incipiency" in this context denotes not the time the stock was acquired, but any time when the acquisition threatens to ripen into a prohibited effect. . . . To accomplish the Congressional aim, the Government may proceed at any time that an acquisition may be said with reasonable probability to contain a threat that it may lead to a restraint of commerce or tend to create a monopoly of a line of commerce. . . .
>
> "[R]eports and other documents written at or near the time of the investment show that du Pont's representatives were well aware that General Motors was a large consumer of products of the kind offered

by du Pont," and that John J. Raskob, du Pont's treasurer and the principal promoter of the investment, "for one, thought that du Pont would ultimately get all that business.". . .

A major consideration was that an expanding General Motors would provide a substantial market needed by the burgeoning du Pont organization. Raskob's summary of reasons in support of the purchase includes this statement: "Our interest in the General Motors Company will undoubtedly secure for us the entire Fabrikoid, Pyralin [celluloid], paint and varnish business of [General Motors], *which is a substantial factor.".* . .

This background of the acquisition, particularly the plain implications of the contemporaneous documents, destroys any basis for a conclusion that the purchase was made "solely for investment.". . .

Thus sprung from the barrier, du Pont quickly swept into a commanding lead over its competitors, who were never afterwards in serious contention. Indeed, General Motors' then principal paint supplier, Flint Varnish and Chemical Works, early in 1918 saw the handwriting on the wall. The Flint president came to [Du Pont] asking to be bought out, telling [Du Pont], as the trial judge found, that he "knew du Pont had bought a substantial interest in General Motors and was interested in the paint industry; [and] that . . . [he] felt he would lose a valuable customer, General Motors." The du Pont Company bought the Flint works and later dissolved it. . . .

The fact that sticks out in this voluminous record is that the bulk of du Pont's production has always supplied the largest part of the requirements of the one customer in the automobile industry connected to du Pont by a stock interest. The inference is overwhelming that du Pont's commanding position was promoted by its stock interest and was not gained solely on competitive merit. . . .

The fire that was kindled in 1917 continues to smolder. It burned briskly to forge the ties that bind the General Motors market to du Pont, and if it has quieted down, it remains hot, and, from past performance, is likely at any time to blaze and make the fusion complete.

Justice Burton wrote a dissenting opinion that attacked the majority's economic logic:

The Court's decision is far reaching. . . . [O]ver 40 years after the enactment of the Clayton Act, it now becomes apparent for the first time that section 7 has been a sleeping giant all along. . . .

The Court, ignoring the many products which General Motors declines to buy from du Pont or which it buys only in small quantities, concentrates on the few products which du Pont has sold in large volume to General Motors for many years — paints and fabrics. . . .

Oldsmobile is the only division which buys antifreeze from du Pont and one of the two car divisions which does not finish its cars with [du Pont finishes]. Buick alone buys du Pont motor enamel, and Cadillac alone uses du Pont's copper electroplating exclusively. . . .

Although du Pont has been General Motors' principal supplier of paint for many years, General Motors continues to buy about 30% of its paint requirements from competitors of du Pont. . . .

Yet the logic of the Court's argument — that the stock relationship between du Pont and General Motors inevitably has or will result in a preference for du Pont products — requires consideration of the total commercial relations between the two companies. Du Pont "influence," if there was any, would be expected to apply to all products which du Pont makes and which General Motors buys.

However, the evidence shows that du Pont has attempted to sell to the various General Motors' divisions a wide range of products in addition to paint and fabrics, and that it has succeeded in doing so only when these divisions, exercising their own independent business judgment, have decided on the basis of quality, service and price that their economic interests would best be served by purchasing from du Pont.

Upon remand, the district court refused to order complete divestiture because of the "consequences to the shareholders of the two companies." In 1961, however, the Supreme Court, by a 4–3 vote, ordered Du Pont to divest itself of its GM stock. By then, forty-three years had elapsed since the original stock acquisition! It is not surprising, therefore, that the case has become known by Justice Burton's phrase as the "sleeping giant case."

***Brown Shoe Company v. United States* 370 U.S. 294 (1962)**   The *Brown Shoe* case involved vertical as well as horizontal elements. In fact, the Supreme Court decision dealt with the vertical elements first.

When Brown acquired Kinney, it involved a merger between the nation's fourth-largest shoe manufacturer and one of the nation's leading retailers. The potential for foreclosure was significant since after the merger Kinney would be expected to purchase an increased percentage of its shoe requirements from Brown. In fact, evidence suggested that Kinney had significantly increased its purchases of Brown shoes following the merger. In a highly competitive market, however, it is doubtful that this had any significant economic impact.

Nevertheless, the Supreme Court ruled that the vertical elements of the merger violated the Clayton Act. The Court, therefore, condemned the Brown-Kinney merger and declared both the horizontal and the vertical elements in violation of the Clayton Act. The Court's majority stated

The present merger involved neither small companies nor failing companies. In 1955, the date of this merger, Brown was the fourth largest manufacturer in the shoe industry with sales of approximately 25 million pairs of shoes and assets of over $72,000,000 while Kinney had sales of about 8 million pairs of shoes and assets of about $18,000,000. Not only was Brown one of the leading manufacturers of men's, women's, and children's shoes, but Kinney, with over 350 retail outlets, owned and operated the largest independent chain of family shoe stores in the Nation. Thus, no merger between a manufacturer and an independent retailer could involve a larger potential market foreclosure. . . .[I]t is apparent both from past behavior of Brown and from the testimony of Brown's President, that Brown would use its ownership of Kinney to force Brown shoes into Kinney stores. Thus, in operation this vertical arrangement would be quite analogous to one involving a tying clause. . . .

Brown argues, however, that the shoe industry is at present composed of a large number of manufacturers and retailers, and that the industry is dynamically competitive. But remaining vigor cannot immunize a merger if the trend in that industry is toward oligopoly. . . .

[T]his merger . . . creates a large national chain which is integrated with a manufacturing operation. The retail outlets of integrated companies, by eliminating wholesalers and by increasing the volume of purchases from the manufacturing division of the enterprise, can market their own brands at prices below those of competing independent retailers. Of course, some of the results of large integrated or chain operations are beneficial to consumers. Their expansion is not rendered unlawful by the mere fact that small independent stores may be adversely affected. It is competition, not competitors, which the Act protects. But we cannot fail to recognize Congress' desire to promote competition through the protection of viable, small, locally owned businesses. Congress appreciated that occasional higher costs and prices might result from the maintenance of fragmented industries and markets. It resolved these competing considerations in favor of decentralization. We must give effect to that decision.

In this last paragraph the Court seemed to be making a purposeful choice in favor of maintaining a large number of firms, regardless of the effect on prices and costs. Such a decision seems to place a priority on social goals (a large number of small firms) instead of efficiency goals (lower prices and costs). In this decision, positive economics seemed to take a backseat to normative economics.

The *Du Pont* and *Brown Shoe* precedents suggested that vertical mergers violated section 7 as long as a reasonable probability of foreclosure existed. That basic precedent has never been explicitly reversed by the Supreme Court.

Ford Motor Company v. United States 405 U.S. 562 (1972)   The *Ford* case is of interest primarily because of the remedy adopted by the district court and later approved by the Supreme Court. In 1961 Ford acquired the Electric Autolite Company (Autolite). Ford, of course, was the nation's second-largest automobile producer, and Autolite was the second-largest producer of automobile spark plugs. Autolite also produced automotive batteries.

Ford was a much more dominant firm in the automobile market than Kinney was in shoe retailing, and Autolite, with a 15 percent market share, controlled a much larger percentage of the spark plug market than Brown Shoe controlled in shoe manufacturing. This was a vertical merger between two firms each with some market power in their respective markets.

The district court ruled against Ford on two grounds. First, the merger eliminated Ford as a potential competitor in the spark plug market, and second, the merger foreclosed Autolite's competitors from the market for Ford's original-equipment spark plugs.

The remedy adopted by the district court, however, was surprising. Rather than simply ordering divestiture of Autolite's assets, the court ordered three additional remedies:

1. Ford was prohibited from manufacturing its own spark plugs for a period of ten years.
2. Ford was *ordered* to purchase 50 percent of its spark plug requirements over the next five years from Autolite.
3. Ford was prohibited from using *its own trademark* on any spark plugs for a period of five years.

The district court's justification for this decree was the necessity of reestablishing Autolite as a viable independent competitor. Ford appealed the decree, but a Supreme Court majority upheld the lower court decision.

Justice Douglas spoke for the majority:

> Divestiture is a start toward restoring the pre-acquisition situation. . . .
> A word should be said about the . . . other injunctive provisions. They are designed to give the divested [firm] an opportunity to establish its competitive position. The divested company needs time so it can obtain a foothold in the industry. The relief ordered should "cure the ill effects of the illegal conduct, and assure the public freedom from its continuance.". . . Moreover, "it is well settled that once the Government has successfully borne the considerable burden of establishing a violation of law, all doubts as to the remedy are to be resolved in its favor.". . .
> The ancillary measures ordered by the District Court are designed to allow Autolite to re-establish itself in the [original-equipment] and replacement markets and to maintain it as a viable competitor until such time as forces already as work within the marketplace weaken the [original-equipment] tie.

This remedy may have been more anticompetitive than the merger! Chief Justice Warren stated that opinion in his dissent:

The remedial provisions are unrelated to restoring the *status quo ante* with respect to the two violations found by the District Court. . . . First, the District Court's order actually undercuts the moderating influence of Ford's position on the edge of the market. . . . By prohibiting Ford from entering the market through internal expansion, . . . the remedy order wipes out, for the duration of the restriction, the pro-competitive influence Ford had on the market prior to its acquisition of Autolite. Second, the Court's order does not fully undo the foreclosure effect of the acquisition. Divestment alone would return the parties to the *status quo ante.* Ford would then be free to deal with Autolite or another plug producer or to enter the market through internal expansion.

In 1973 Ford sold Autolite to Bendix, a large, diversified firm that probably could have reestablished Autolite without the restrictive provisions of the decree. Ten years later, Bendix-Autolite was a strong competitor in the spark plug market.

International Telephone and Telegraph Corporation v. General Telephone and Electronics Corporation and Hawaiian Telephone Company 518 F.2d 913 (1975)   The *ITT v. GTE* case is of interest primarily because it was a private rather than government suit in which the district court awarded the plaintiff divestiture as a remedy. The case stemmed from GTE's purchase of a number of telephone operating companies, including Hawaiian Telephone. ITT argued that GTE's purchases foreclosed ITT from the market for telephone equipment in many parts of the country. The district court sided with ITT and ordered GTE to divest itself of one of its major telephone equipment manufacturing subsidiaries, Automatic Electric, and a number of operating companies. GTE appealed the decision, with the appeal centering in large part around the use of divestiture in a *private* antitrust action.

The Ninth Circuit Court of Appeals held that even if GTE had violated section 7, divestiture was not an available remedy in private antitrust cases. Judge Goodwin wrote the opinion:

We hold that divestiture is not an available remedy in private antitrust actions under . . . the Clayton Act. . . . While we agree that the prior judicial decisions on this issue do not furnish persuasive authority, we conclude from the legislative history of [the Clayton Act] that Congress did not intend to permit private divestiture suits. . . .

During . . . hearings, members of the House Judiciary Committee referred several times to proposals to broaden the section by permitting private individuals to bring dissolution suits. . . .

[I]n an exchange with Samuel Untermeyer, an antitrust attorney who advocated private dissolution suits, Congressman John Floyd stated:

"We did not intend . . . to give the individual the same power to bring a suit to dissolve the corporation that the Government has. . . . We discussed that very thoroughly among ourselves and we decided he should not have [it]."

Since it viewed dissolution as an equitable remedy distinct from "injunctive relief," the committee would have had to broaden the language of the proposed bill along the lines suggested by Mr. Untermeyer in order to demonstrate an intent to permit private dissolution suits. No such amendment was made. The inescapable conclusion is that the committee chose to reject the proposed amendments and permit "injunctive relief only." Whether Congress shared this intention is not subject to proof. However, the Congressional debates reveal no indication of an intent to broaden the meaning of "injunctive relief" to include dissolution suits. . . .

In holding that the remedy of divestiture is not available we do not jeopardize the district court's ability to restrain GTE from violating the antitrust laws. . . .

[W]e are confident that the pernicious manifestations or tendencies of an illegal vertical combination — such as an anticompetitive purchasing policy — are susceptible to direct injunctive restraint. Relief — such as an "open purchasing agreement" — directed at the symptom rather than the underlying cause may indeed prove somewhat burdensome to the enjoined party. . . . If this threat is sufficiently serious, then a possible recourse for GTE is to stipulate to the remedy of divestiture as an alternative.

The court of appeals remanded the case to the district court with three major provisions. First, divestiture was barred as a remedy. Second, the court changed the district court's market definition. The district court had defined the relevant market as telephone equipment, but had excluded both the purchases by the Bell system from its subsidiary Western Electric and purchases by nonoperating companies. The court of appeals ordered that these purchases should be included in the relevant market. Finally, the court of appeals ordered that the competitive effects of each of GTE's acquisitions had to be considered separately rather than as a group. Each of these provisions favored GTE's defense.

In summarizing these vertical merger cases, several points should be emphasized. First, the courts have accepted even a moderate degree of foreclosure as sufficient grounds for condemning a vertical merger. Second, the "sleeping giant case" suggests that there is virtually no statute of limitations with regard to section 7 cases. Third, it appears that divestiture is not an available remedy in *private* Clayton Act cases. Finally, in vertical merger cases the courts have virtually ignored the potential cost savings associated with vertical mergers and instead have concentrated on one legal issue: foreclosure.

V   CONGLOMERATE MERGERS

When the courts' interpretation became strict with regard to horizontal and vertical mergers, there was an incentive for firms to avoid antitrust problems by engaging in conglomerate mergers. Generally, this strategy was successful because conglomerate mergers have been treated much more cautiously in the courts than either horizontal or vertical mergers. The government has based its relatively few attacks primarily on two issues: the elimination of potential competition and the possibility of reciprocal buying arrangements. Each of these issues is considered separately.

Potential Competition Cases

United States v. Penn-Olin Chemical Co. 378 U.S. 158 (1964)   The first potential competition case to reach the Supreme Court was not a merger case, but a joint-venture case. In a joint venture, two companies combine to form a third company for the explicit purpose of producing and marketing one product.

In 1960, Pennsalt Chemical and Olin Mathieson combined to form a new company, Penn-Olin, to produce and market sodium chlorate in the Southeastern United States. Sodium chlorate (a chemical used primarily to bleach wood pulp and brighten paper) was produced in a highly concentrated market. Between 1957 and 1961 there were only three firms producing sodium chlorate, Hooker Chemical, American Potash, and Pennsalt. Pennsalt controlled 57.8 percent of the sodium chlorate market west of the Rockies and had entered the Southeastern market on a limited basis in 1957. Prior to 1961, Pennsalt's sodium chlorate was marketed in the Southeast by Olin through an agreement reached in December 1957. In the Southeast, Hooker and American Potash controlled over a 90 percent market share.

On February 11, 1960, Penn-Olin was formed. The new company began producing at Calvert City, Kentucky, in 1961. The government contended that the joint venture eliminated the possibility that *either* both companies would have entered independently *or* that one company would have entered while the other would have remained a potential entrant. The district court found no significant probability that *both would have entered de novo,* and it dismissed the complaint. By 5–4, the Supreme Court remanded the case to the district court for a more thorough investigation of the potential competition argument.

Justice Clark spoke for the majority:

> As early as 1951 Pennsalt had considered building a plant at Calvert
> City and starting in 1955 it initiated several cost studies for a sodium

chlorate plant in the southeast. . . . However, in December 1957 the management decided that the estimated rate of return was unattractive and considered it "unlikely" that Pennsalt would go it alone. It was suggested that Olin would be a "logical partner" in a joint venture and might in the interim be interested in distributing in the East. . . .

During the same period — beginning slightly earlier — Olin began investigating the possibility of entering the sodium chlorate industry. . . . Olin's engineering supervisor concluded that entry into sodium chlorate production was "an attractive venture" since it "represents a logical expansion of the product line of the Industrial Chemicals Division.". . .

Overall, the same considerations apply to joint ventures as to mergers, for in each instance we are but expounding a national policy enunciated by the Congress to preserve and premote a free competitive economy. . . .

[T]he [District] Court found it "impossible to conclude that as a matter of reasonable probability *both* Pennsalt and Olin would have built plants in the southeast if Penn-Olin had not been created." The court made no decision concerning the probability that one would have built "while the other continued to ponder.". . .

We believe that the court erred in this regard. Certainly the sole test would not be the probability that *both* companies would have entered the market. Nor would the consideration be limited to the probability that one entered alone. There still remained for consideration the fact that Penn-Olin elminated the potential competition of the corporation that might have remained at the edge of the market, continually threatening to enter. . . . The existence of an aggressive, well equipped and well financed corporation engaged in the same or related lines of commerce waiting anxiously to enter an oligopolistic market would be a substantial incentive to competition which cannot be underestimated.

Upon remand, the district court concluded that entry by just one of the firms was highly improbable, and it once again ruled in favor of Penn-Olin. The government appealed, and in 1967 a divided Supreme Court affirmed the district court's decision by a 4–4 vote. The district court's reasoning seems questionable since the market for sodium chlorate in the Southeast was expanding very rapidly and other companies had entered the market while the case was being litigated. In any event, the *Penn-Olin* case established potential competition as a legitimate basis for attacking conglomerate mergers. A few years later, the government claimed its first victory.

***Federal Trade Commission v. Procter & Gamble Co.* 386 U.S. 568 (1967)** In 1957, Procter & Gamble, the nation's leading producer of soaps and detergents, acquired Clorox, the nation's leading producer of liquid bleach. Both firms held dominant positions in their respective markets. Procter & Gamble held a 54.4 percent share of the detergent market, and Clorox held a 48.8 percent share of the liquid bleach market. The four-firm concentration ratio was over 80 percent in *both* markets; therefore, the merger involved the two leading firms in two highly concentrated and complementary markets.

The government complaint charged three major negative effects of the merger. First, it eliminated Procter & Gamble as a potential competitor in the liquid bleach market. Second, it further entrenched Clorox as the industry leader because Procter & Gamble, as the nation's leading advertiser, would greatly increase the advertising capability of Clorox. Finally, the FTC argued that smaller competitors would be much more hesitant to compete aggressively against large, diversified Procter & Gamble.

By a 7–0 vote, the Supreme Court ordered the merger dissolved. Justice Douglas wrote as follows:

> The interjection of Procter into the market considerably changed the [competitive] situation. There is every reason to assume that the smaller firms would become more cautious in competing due to their fear of retaliation by Procter. It is probable that Procter would become the price leader and that oligopoly would become more rigid. . . .
>
> The acquisition may also have the tendency of raising the barriers to new entry. The major competitive weapon in the successful marketing of bleach is advertising. Clorox was limited in this area by its relatively small budget and its inability to obtain substantial discounts. By contrast, Procter's budget was much larger and, although it would not devote its entire budget to advertising Clorox, it could divert a large portion to meet the short-term threat of a new entrant. . . . Thus, a new entrant would be much more reluctant to face the giant Procter than it would have been to face the smaller Clorox. . . .
>
> The evidence . . . clearly shows that Procter was the most likely entrant. Procter had recently launched a new abrasive cleaner in an industry similar to the liquid bleach industry, and had wrested leadership from a brand [Lestoil] that had enjoyed even a larger market share than had Clorox. Procter was engaged in a vigorous program of diversifying into product lines closely related to its basic products. Liquid bleach was a natural avenue of diversification since it is complementary to Procter's products, is sold to the same customers through the same channels, and is advertised and merchandised in the same manner. . . .

One interesting sidelight to this case was Clorox's behavior after being separated from Procter & Gamble. Clorox was spun off as an independent firm and immediately began diversifying into new products through merger. By 1974 Clorox produced liquid drain openers, oven cleaners, mushrooms, salad dressings, soft drink concentrates, packaging products, food preparation equipment for fast food chains, charcoal briquets, skiing equipment, and wet suits for divers! After a decade under Procter & Gamble's control, Clorox's management certainly must have believed that there were some advantages associated with diversification.

There may have been some real economies in advertising associated with the Procter & Gamble–Clorox merger. The potential real-cost savings however, were probably small, and there were probably few potential economic benefits associated with the merger. Furthermore, the merger could not be defended as being procompetitive since Procter & Gamble was acquiring a dominant firm. If Procter & Gamble had acquired a small bleach producer and then competed aggressively with Clorox, such a merger might have significantly increased the level of effective competition. A few years later, the FTC addressed this type of toehold merger in the *Bendix* case.

***In the Matter of the Bendix Corporation* 77 F.T.C. 731 (1970)**   In 1967 Bendix, a large diversified firm specializing in the aerospace, automotive, automation, and scientific industries, acquired Fram, a leading producer of filters, including automotive, aerospace, and water filters. The complaint revolved around the automobile filter market, which was highly concentrated, with General Motors controlling 32.4 percent, Purolator 21.7 percent, and Fram 17.2 percent. Bendix held a very small 0.35 percent market share and decided that it wanted to expand into the market on a much larger scale. After some deliberation, Bendix decided it would expand only through merger, not through internal expansion.

The FTC staff argued that the Bendix-Fram merger eliminated potential competition. The full commission agreed, but in the process handed down an important ruling, which stated that the FTC would be inclined to permit toehold mergers between a large potential competitor and a small, nondominant firm.

Commissioner Elman wrote the decision:

> Bendix was already a minor participant in the automobile filter industry. . . .
>
> As the hearing examiner found:
>
>> At various times during the period from 1961 to 1966 Bendix gave consideration to acquiring an interest in one of several filter manufacturers. In 1961 it acquired a small stock interest in Wix Corporation, which was then manufacturing certain types of air filters for it. . . . Consideration was given at various times to the acquisition of Walker Manufacturing Company, Donaldson Company, Inc., Hastings Manufacturing Company, and Purolator Products, Inc. . . . Meetings were held with Purolator in March 1966 to consider the possibility of a merger or acquisition, but nothing came of the effort.

In short, its management was convinced that Bendix should make a substantial entry into the passenger car filter aftermarket, in an attempt to salvage the current Bendix investment in filters, and to bring greater profits and stability to the corporation as a whole. . . .

Various forms of merger entry other than through acquisition of a leading company — for example, a "toehold" acquisition of a small company capable of expansion into a substantial competitive force — may be as economically desirable and beneficial to competition as internal expansion into a relevant market, and must be considered in addressing the potential competition of the acquiring firm which had been eliminated as a result of the challenged merger. . . .

Indeed, where entry into some markets by internal expansion is foreclosed and/or restricted, entry by toehold acquisition may be the most feasible route for developing new competition. Furthermore, in an age of mergers and acquisitions, the threat of a toehold merger by a powerful firm may often serve as a much greater incentive to competitive performance in the affected market than does that prospect of more costly and slower internal, *de novo* expansion. . . .

[T]he record indicates that few, if any, firms were likely to be as imminent or as substantial potential entrants as Bendix. Thus, the disappearance of Bendix from the market's edge was particularly significant. . . .

In conclusion, while we do not find nor believe that Bendix was the only potential entrant, . . . Bendix was among the most likely of a limited number of possible entrants capable of making a significant entry by acquisition and expansion of a smaller firm. Consequently, the elimination of that potential entrant and competitor is even more significant for its effect upon competition. . . .

In 1971, the Sixth Circuit Court of Appeals overturned the commission's ruling, not on substance, but on a legal technicality [see 450 F.2d 534 (1971)]. The court of appeals ruled that since the FTC had failed to inform Bendix of its intention to use the toehold theory in its case, Bendix had not been given the opportunity to prepare an adequate defense. The court of appeals, however, did not rule on the legitimacy of the toehold theory.

United States v. Falstaff Brewing Corporation 410 U.S. 526 (1973) In 1965 the Falstaff Brewing Company acquired the Narrangansett Brewing Company. Falstaff was the nation's fourth-largest producer of beer with a 5.4 percent national market share, but Falstaff did not compete in the Northeast; therefore, this was a geographic extension merger. Furthermore, Narragasett was the largest producer in the New England market, with a 20 percent share; therefore, Narragansett was not a toehold acquisition.

The Justice Department filed a complaint, which the district court dismissed on the grounds that the New England beer market was highly competitive. District Judge Day's opinion certainly was not an outstanding example of American jurisprudence. Most district court decisions in major antitrust cases provide a detailed analysis of the facts and economic conditions in the industry, as well as an analysis of legal precedents. Judge Day's entire decision, however, covered only *two* pages! Furthermore, the judge virtually ignored the key economic issue in the case, potential competition.

The Supreme Court, handicapped by the lack of a significant district court opinion, remanded the case for reconsideration. Justice White delivered the opinion:

> For several years Falstaff publicly expressed its desire for national distribution and after making several efforts in the early 1960's to enter the Northeast by acquisition, agreed to acquire Narragansett in 1965. . . .
>
> [T]he District Court found that the geographic market was highly competitive; that Falstaff was desirous of becoming a national brewer by entering the Northeast; that its management was committed against *de novo* entry; and that competition had not diminished since the acquisition. . . .
>
> The District Court erred as a matter of law. The error lay in the assumption that because Falstaff, as a matter of fact, would never have entered the market *de novo,* it could in no sense be considered a potential competitor. . . .
>
> The specific question with respect to this phase of the case is not what Falstaff's internal company decisions were but whether, given its financial capabilities and conditions in the New England market, it would be reasonable to consider it a potential entrant into that market. Surely, it could not be said on this record that Falstaff's general interest in the New England market was unknown and if it would appear to rational beer merchants in New England that Falstaff might well build a new brewery to supply the northeastern market then its entry by merger becomes suspect under section 7. The District Court should therefore have appraised the economic facts about Falstaff and the New England market in order to determine whether in any realistic sense Falstaff could be said to be a potential competitor on the fringe of the market with likely influence on existing competition. . . .
>
> We leave for another day the question of the applicability of section 7 to a merger that will leave competition in the marketplace exactly as it was, neither hurt not helped, and that is challengeable under section 7 only on grounds that the company could, but did not, enter *de novo* or through "toe-hold" acquisition and that there is less competition than there would have been had entry been in such a manner.

Not surprisingly, upon remand Judge Day found that Falstaff was not *perceived* as a potential entrant and let the merger stand. Actually, Falstaff probably would have been better off had the merger been dissolved. Narragansett was an old, inefficient firm. After the merger, Falstaff's position in New England deteriorated relative to its major competitors, Anheuser-Busch and Schlitz, both of which built new plants in the area rather than acquiring old, run-down breweries such as Narragansett.

In the *Falstaff* decision the district court seemed to imply that the government had to prove that a firm was *actually perceived* as a potential entrant by competitors. This is a rather heavy legal burden, that the Supreme Court imposed on the government the following year in the *Marine Bancorporation* case.

United States v. Marine Bancorporation, Inc. **418 U.S. 602 (1974)** The *Marine Bancorporation* case involved a geographic extention merger by one of Washington State's largest banks. In February 1971 the National Bank of Commerce (NBC), which was a wholly owned subsidiary of Marine Bancorporation, acquired the Washington Trust Bank (WTB). The two banks operated on opposite sides of Washington, almost 300 miles apart. NBC, located in Seattle, was the state's second-largest bank; when combined with Seattle-First National Bank, the state's largest bank, the two top banks controlled 51.3 percent of Washington's total deposits. WTB was the third-largest bank in the Spokane area, with an 18.6 percent market share. The top three banks in Spokane held a 92.3 percent market share.

Entry and expansion in the banking industry was tightly regulated in Washington. Some of the regulations made little economic sense, except to protect banks from competition. Banks were forbidden from operating or establishing new branches outside of the city or town in which they operated, *except* by merger with another bank in another town. Furthermore, once a bank acquired another bank's assets, it was prohibited from branching. Washington also forbad a new bank, for a period of ten years after its establishment, from merging with any company.

The state controller examined the NBC-WTB merger and decided to permit it. The Justice Department, however, appealed the controller's decision. By 5–3, the Supreme Court agreed to permit the merger. The major issue was potential competition. Justice Powell stated the majority opinion as follows:

> It is undisputed that under state law NBC cannot establish *de novo* branches in Spokane. . . . The Government contends that NBC has two distinct alternatives for acquisition of banks smaller than WTB. . . .

First, the Government contends that NBC could arrange for the formation of a new bank (a concept known as "sponsorship"), insure that the stock for such a new bank is placed in friendly hands, and then ultimately acquire that bank. Appellees respond that this approach would violate the spirit if not the letter of state-law restrictions on bank branching. . . .

[W]e will assume, *arguendo,* that NBC conceivably could succeed in sponsoring and then acquiring a new bank in Spokane at some indefinite time in the future. It does not follow from this assumption, however, that this method of entry would be reasonably likely to produce any significant procompetitive benefits in the Spokane commercial banking market. To the contrary, it appears likely that such a method of entry would not significantly affect that market.

State law would not allow NBC to branch from a sponsored bank after it was acquired. NBC's entry into Spokane therefore would be frozen at the level of its initial acquisition. Thus, if NBC were to enter Spokane by sponsoring and acquiring a small bank, it would be trapped into a position of operating a single branch office in a large metropolitan area with no reasonable likelihood of developing a significant share of that market. . . .

As a second alternative method of entry, the Government proposed that NBC could enter by a foothold acquisition of one of two small, state-chartered commercial banks that operate in the Spokane metropolitan area. . . .

Once NBC acquired either of these banks, it could not branch from the acquired bank. This limitation strongly suggested that NBC would not develop into a significant participant in the Spokane market, a prospect that finds support in the record. . . .

Rational commercial bankers in Spokane, it must be assumed, are aware of the regulatory barriers that render NBC an unlikely or an insignificant potential entrant except by merger with WBT. In light of those barriers, it is improbable that NBC exerts any meaningful procompetitive influence over Spokane banks by "standing in the wings."

It is interesting to note that the *Marine Bancorporation* decision was handed down at the same time as the *General Dynamics–United Electric* decision. The two decisions point clearly toward a more lenient attitude toward mergers by a more conservative Supreme Court during the 1970s. The FTC also became more cautious in its potential competition decisions during the 1970s, as suggested by the commission's ruling in the *Budd* case.

In the Matter of the Budd Company 86 F.T.C. 518 (1975)   In 1968, the Budd Company acquired the Gindy Manufacturing Corporation (Gindy). Budd was the nation's 250th-largest company and the leading independent supplier of body parts to the automobile industry. Budd manufactured automotive bodies, wheels, rims, hubs, drums, brakes, and railroad and mass transit cars. Gindy manufactured van trailers, containers, and container chassis. Van trailers are the large box-type trailers that are attached to truck chassis. Containers refer to the closed boxed structures that are detachable from truck chassis and can be easily transferred from a truck to a train and then back to a truck.

The administrative law judge ruled that the merger violated section 7. The full commission, however, permitted the merger by a 3–2 vote.

Commissioner Engman wrote the majority decision:

> On the question of whether Budd was a perceived potential entrant, we disagree with the [administrative law judge]. A large number of industry witnesses testified in this proceeding when asked whether they had viewed Budd as a potential entrant before the Gindy acquisition, the response was uniformly "no.". . .
>
> Nor is there any reason to believe that had the Gindy acquisition not taken place Budd's continued presence outside the market would have influenced industry prices. . . . No witness testified that their prices or practices were affected by these firms. The only conclusion that can be reasonably drawn from the evidence is that there is no basis upon which to believe that *Budd's* continued presence at the edge of the market would have any greater effect on market performance. . . .
>
> In the overall trailer market Gindy's share fluctuated between 4.9 percent and 6.5 percent during the three years prior to the merger. In the van trailer market, where Gindy's share was highest, it never rose appreciably above 7–8 percent as compared to Fruehauf's [the industry leader], 27 percent and Trailmobile's 17 percent. . . . In the container-and-chassis market, Gindy ranked number 6 with only 3.8 percent of the market. . . .
>
> We believe it to be desirable to observe a general rule in potential competition cases that firms possessing no more than 10 percent in a target market . . . should ordinarily be presumed to be toehold or foothold firms. This presumption by no means is conclusive and the inference of lack of anticompetitive effects flowing from the acquisition of such a firm can be rebutted in particular cases. . . .
>
> Subsequent to the acquisition, Budd established a financial corporation to help finance the van trailers sold by Gindy as well as sales by other Budd divisions. By virtue of this finance subsidiary Gindy was able to finance trailer sales on more competitive terms. . . .
>
> In addition, Budd enlarged Gindy's Eagle plant and increased its capacity by 40 percent at a cost to Budd of $1.75 million. [Thus the merger made Gindy a more effective competitor.]. . .
>
> In view of our finding that the acquisition did not lessen competition, the initial decision will be vacated and the complaint dismissed. . . .

Under the present Supreme Court interpretation, the government's burden of proof in potential competition cases is very difficult to sustain. First, the market must be highly concentrated with high entry barriers. Second, the acquiring firm must be an *actual perceived* potential entrant. This latter requirement is particularly difficult to prove.

Despite the current Court attitude, since 1975 there have been occasional government actions based on the potential competition doctrine. In 1977 the FTC complained when BIC Pen attempted to acquire Philip Morris's American Safety Razor Division. The commission argued that BIC was both an actual and a potential competitor. [See *In the Matter of BIC Pen Corporation* 89 F.T.C. 139 (1977).] As a result of the complaint, BIC decided to withdraw its offer for American Safety Razor, and today the two companies compete against each other. The potential competition doctrine, therefore, can still have an occasional impact.

Reciprocal Buying Cases

Federal Trade Commission v. Consolidated Foods Corporation **380 U.S. 592 (1964)**   The *Consolidated Foods* case is the classic reciprocal buying case. In 1951 Consolidated Foods acquired Gentry. Consolidated Foods was a food processor, wholesaler, and retailer. Gentry produced dehydrated onions and garlic in a highly concentrated market. In 1951 Basic Vegetable was the industry leader with a 58 percent share, and Gentry controlled 32 percent.

The FTC complained that Consolidated Foods had attempted to expand Gentry's market share by suggesting to its suppliers that they purchase their requirements of dehydrated onions and garlic from Gentry. By 1958 Gentry had succeeded in raising its market share to only 35 percent, hardly evidence of an overwhelmingly successful campaign. In a rare unanimous decision, however, the Supreme Court sided with the FTC.

Justice Douglas wrote

> We hold at the outset, that the "reciprocity" made possible by such an acquisition is one of the [large number] of anticompetitive practices at which the antitrust laws are aimed. . . .
>
> After the acquisition Consolidated (though later disclaiming adherence to any policy of reciprocity) did undertake to assist Gentry in selling. An official of Consolidated wrote as follows to its distributing divisions:
>
>> . . . Everyone believes in reciprocity providing all things are equal.
>> "Attached is a list of prospects for our Gentry products. We would like to have you indicate on the list whether or not you are purchasing any supplies from them."

Food processors who sold to Consolidated stated they would give their onion and garlic business to Gentry for reciprocity reasons if it could meet the price and quality of its competitors' products. . . .

Some suppliers responded and gave reciprocal orders. Some who first gave generous orders later reduced them or abandoned the practice. . . .

The Commission found that Basic's product was superior to Gentry's — as Gentry's president freely and repeatedly admitted. Yet Gentry, in a rapidly expanding market, was able to increase its share of onion sales by 7% and to hold its losses in garlic to a 12% decrease. . . .

The evidence is in our view plainly substantial. Reciprocity was tried over and again and it sometimes worked.

Gentry's behavior was so overtly an attempt to influence its suppliers that the Court declared the merger illegal. Given the admission of Gentry's President that Gentry's product was inferior, it is questionable whether Consolidated Food's behavior had much of an impact on the market. The *Gentry* case suggests that overt attempts to influence purchasers buying habits may be enough to condemn a merger.

***United States v. International Telephone and Telegraph Corporation* 324 F. Supp. 19 (1970)**   It is difficult to decide where this case fits in an analysis of merger policy. The case involved ITT's acquisition of Grinnell, but the Justice Department simultaneously had two other suits pending against ITT for its acquisitions of Hartford Insurance and Canteen Corporation. The *ITT-Grinnell* case involved a charge of reciprocal buying; therefore, it is included here. The case also involved many other charges, however, including a charge that large conglomerate mergers are likely to have general anticompetitive effects and should be prohibited.

On December 31, 1969, ITT acquired Grinnell. ITT was one of the nation's leading conglomerate firms; it controlled over 200 subsidiaries and ranked as the nation's ninth-largest industrial corporation. The government contended that the merger significantly reduced competition in the automatic sprinkler devices and systems market. The complaint charged eight specific anticompetitive effects, but the district court ruled that Grinnell did not have sufficient market power in *any* market to warrant a conviction. This is somewhat surprising since Grinnell (with a 23 percent share) was the largest of only fourteen manufacturers of automatic sprinkler devices. Furthermore, Grinnell held a 44.3 percent share in one submarket accepted by the district court, the state of Utah.

Chief Judge Timbers delivered the district court opinion:

The Court having concluded, upon the entire record, that the evidence does not support the government's claim that Grinnell is the dominant competitor in any of the relevant markets, that should end the case. A bolder Court would enter judgment for defendant and proceed no further. . . .

Affiliation with Hartford [Insurance Company]

A large portion of the evidence upon this issue focused upon the government's contention that Grinnell will gain a competitive advantage from its affiliation with Hartford by receiving leads for sprinkler business from Hartford and from Hartford agents. . . .

Sprinkler contracts are awarded for the most part on the basis of competitive bids. Recommendations of an insurance company or its agents accordingly have little or no effect. . . .

[T]he evidence overwhelmingly demonstrates that Grinnell would stand to lose far more than it could gain from any exploitation of the Hartford affiliation.

The evidence on this is concise but convincing. While Hartford is a large insurance company, its total share of the domestic fire insurance market is only 4.4% and its total share of the sprinklered risk market is approximately 2.4%. . . . The evidence shows that too close an alliance between Hartford and Grinnell would cause other insurance interests to be less friendly with Grinnell; testimony by witnesses called by both sides established beyond any question that the result of any such relationship would be to deter non-Hartford agents from recommending Grinnell sprinklers, although under other circumstances they might have made such a recommendation. . . .

Access to ITT's Financial Resources and Advertising

The evidence is uncontroverted that Grinnell already is in a position to offer credit and leasing arrangements to sprinkler customers without financing assistance from ITT and is capable itself of expanding such financing as broadly as is desirable commercially. . . .

With respect to advertising, the Court finds that it simply is not a significant factor in the sprinkler industry. . . .

Vertical Foreclosure

The short and conclusive answer to the government's vertical foreclosure claim is that ITT's purchases of sprinklers represent a *de minimis* part of the market. While the government points out that 55 sprinkler systems were installed in ITT facilities during the past five years and that ITT contemplates installing approximately 22 new sprinkler systems during the next year, . . .[this] represents less that 1/10 of 1% of the total prospective sprinkler system business for those years. . . .

Reciprocal Dealing

Most sprinkler work, for all classes of customers, is awarded on a competitive bidding basis, thus minimizing reciprocity and reciprocity effect potential. . . .

The evidence upon which the government relies to show reciprocity in the sprinkler industry relates for the most part to a period of time more than five years ago and involves alleged reciprocity between Grinnell and certain steel companies. As to the latter, five of the companies which allegedly had reciprocity interest in Grinnell . . . have entered into antireciprocity consent decrees designed to assure against future reciprocity or reciprocity effect in their business conduct. Moreover, as indicated below, the consensus of those in the best position to know is that the focus upon the illegality of reciprocity practices in recent years has brought about a substantial decline in the incidence of such practices — a trend which the record in the instant case indicates is more likely to continue than to abate. . . .

Claim of Economic Concentration

At the preliminary injunction hearing in this case the government raised, and the Court ruled upon, a claim of economic concentration. . . . At the trial on the merits the government . . . again raised the same issue but with a different and somewhat ingenious twist.

The new twist to the government's economic concentration claim is that in the wake of a "trend among large diversified industrial firms to acquire other large corporations," it can be established that "anticompetitive consequences will appear in numerous though *undesignated individual 'lines of commerce'.*"

The Court's short answer to this claim . . . is that the legislative history, the statute itself and the controlling decisional law all make it clear beyond a . . . doubt that in a Section 7 case the alleged anticompetitive effects of a merger must be examined in the context of *specified product and geographic markets.* . . .

The defendant is entitled to judgment dismissing the complaint on the merits.

The *ITT* case was the last major conglomerate merger case filed by the Justice Department. Unfortunately, it was never appealed to a higher court. Attorney General Mitchell and President Nixon were both strongly against an appeal. Just how strongly the president felt is indicated by the following statement excerpted from the famous White House tapes. On April 19, 1971, President Nixon told Deputy Attorney General Kleindienst, "The IT&T thing — stay the hell out of it. Is that clear? . . . Your — my order is to drop the God damn thing. Is that clear?" [8].

Given the president's sentiments, it is not surprising that the Justice Department withdrew all three pending cases in exchange for a consent decree. Under the decree, ITT agreed to divest itself of Grinnell's fire protection division and Canteen Corporation. It is unfortunate that the Supreme Court never had an opportunity to rule on the major issues involved in these cases.

One final case, although difficult to categorize, deserves mention. It contains some elements of a horizontal merger case and some elements of a conglomerate merger case.

United States v. Continental Can Company 378 U.S. 441 (1964)   In 1956 Continental Can acquired Hazel-Atlas Glass. At the time, Continental Can ranked as the nation's second-largest producer of metal containers with a 33 percent market share. Hazel-Atlas ranked as the third-largest producer of glass containers with a 9.6 percent market share, but its market share had been declining. At first, this merger appears to be a typical market extension conglomerate merger. The Supreme Court, however, essentially turned it into a horizontal merger by combining the metal container and glass container markets into one market for metal and glass containers.

Justice White delivered the 7–2 majority opinion:

> It is quite true that glass and metal containers have different characteristics which may disqualify one or the other, at least in their present form, from this or that particular use[.]. . . These are relevant and important considerations but they are not sufficient to obscure the competitive relationships which this record so compellingly reveals. . . .
>
> Baby food was at one time packed entirely in metal cans. Hazel-Atlas played a significant role in inducing the shift to glass as the dominant container by designing "what has become the typical baby food jar.". . .
>
> In the soft drink business, a field which has been, and is, predominantly glass territory, the court recognized that the metal can industry had "[a]fter considerable initial difficulty . . . developed a can strong enough to resist the pressures generated by carbonated beverages" and "made strenuous efforts to promote the use of metal cans for carbonated beverages as against glass bottles.". . .
>
> The District Court found that "[a]lthough at one time almost all packaged beer was sold in bottles, in a relatively short period the beer can made great headway and may well have become the dominant beer container.". . .
>
> In light of this record and these findings, we think the District Court employed an unduly narrow construction of the "competition" protected by section 7 and of "reasonable interchangeability of use of the cross-elasticity of demand" in judging the facts in this case. . . .
>
> Continental's major position in the relevant product market — the combined metal and glass container industry — prior to the merger is undeniable. . . . Of the six largest firms in the product market, it ranked second. . . . In terms of total containers shipped, Hazel-Atlas ranked sixth in the relevant line of commerce, its almost 2 billion containers being 3.1% of the product market total. . . .
>
> The product market embracing the combined metal and glass container industries was dominated by six firms having a total of 70.1% of the

business. . . . By the acquisition of Hazel-Atlas stock Continental not only increased its own share more than 14% from 21.9% to 25%, but also reduced from five to four the most significant competitors who might have threatened its dominant position. . . . The case falls squarely within the principle that where there has been a "history of tendency toward concentration in the industry" tendencies toward further concentration "are to be curbed in their incipiency.". . .

As usual in the 1960s, Justice Harlan delivered the dissent:

> The bizarre result of the Court's approach is that market percentages of a nonexistent market enable the Court to dispense with "elaborate proof of market structure, market behavior and probable anticompetitive effects.". . .
>
> The truth is that "glass and metal containers" form a distinct line of commerce only in the mind of this Court. . . .
>
> The Court's spurious market-share analysis should not obscure the fact that the Court is, in effect, laying down a "*per se*" rule that mergers between two large companies in related industries are presumptively unlawful under section 7. . . .
>
> Hereafter, however slight (or even nonexistent) the competitive impact of a merger on any actual market, businessmen must rest uneasy lest the Court create some "market," in which the merger presumptively dampens competition, out of bits and pieces of real ones.

Justice Harlan's fears never came to fruition. The current Supreme Court certainly does not follow a policy that suggests a *per se* ban on any merger involving two large companies. In fact, it is almost impossible to imagine the *Continental Can* case being decided in a similar manner by the current Supreme Court.

One of the ironies of the *Continental Can* case was the remedy adopted. Hazel-Atlas was purchased by Brockway Glass, a medium-sized glass container producer. As a result, the glass container industry became more concentrated. In essence, the Supreme Court dissolved a conglomerate merger, but the government permitted a horizontal merger to take its place. The permitted merger may well have been more anticompetitive than the prohibited merger.

VI   MERGER GUIDELINES AND THE HART-SCOTT-RODINO ACT

Having analyzed the courts' position with regard to mergers, it is useful to analyze the criteria used by the government to decide which mergers to challenge. In 1968 the Justice Department issued its first set of merger guidelines. The guidelines were meant to reduce the uncertainty regarding the legality or illegality of a particular merger. Especially with regard to *horizontal mergers,* the 1968 guidelines tended to be quite strict. In an industry with a four-firm concentration ratio of over 75 percent, the guidelines suggested that the antitrust authorities would challenge any of the mergers in Table 4–1.

With regard to *vertical mergers,* the 1968 guidelines suggested that a challenge would be forthcoming if the buyer of an input made 6 percent of the total purchases of the input *and* the supplier of the input made 10 percent of total input sales, or if the supplier of the input made 20 percent of total input sales, or if the buyer of the input controlled 10 percent of its market, or if there was a significant *trend* toward vertical integration in the industry.

With regard to *conglomerate mergers,* the 1968 guidelines suggested that a merger would be challenged if the merger eliminated a main potential entrant, or the merger created a substantial possibility of reciprocal buying arrangements, or the merger created increased leverage for the acquired firm, such as an increased advertising advantage, or *any* of the largest 200 firms tried to acquire any other significant firm.

In keeping with the main line of economic thinking during the 1960s and the fairly tough policy toward mergers of the Warren court, the 1968 guidelines were quite strict. By the time President Reagan took office in 1980, however, both economic thinking and the Supreme Court's position had changed. Both economists and the Court had become more accepting of the economic advantages associated with many mergers and less suspicious of the potential negative impacts of mergers, particularly vertical and conglomerate mergers. Partially as a result of this new attitude and partially as a result of a conservative presidential administration, Assistant Attorney General William Baxter presided over the rewriting of the merger guidelines in 1982.

The new guidelines were released in June 1982 and revised slightly in 1984. The new guidelines represented a major policy change. With regard to *horizontal mergers,* the new guidelines were significantly more lenient. Instead of basing the standard on traditional concentra-

Table 4–1

Acquiring Firm's Market Share	Acquired Firm's Market Share
4 percent	4 percent
10 percent	2 percent
15 percent	1 percent

tion ratio measures, the 1982 guidelines were based on a different and superior measure of market power, the *Herfindahl-Hirshman index* (HHI). The Herfindahl-Hirshman index is defined as follows:

$$HHI = \sum_{i=1}^{n} S_i^2$$

where S_i is the market share of the ith firm in the industry and n is the total number of firms in the industry. The HHI is the sum of the squares of the market shares of *all* firms in an industry. The HHI increases if *either* concentration increases *or* the degree of market share inequality increases; therefore, the HHI generally is considered a better measure of market power than the simple four-firm concentration ratio.

To better understand the advantage of the HHI over the four-firm concentration ratio, consider two hypothetical industries. In industry 1, each of five firms has a market share of 20 percent; therefore, the four-firm concentration ratio is 80 percent. In industry 1, the HHI = 400 + 400 + 400 + 400 + 400 = 2,000. In industry 2, the respective rank and market share of each firm is first, 50 percent; second, 20 percent; and third through eighth, 5 percent each. The four-firm concentration ratio in industry 2 is also 80 percent, but the HHI = 2,500 + 400 + 25 + 25 + 25 + 25 + 25 + 25 = 3,050. The HHI identifies a difference in market structure between industry 1 and industry 2 that the four-firm concentration ratio fails to identify. Furthermore, as can be seen in this illustration, the HHI is particularly sensitive to large market shares held by the top firm or firms.

The 1982 *horizontal merger* guidelines suggest that the Justice Department will not challenge a merger if the postmerger industry HHI will be less than 1,000. If the postmerger HHI falls between 1,000 and 1,800, mergers causing an increase in the HHI of less than 100 are unlikely to be challenged, but mergers causing an increase in the HHI of more than 100 are likely to be challenged *subject to* an analysis of the effects of the merger on entry barriers, the probability of collusion, and other competitive conditions. If a merger results in a postmerger HHI of over 1,800 and causes an increase in the HHI of 100, it is very likely to be challenged. If a merger results in a postmerger HHI of over 1,800 and causes an increase in the HHI of between 50 and 100, it is likely to be challenged *subject to* a consideration of its competitive effects. Finally, if a merger results in a postmerger HHI of over 1,800 and causes an increase in the HHI of less than 50, it is unlikely to be challenged.

These new guidelines are significantly more lenient than the 1968 guidelines. Under the old guidelines, the Von's Grocery–Shopping Bag merger would have been a borderline case for challenge. Under the new guidelines, it would not even come close to being challenged.

With regard to *vertical mergers,* the 1982 guidelines eliminate all mention of specific market-share limitations. Instead, the new guidelines list three requirements for *consideration* of a challenge to a vertical merger. First, the merger must make it unlikely that any entrant would enter one market (the primary market) without entering the other market (the secondary market) involved in the merger. Second, the merger must make entry into the *primary market* much less likely. Third, entry barriers and other characteristics of *noncompetitive* performance must exist in the *primary market*. The combined effect of these requirements is to make a challenge to *any* vertical merger extremely unlikely. Under these guidelines, the Brown Shoe–Kinney Shoe merger and the Du Pont–General Motors merger would almost certainly have been permitted.

As for *conglomerate mergers,* the 1982 guidelines mention only one reason for challenging a conglomerate merger — the elimination of potential competition. With regard to potential competition challenges, the new guidelines create a tough standard for challenging a merger. First, the market must be highly concentrated with an HHI of over 1,800. This requirement alone puts the overwhelming majority of conglomerate mergers beyond the reach of the guidelines. Second, entry into the market must be difficult. Third, there must be only a few other potential entrants into the market. Fourth, the market share of the acquired firm must be at least 5 percent. Under these guidelines very few conglomerate mergers will be challenged.

Compared with the 1968 guidelines, the 1982 guidelines leave relatively few mergers open for serious challenge. The guidelines clearly suggest a retreat from an aggressive antimerger policy and an advance toward a view that most mergers result in *net* economic benefits. This view of mergers as being primarily *efficiency promoting* is inconsistent with most economic evidence on the subject, but is the view of the Reagan administration and its appointed leaders at the Justice Department [9].

The new guidelines also suggest a short-run rather than a long-run perspective toward mergers. Under the previous guidelines, the Justice Department was concerned with "mergers which alter market structure in ways likely to prevent now or eventually to encourage or permit non-competitive conduct." Preventing market power in its incipiency, therefore, was an explicit goal of the 1968 guidelines. The 1982 guidelines, however, appear to be concerned only with present economic conditions and certainly are not concerned with incipiency arguments against mergers. Unfortunately, the impact that this change in merger policy will not be known for many years, and it is far too early to evaluate whether or not the new guidelines will yield net economic benefits or net economic costs.

In 1984 the Justice Department revised the 1982 guidelines. The revision was relatively minor, except for one major change. The 1982 guidelines stated that the department generally would not consider the potential efficiency gains before deciding whether or not to challenge a particular merger. The 1984 guidelines, however, explicitly recognize efficiency gains as a relevant factor in the department's decision-making process. The 1984 guidelines make it clear, however, that efficiencies are not to be considered an *absolute defense,* but merely one factor to be considered before a final decision is reached on a particular merger. This explicit policy change actually has had very little effect since under the Reagan administration the Justice Department was already considering efficiencies as a factor before proceeding against a merger.

Before concluding our discussion of merger policy, it is important to note one major change in antitrust enforcement procedure that went into effect with the passage of the *Hart-Scott-Rodino Act* (also known as the Antitrust Improvements Act) in 1976. The Hart-Scott-Rodino Act amended section 7 of the Clayton Act to *require* advance notification to the Justice Department and the FTC of any major merger. Any merger where one firm has sales or assets of at least $100 million and the other firm has sales or assets of at least $10 million must be reported to the government at least thirty days in advance. The act requires the provision of extensive data concerning the proposed merger and gives the government time to report to the potential merger partners whether or not a challenge will be forthcoming.

There are several major benefits associated with the Hart-Scott-Rodino Act. First, it gives the government a chance to seek an injunction halting a proposed merger before it is consummated. The merging partners, therefore, are prevented from quickly consolidating their activities and thereby making it difficult to dissolve the merger at a later date. Second, from the merging firms' point of view, it eliminates much of the uncertainty surrounding a proposed merger. Prior to the act, it was often difficult to predict whether or not a particular merger would be challenged. Under the Hart-Scott-Rodino Act, firms know prior to the completion of a merger whether it will be challenged. Finally, the act enables the government to seek modifications of a proposed merger. The government has initially objected to some mergers under the act, but later accepted these mergers subject to the acquiring firm's agreement to divest itself of a portion of its new acquisition. The Standard Oil of California–Gulf merger was approved only after Standard Oil agreed to divestiture of some of Gulf's assets.

Although compliance with the Hart-Scott-Rodino Act is expensive, the act has probably resulted in improved enforcement by enabling the government to act quickly and before the fact against many proposed mergers. In fact, it is probably more than a coincidence that no major merger case has worked its way to the Supreme Court since the passage of the Hart-Scott-Rodino Act.

VII   SUMMARY

In the 1960s a liberal Supreme Court took a tough position against most mergers. That Court believed that a major objective of section 7 was the prevention of concentration in its incipiency. In the 1970s, a more conservative Supreme Court adopted a more lenient view toward mergers, especially conglomerate mergers.

Some of the basic precedents of the 1960s have never been *explicitly* overturned. Horizontal mergers are still subject to sanction if the two firms hold a significant market share, and vertical mergers can still be attacked on the basis of a relatively moderate degree of foreclosure. In the area of conglomerate mergers, the Supreme Court has yet to address some of the major issues, particularly the toehold theory that would forbid a potential competitor from acquiring a major firm but permit it to acquire a small firm.

Given the present makeup of the Supreme Court and the conservative Reagan administration, it is doubtful that the administration will press a very aggressive antimerger policy. Under the Reagan administration, the Justice Department has liberalized its merger guidelines in all areas, and so long as Reagan is president, it is safe to assume that there will be little activity in this area. This could change dramatically if the makeup of the Supreme Court changed, and/or a new administration were elected that was more sympathetic toward the antitrust laws in general and section 7 in particular.

NOTES

1. For an excellent statement of this position see R. A. Posner, *Antitrust Law: An Economic Perspective* (Chicago: University of Chicago Press, 1976), pages 196–201; see also J. J. Spengler, "Vertical Integration and Antitrust Policy," *Journal of Political Economy,* August 1950, pages 347–352.

2. W. B. Hickman, *Corporate Bond Quality and Investor Experience* (Princeton, N.J.: Princeton University Press, 1958); for a differing opinion see D. J. Smyth, W. J. Boyes, and D. E. Peseau, *Size, Growth, Profits, and Executive Compensation in the Large Corporation* (New York: Holmes and Meier, 1975), pages 60–66.

3. F. R. Edwards, "Concentration in Banking and Its Effects on Business Loan Rates," *Review of Economics and Statistics,* August 1964, pages 294–300; P. A. Meyer, "Price Discrimination, Regional Loan Rates, and the Structure of the Banking Industry," *Journal of Finance,* March 1967, pages 37–48; and D. Jacobs, *Business Loan Costs and Bank Market Structure* (New York: Columbia University Press, 1971).

4. G. A. Hay and D. Kelley, "An Empirical Survey of Price Fixing Conspiracies," *Journal of Law and Economics,* April 1974, pages 13–38; and A. G. Fraas and D. F. Greer, "Market Structure and Price Collusion: An Empirical Analysis," *Journal of Industrial Economics,* September 1977, pages 21–44.

5. F. M. Scherer, *Industrial Market Structure and Economic Performance* (Chicago: Rand-McNally, 1980), page 137.

6. D. F. Greer, *Business, Government, and Society* (New York: Macmillan, 1983), page 173.

7. Scherer, *Industrial Market Structure and Economic Performance,* page 546.

8. W. F. Mueller, "The Anti-Antitrust Movement" in John V. Craven (ed.), *Industrial Organization, Antitrust, and Public Policy* (Boston: Kluwer-Nijhoff Publishing, 1983), page 23.

9. D. C. Mueller, "The Effects of Conglomerate Mergers," *Journal of Banking and Finance,* December 1977, pages 315 – 344; D. F. Greer, *Industrial Organization and Public Policy* (New York: Macmillan, 1984), pages 135 –136; and Scherer, *Industrial Market Structure and Economic Performance,* page 137.

CHAPTER

FIVE

Horizontal Agreements

Section 1 of the Sherman Act declares

> Every contract, combination in the form of trust or otherwise, or conspiracy, in restraint of trade or commerce among the several states, or with foreign nations, is hereby declared illegal.

Explicit price-fixing agreements are the most obvious restraints of trade. In addition to direct price-fixing agreements, however, there are a number of more subtle restraints, including tacit agreements among oligopolists, trade association behavior, and ethical codes in professional organizations. Each of these restraints will be examined in this chapter.

I OVERT PRICE-FIXING AGREEMENTS

Whenever firms collude to fix prices, the objective is always the same: to increase and/or stabilize prices. Typically, a conspiracy attempts to bring prices closer to the joint profit-maximizing, or monopoly, level. In theory, all conspiracies attempt to widen the gap between price and marginal cost; therefore, they should all reduce economic efficiency. It is necessary, however, to question whether or not there are any valid justifications for price-fixing.

Several justifications have been advanced by defendant firms. First, it has been argued that price-fixing prevents cutthroat competition. This argument is particularly popular in industries characterized by high *fixed* costs relative to *variable* costs, such as the steel and railroad industries. When demand declines in these industries, marginal cost is likely to be less than average cost, because each firm operates on the downward-sloping portion of its average-cost curve. Under these conditions, a firm's demand curve may be everywhere below its average-cost curve, such as the situation depicted in Figure 5-1. In this case, no single, *nondiscriminatory* price will cover average cost, and the firm may attempt to attract new business by offering discriminatory price discounts to some purchasers. So long as price is above *marginal* cost to *all* buyers and the firm is able to maintain its high price to *all* of its *original* customers, its losses will be reduced as it attracts additional customers by cutting prices. If a firm's discriminatory price-cutting remains secret, this strategy may work, as the price cutter is able to attract new customers *away from* its competitors. Secret price cuts, however, usually become public and lead to matching cuts by other firms. If this occurs, prices may fall to very low levels as each firm matches its competitors' lower prices. If the price-cutting becomes widespread throughout the industry and leads to a downward price spiral, significant economic losses will result for all firms.

In Figure 5-1, suppose that price is initially stable at the firm's loss-minimizing price P_1 and the firm is sustaining an economic loss equal to area P_1abC_1. If cutthroat competition developed, prices might fall below P_1 on *all* sales. In fact, prices might decline to marginal cost P_2, and the firm would then sustain a much greater economic loss equal to area P_2cdC_2.

A price decline to P_2 would certainly result in economic losses and serious problems for firms in the industry, but the price decline should not be a major cause for society's concern or used as a justification for permitting price-fixing. When price equals P_2, price equals marginal cost, which is the allocatively efficient price. The profit issue is a normative issue, not a positive issue. From a positive viewpoint, the short-run

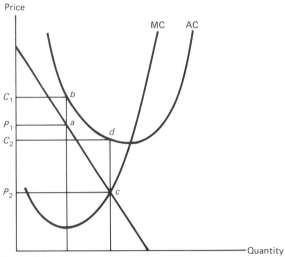

Figure 5-1

socially optimal price is P_2, and price-fixing to maintain prices above P_2 should not be permitted.

With regard to profits, the theory of competitive markets implies that long-run profits will be normal. In the short run, profits will vary. During expansion periods, excess profits are likely to exist (as they often did in the railroad and steel industries); during recessions and depressions, economic losses are likely to occur. True competition, therefore, is often cruel, and in highly competitive markets firms periodically sustain economic losses and are forced to leave. The exit of firms suggests that the competitive process is working, not that it is failing. One can be fairly confident that in most instances when firms complain about cutthroat competition, they are really complaining about just plain old competition.

It has also been argued that price-fixing reduces risk and results in a more stable economy. According to this argument, high risk discourages investment, reduces supply, and results in higher prices. Price-fixing, by reducing risk, may in fact encourage investment, but collusion that artificially reduces risk may create economic problems. If risk is artificially reduced through collusion, it may result in a sluggish rate of technological advance as firms lose some of their incentive to produce new products. Furthermore, artificially reduced risk may encourage entry and capacity expansion beyond the socially optimal level [1]. An artificial reduction in risk caused by collusion, therefore, is likely to result in excess capacity and economic inefficiencies.

Finally, it has been suggested that the higher profits associated with collusion are necessary to encourage research and development. This argument seems foolish in light of the fact that price-fixing, by encouraging cooperation among competitors, seems unlikely to spur firms to attempt to produce new products that would make it more difficult to continue a policy of successful collusion. Furthermore, in technologically advanced industries, where research and development expenditures are high, price-fixing agreements rarely work, because new products are developed too rapidly. It would be impossible to form a cartel in the computer industry, because new technology is developed almost daily.

Despite the preceding analysis, a few price-fixing agreements might be justified on efficiency grounds [2]. These exceptions, however, are so few and far between that an absolute ban on direct price-fixing agreements represents the best public policy.

United States v. Trans-Missouri Freight Association **166 U.S. 290 (1897)**   The first major price-fixing case to reach the Supreme Court was the *Trans-Missouri Freight Association* case. On March 15, 1889, fifteen Western railroads combined to form the Trans-Missouri Freight Association. Three additional railroads joined later. The stated objective of the association was to establish rates. Meetings were held to set rates, and penalties were imposed upon carriers who broke the agreement. Penalties were even imposed for simply missing a rate-setting meeting! After the passage of the Sherman Act, the association continued to operate until December 6, 1892. On that date the association was disbanded, but it was replaced by a seven-member committee that continued to set rates.

The defendants never denied that they had an agreement to set rates. Instead, the association's defense centered around two arguments. First, since railroads were regulated by the Interstate Commerce Commission, the association argued that it was not subject to the Sherman Act. The Supreme Court quickly dismissed this argument. Second, and of more economic significance, the association contended that rates were always reasonable and that in the absence of the association cutthroat competition would ruin the industry.

By 5–4, the Supreme Court overturned two lower court rulings and found for the government. Justice Peckman delivered an opinion that implied that price-fixing agreements were illegal *per se,* regardless of the reasonableness of the prices established:

> The . . . [next] question to be discussed is as to what is the true construction of the statute. . . . Is it confined to a contract or combination which is only in unreasonable restraint of trade or commerce, or does it include what the language of the act plainly and in terms covers, all contracts of that nature? . . .
>
> When . . . the body of an act pronounces as illegal every contract or combination in restraint of trade or commerce among the several States, etc., the plain and ordinary meaning of such language is not limited to that

kind of contract alone which is in unreasonable restraint of trade, but all contracts are included in such language, and no exception or limitation can be added without placing in the act that which has been omitted by Congress. . . .

[The defendants contend that] if competing railroad companies be left subject to the sway of free and unrestricted competition . . . each company will seek business to the extent of its power and will underbid its rival in order to get the business, and such underbidding will act and react upon each company until the prices are so reduced as to make it impossible to prosper or live under them. . . . The only refuge, it is said, from this wretched end lies in the power of competing roads agreeing among themselves to keep up prices for transportation to such sums as shall be reasonable in themselves, so that companies may be allowed to save themselves from themselves, and to agree not to attack each other, but to keep up reasonable and living rates for the services performed. . . .

If only that kind of contract which is in unreasonable restraint of trade be within the meaning of the statute, and declared therein to be illegal, it is at once apparent that the subject of what is a reasonable rate is attended with great uncertainty. What is a proper standard by which to judge the fact of reasonable rates? Must the rate be so high as to enable the return for the whole business done to amount to a sum sufficient to afford the shareholder a fair and reasonable profit upon his investment? If so, what is a fair and reasonable profit? . . . Or is the reasonableness of the profit to be limited to a fair return upon the capital that would have been sufficient to build and equip the road, if honestly expended? . . . It is quite apparent, therefore, that it is exceedingly difficult to formulate even the terms of the rule itself which should govern in the matter of determining what would be reasonable rates for transportation. . . .

The claim that the company had the right to charge reasonable rates, and that, therefore, it has the right to enter into a combination with competing roads to maintain such rates, cannot be admitted. . . . Competition will itself bring charges down to what may be reasonable, while in the case of an agreement to keep prices up, competition is allowed no play; it is shut out, and the rate is practically fixed by the companies themselves by virtue of the agreement, so long as they abide by it. . . .

It may be that the policy evidenced by the passage of the act itself will, if carried out, result in disaster to the roads and in a failure to secure the advantages sought from such legislation. Whether that will be the result or not we do not know and cannot predict. These considerations are, however, not for us. If the act ought to read as contended for by defendants, Congress is the body to amend it and not this court, by a process of judicial legislation wholly unjustifiable.

The *Trans-Missouri Freight* case seemed to establish a *per se* ban on price-fixing, but just two years later the Supreme Court seemed to waver a bit on this per se ruling in the *Addyston Pipe* case.

Addyston Pipe and Steel Company v. United States 175 U.S. 211
(1899) The *Addyston Pipe* case involved six large producers of cast-iron pipe in the Midwest and South. Beginning in 1894 the six firms, which controlled over 65 percent of the market, entered into agreements that divided the market into exclusive pay territories and free territories. In pay territories it was agreed that one firm would be the low bidder on all jobs. Addyston Pipe was located in Cincinnati and was awarded the pay territories of Cincinnati, Ohio; Covington, Kentucky; and Newport, Kentucky. Each of the six agreed to pay bonuses into a common pool on all sales made in pay territories. These bonuses were then divided among the six firms.

Under the arrangement, the defendants offered pipe in free territories, which were more that 500 miles away from their manufacturing facilities, at prices well below the prices offered in pay territories, which were much closer to their manufacturing plants. The conspirators set prices in pay territories at levels that just prevented firms located in the Northeast from shipping pipe into the Midwest and South, but at times prices were set too high, and orders were lost to Northeastern firms. The defense argued that prices were reasonable and prevented ruinous competition in an industry characterized by high fixed costs relative to variable costs.

The Supreme Court ruled unanimously against Addyston Pipe, but in the process appeared to leave open the possibility that firms could sometimes use a reasonableness defense. Justice Peckman again wrote the decision:

> [W]e are of [the] opinion that the agreement or combination was not one which simply secured for its members fair and reasonable prices for the article dealt in by them. . . . [W]e agree with the Circuit Court of Appeals in its statement of the special facts upon this branch of the case and with its opinion thereon as set forth by Circuit Judge [later President] Taft, as follows:
>
>> "The defendants were by their combination . . . able to deprive the public in a large territory of the advantages otherwise accruing to them from the proximity of defendants' pipe factories and, by keeping prices just low enough to prevent competition by Eastern manufacturers, to compel the public to pay an increase over what the price would have been if fixed by competition between defendants, nearly equal to the advantage in freight rates enjoyed by defendants over Eastern competitors. The defendants acquired this power by voluntarily agreeing to sell only at prices fixed by their committee and by allowing the highest bidder at the secret 'auction pool' to become the lowest bidder of them at the public letting." . . .
>>
>> "It has been earnestly pressed upon us that the prices at which the cast-iron pipe sold in 'pay' territory were reasonable." . . .

"We do not think the issue an important one, because, as already stated, we do not think that at common law there is any question of reasonableness open to the courts with reference to such a contract. Its tendency was certainly to give defendants the power to charge unreasonable prices, had they chosen to do so. But if it were important we should unhesitatingly find that the prices charged in the instances which were in evidence were unreasonable. . . . The cost of producing pipe at Chattanooga, together with a reasonable profit, did not exceed $15 a ton. It could have been delivered at Atlanta at $17 to $18 a ton, and yet the lowest price which a foundry was permitted by the rules of the association to bid was $24.25. The same thing was true all through 'pay' territory to a greater or less degree, and especially at 'reserved' cities."

We have no doubt that where the direct and immediate effect of a contract or combination among particular dealers in a commodity is to destroy competition between them and others, so that the parties to the contract or combination may obtain increased prices for themselves, such contract or combination amounts to a restraint of trade in the commodity. . . . All the facts and circumstances are, however, to be considered in order to determine the fundamental question — whether the necessary effect of the combination is to restrain interstate commerce.

If iron pipe cost one hundred dollars a ton instead of the prices which the record shows were paid for it, no one, we think, would contend that the trade in it would amount to as much as if the lower prices prevailed. The higher price would operate as a direct restraint upon the trade, and therefore any contract or combination which enhanced the price might in some degree restrain the trade in the article. . . . The question is as to the effect of [a] combination upon the trade in the article, and if that effect be to destroy competition and thus advance the price, the combination is one in restraint of trade.

In the last section of the *Addyston Pipe* decision there was a great emphasis placed on the fact that higher prices act as a restraint of trade. It is possible to derive a corollary from this position: Agreements that do not raise prices do not result in a restraint of trade and, therefore, do not violate the Sherman Act. The issue was further complicated in 1911 with the handing down of the Rule of Reason in the *Standard Oil* and *American Tobacco* cases. In 1927, however, the Supreme Court appeared to remove any doubt concerning the *per se* ban on direct price-fixing agreements in the *Trenton Potteries* case.

United States v. Trenton Potteries Company 273 U.S. 392

(1927) The *Trenton Potteries* case involved twenty-three members of the Sanitary Potters' Association. The defendants controlled over 80 percent of the vitreous pottery fixture market (better known as bathroom bowls and tubs). Through the association, competitors met and set standard price lists and attempted to persuade each other not to sell below list price. Evidence suggested that the agreements often broke down and that many sales took place at prices below list. The Supreme Court, however, stated its strong support for a *per se* ban on all price-fixing agreements in a 5–3 decision.

Justice Stone delivered the majority opinion:

> There is no contention here that the verdict was not supported by sufficient evidence that respondents, controlling some 82 percent of the business of manufacturing and distributing in the United States vitreous pottery of the type described, combined to fix prices and to limit sales in interstate commerce to jobbers. . . .
>
> It is urged [by the government] that the court below erred in holding in effect . . . that the trial [court] should have submitted to the jury the question whether the price agreement complained of constituted an unreasonable restraint of trade. . . .
>
> The trial court charged, in submitting the case to the jury, that if it found the agreements or combination complained of, it might return a verdict of guilty without regard to the reasonableness of the prices fixed, or the good intentions of the combining units, whether prices were actually lowered or raised or whether sales were restricted to the special jobbers, since both agreements of themselves were unreasonable restraints. . . . In particular the court refused the request to charge the following:
>
>> "The essence of the law is injury to the public. It is not every restraint of competition and not every restraint of trade that works an injury to the public; it is only an undue and unreasonable restraint of trade that had such an effect and is deemed to be unlawful."
>
> That only those restraints upon interstate commerce which are unreasonable are prohibited by the Sherman Law was the rule laid down by the opinions of this Court in the *Standard Oil* and *American Tobacco* cases. But it does not follow that agreements to fix or maintain prices are reasonable restraints and therefore permitted by the statute merely because the prices themselves are reasonable. . . .
>
> The aim and result of every price-fixing agreement, if effective, is the elimination of one form of competition. The power to fix prices, whether reasonably exercised or not, involves power to control the market and to fix arbitrary and unreasonable prices. The reasonable price fixed today may through economic and business changes become the unreasonable price of tomorrow. Once established, it may be maintained unchanged because of the absence of competition secured by the agreement for a price reasonable when fixed. Agreements which create such potential power may well be held to be in themselves unreasonable or unlawful restraints, without the

necessity of minute inquiry whether a particular price is reasonable or unreasonable as fixed and without placing on the government in enforcing the Sherman Law the burden of ascertaining from day to day whether it has become unreasonable through the mere variation of economic conditions. . . .

It follows that the judgment of the circuit court of appeals must be reversed and the judgment of the district court reinstated.

In the *Trenton Potteries* case, the price-fixing agreements probably had little, if any, effect on price, yet the Supreme Court majority forcefully condemned the attempt to fix prices. This remains the basic precedent today: Any overt attempt to fix prices is illegal *per se*.

Appalachian Coals, Inc. v. United States **288 U.S. 344 (1933)**   In the years immediately following the *Trenton Potteries* decision, the Great Depression struck. Industrial output collapsed, and the Roosevelt administration tried to legalize price-fixing through the National Industrial Recovery Act. As a direct result of the depressed conditions, the Supreme Court handed down a decision in 1933 that appeared to overturn the *Trenton Potteries* precedent. The *Appalachian Coals* case now stands as a strange aberration in antitrust history. It is important to understand this decision in its historical context because it suggests how strongly judicial interpretation may be dependent upon contemporary attitudes and circumstances.

In 1929, 137 firms combined to form a new firm, Appalachian Coals, Inc., for the express purpose of acting as their exclusive selling agent. Appalachian Coals controlled 11.96 percent of total bituminous coal production east of the Mississippi River, and 54.21 percent of total production in the Appalachian territory (lying in Virginia, West Virginia, Kentucky, and Tennessee). Before the agreements were even put into practice, the government filed a Sherman Act suit.

The creation of Appalachian Coals eliminated competition among 137 independent coal producers. The defendants argued that the purpose of the agreement was to increase sales through "better methods of distribution, intensive advertising and research; to achieve economies in marketing, and eliminate abnormal, deceptive and destructive trade practices." This defense makes little economic sense since increased sales would reduce prices further in a severely depressed industry with a highly inelastic demand. There can be little doubt that the *true* purpose of the agreement was to raise prices by controlling the output of 137 firms. The Supreme Court, however, ruled in favor of Appalachian Coals.

Chief Justice Hughes spoke for an overwhelming 8–1 majority:

The restrictions the Act imposes are not mechanical or artificial. Its general phrases, interpreted to attain its fundamental objects, set up the essential standard of reasonableness. . . .

The findings of the District Court, upon abundant evidence, leave no room for doubt as to the economic condition of the coal industry. That condition, as the District Court states, "for many years has been indeed deplorable." . . .

There are 130 producers of coal other than defendants in Appalachian territory who sell coal commercially. . . . Competing producers testified that the operation of the selling agency, as proposed by defendants, would not restrain competition and would not hurt their business. . . .

The unfortunate state of the industry would not justify any attempt unduly to restrain competition or to monopolize, but the existing situation prompted defendants to make, and the statute did not preclude them from making, an honest effort to remove abuses, to make competition fairer, and thus to promote the essential interests of commerce. The interests of producers and consumers are linked. When industry is grievously hurt, when producing concerns fail, when unemployment mounts and communities dependent upon profitable production are prostrated, the wells of commerce go dry. So far as actual purposes are concerned, the conclusion of the court below was amply supported that defendants were engaged in a fair and open endeavor to aid the industry in a measurable recovery from its plight. . . .

Defendants' coal will continue to be subject to active competition. In addition to the coal actually produced and seeking markets in competition with defendants' coal, enormous additional quantities will be within reach and can readily be turned into the channels of trade if an advance of price invites that course. . . . The plan cannot be said either to contemplate or to involve the fixing of market prices. . . .

The question remains whether, despite the foregoing conclusions, the fact that the defendants' plan eliminated competition between themselves is alone sufficient to condemn it. . . .[N]o valid objection could have been interposed under the Sherman Act if the defendants had eliminated competition between themselves by a complete integration of their mining properties in a single ownership. . . . We agree that there is no ground for holding defendants' plan illegal merely because they have not integrated their properties and have chosen to maintain their independent plants, seeking not to limit but rather to facilitate production. . . . If the mere size of a single, embracing entity is not enough to bring a combination in corporate form within the statutory inhibition, the mere number and extent of the production of those engaged in a cooperative endeavor to remedy evils which may exist in an industry, and to improve competitive conditions, should not be regarded as producing illegality.

There is a clear statement in the *Appalachian Coals* decision that price-fixing agreements come under a Rule of Reason interpretation. Furthermore, there is the rather strange logic that because a merger of 137 firms would have been legal in 1933, a price-fixing agreement between 137 firms must also have been legal. If carried to its logical conclusion, this argument implies that almost all price-fixing agreements would have been legal in 1933 because at that time there was no effective antimerger law. Fortunately, the Supreme Court quickly forgot about this decision, and in 1940 the Court reestablished the *per se* rule against overt collusion in the *Socony-Vacuum* case.

***United States v. Socony-Vacuum Oil Company* 310 U.S. 150 (1940)** In the *Socony-Vacuum* case, twelve Midwestern oil refiners were charged with purchasing large volumes of gasoline from independent refiners for the purpose of keeping the gasoline off the market. The twelve defendants included such large companies as Socony-Vacuum (now Mobil), Shell, and Continental Oil.

The facts in this case were remarkably similar to those in the *Appalachian Coals* case. In the early and mid-1930s, economic conditions in the oil industry were deplorable. There was a tremendous glut of gasoline, and wholesale prices often fell below average cost. In February 1935 the major Midwestern refiners developed a plan to prevent tank cars of excess gasoline from coming into the market. There was no explicit agreement to fix price at a particular level; however, each of the major companies was selected to purchase excess gasoline from one particular independent refiner, known as its "dancing partner." Defendants typically purchased 10 to 15 percent of their dancing partner's output, and evidence suggested that the plan helped to raise and stabilize prices during 1935 and early 1936.

Naturally, the defense relied on the *Appalachian Coals* precedent. The Supreme Court made a weak attempt to rationalize the *Appalachian Coals* decision. It then proceeded to repudiate it completely and reestablish the *per se* rule.

Justice Douglas spoke for a 6–1 majority:

> The [district] court charged the jury that it was a violation of the Sherman Act for a group of individuals or corporations to act together to raise the prices to be charged for the commodity which they manufactured where they controlled a substantial part of the interstate trade and commerce in that commodity. The court stated that where the members of a combination had the power to raise prices and acted together for that purpose, the combination was illegal; and that it was immaterial how reasonable or unreasonable those prices were or to what extent they had been affected by the combination. . . .
>
> The Circuit Court of Appeals held this charge to be reversible error, since it was based upon the theory that such a combination was illegal *per se*. In its view respondents' activities were not unlawful unless they constituted an unreasonable restraint of trade. . . .
>
> In *United States v. Trenton Potteries* . . . [t]his Court pointed out that the so-called "rule of reason" announced in *Standard Oil Co. v. United States*

and in *United States v. American Tobacco* had not affected [its] view of the illegality of price-fixing agreements. . . .[A]greements "to fix or maintain prices" are not reasonable restraints of trade under the statute merely because the prices themselves are reasonable. . . .

But respondents claim that other decisions of this Court afford them adequate defenses to the indictment. Among those on which they place reliance [is] *Appalachian Coals, Inc. v. United States.* . . .

[T]he only essential thing in common between the instant case and the *Appalachian Coals* case is the presence in each of so-called demoralizing or injurious practices. The methods of dealing with them were quite divergent. In the instant case there were buying programs of distress gasoline which had as their direct purpose and aim the raising and maintenance of spot market prices and of prices to jobbers and consumers in the Mid-Western area, by the elimination of distress gasoline as a market factor. . . . Unlike the plan in the instant case, the plan in the *Appalachian Coals* case was not designed to operate *vis-à-vis* the general consuming market and to fix the prices on that market. Furthermore, the effect, if any, of that plan on prices was not only wholly incidental but also highly conjectural. For the plan had not then been put into operation. . . .

[F]or over forty years this Court ha[s] consistently and without deviation adhered to the principle that price-fixing agreements are unlawful *per se* under the Sherman Act and that no showing of so-called competitive abuses or evils which those agreements were designed to eliminate or alleviate may be interposed as a defense. . . .

Proof that there was a conspiracy, that its purpose was to raise prices, and that it caused or contributed to a price rise is proof of the actual consummation or execution of a conspiracy under section 1 of the Sherman Act. . . .

The elimination of so-called competitive evils is no legal justification for such buying programs. . . . Fairer competitive prices, it is claimed, resulted when distress gasoline was removed from the market. But such defense is typical of the protestations usually made in price-fixing cases. Ruinous competition, financial disaster, evils of price cutting and the like appear throughout our history as ostensible justifications for price-fixing. If the so-called competitive abuses were to be appraised here, the reasonableness of prices would necessarily become an issue in every price-fixing case. In that event the Sherman Act would soon be emasculated; its philosophy would be supplanted by one which is wholly alien to a system of free competition; it would not be the charter of freedom which its framers intended. . . .

Any combination which tampers with price structures is engaged in an unlawful activity. Even though the members of the price-fixing group were in no position to control the market, to the extent that they raised, lowered, or stabilized prices they would be directly interfering with the free play of market forces. . . .

> Under the Sherman Act a combination formed for the purpose and with the effect of raising, depressing, fixing, pegging, or stabilizing the price of a commodity in interstate or foreign commerce is illegal *per se.*

The *Socony-Vacuum* precedent is now accepted as policy. Today any direct attempt to affect prices is illegal *per se,* and direct price-fixing conspiracies almost inevitably end with the defendants pleading nolo contendere.

Price-Exchange Agreements

The *Socony-Vacuum* decision put an end to the basic issue of direct price-fixing agreements but left open for future consideration certain types of behavior, including price exchanges between competitors. The Supreme Court first addressed this issue in the 1969 *Container Corporation* case.

United States v. Container Corporation of America 393 U.S. 333 (1969)

The *Container Corporation* case involved an agreement between eighteen manufacturers of cardboard containers in the Southeastern United States. These firms controlled 90 percent of the relevant market. Under the agreement each firm agreed to supply its competitors with price information on its most recent sales in exchange for a reciprocal agreement from each of its competitors. Price was particularly crucial in the cardboard container industry because the product was perfectly homogeneous, and firms were forced to match their competitors' price reductions. Despite the information exchanges, prices were generally *declining* throughout the period. Furthermore, there was a large increase, from thirty to fifty-one, in the number of firms in the market.

A 6–3 majority of the Supreme Court ruled for the government. Justice Douglas wrote

> The case as proved is unlike any other price decisions we have rendered. There was here an exchange of price information but no agreement to adhere to a price schedule. . . .
>
> Here all that was present was a request by each defendant of its competitor for information as to the most recent price charged or quoted, whenever it needed such information and whenever it was not available from another source. Each defendant on receiving that request usually furnished the data with the expectation that it would be furnished reciprocal information when it wanted it. That concerted action is of course sufficient to establish the combination or conspiracy, the initial ingredient of a violation of section 1 of the Sherman Act. . . .

The result of this reciprocal exchange of prices was to stabilize prices though at a downward level. Knowledge of a competitor's price usually meant matching that price. The continuation of some price competition is not fatal to the Government's case. The limitation or reduction of price competition brings the case within the ban, for as we held in *United States v. Socony-Vacuum,* interference with the setting of price by free market forces is unlawful *per se.* Price information exchanged in some markets may have no effect on a truly competitive price. But the corrugated container industry is dominated by relatively few sellers. The product is fungible and the competition for sales is price. The demand is inelastic, as buyers place orders only for immediate, short-run needs. The exchange of price data tends toward price uniformity. For a lower price does not mean a larger share of the available business but a sharing of the existing business at a lower return. Stabilizing prices as well as raising them is within the ban of section 1 of the Sherman Act. . . . The inferences are irresistible that the exchange of price information has had an anticompetitive effect in the industry, chilling the vigor of price competition. . . .

Price is too critical, too sensitive a control to allow it to be used even in an informal manner to restrain competition.

Both Justice Douglas's opinion and a concurring opinion written by Justice Fortas made it clear that price exchanges were not illegal *per se*, but were illegal in cases where the structural characteristics of an industry led to the conclusion that prices would be affected by the price exchanges. In their dissent, Justices Marshall, Harlan, and Stewart held that this particular price exchange had not restrained competition.

Justice Marshall wrote the dissenting opinion:

I agree with the Court's holding that there existed an agreement among defendants to exchange price information whenever requested. However, I cannot agree that that agreement should be condemned, either as illegal *per se,* or as having had the purpose or effect of restricting price competition in the corrugated container industry in the Southeastern United States. . . .

Complete market knowledge is certainly not an evil in perfectly competitive markets. This is not, however, such a market, and there is admittedly some danger that price information will be used for anticompetitive purposes, particularly the maintenance of prices at a high level. . . .

I do not think, [however,] it can be concluded that this particular market is sufficiently oligopolistic, especially in light of the ease of entry, to justify the inference that price information will necessarily be used to stabilize prices. . . .

Given the uncertainty about the probable effect of an exchange of price information in this context, I would require that the Government prove that the exchange was entered into for the purpose of, or that it had the effect of, restraining price competition. . . .

The Government admits that the price trend was down, but asks the Court to assume that the trend would have been accelerated with less informed, and hence more vigorous, price competition. . . .

The trial judge found that price decisions were individual decisions, and that defendants frequently did cut prices in order to obtain a particular order. . . .

The Government is ultimately forced to fall back on the theoretical argument that prices would have been more unstable and would have fallen faster without price information. . . .

The District Court's finding that this was a competitive industry, lacking any price parallelism or uniformity, effectively refute[s] the Government's assertion that the result of those decisions was to maintain or tend to maintain prices at other than a competitive level. Accordingly, I would affirm the decision of the court below.

Neither the majority nor the dissenting opinion addressed the reasons why prices declined during the price-exchange period. This is an important issue because the downward price trend may actually have been accelerated by the price-exchange agreement. By artificially stabilizing the industry and reducing risk, the agreement may have encouraged some firms to expand their capacity and others to enter the market. Artificially reduced risk, therefore, may have induced the observed continuous entry and excess capacity, both of which placed downward pressure on prices. Lower prices, therefore, may have been symptomatic of economic inefficiency in the form of excess capacity. This suggests that the full economic impact of a conspiracy may not be revealed by simply examining an industry's pricing trend.

Even after the government victory in 1969, members of the cardboard container industry continued to follow similar practices, which resulted in new antitrust cases during the 1970s. As a result of these cases, twenty-three container companies were eventually indicted, and fourteen executives were sentenced to jail, including the president of Container Corporation. Despite Justice Marshall's dissenting opinion, therefore, the cardboard container producers must have perceived some benefits from the price exchanges, or else they were acting very irrationally by continuing a practice that eventually ended up sending executives to jail.

United States v. United States Gypsum Company 438 U.S. 422 **(1978)** The apparently strong ban on price-exchange agreements in the *Container Corporation* decision appeared to be modified a bit in the 1978 *U.S. Gypsum* case. Gypsum board was sold in a highly concentrated market, where the eight-firm concentration ratio was 94 percent. The eight leading producers had followed the same price-exchange practices as the cardboard container manufacturers, but their defense had a somewhat different twist: They argued that price verification was *necessary* in order to prevent them from violating the Robinson-Patman Act! According to this defense, price verification was simply a method of preventing illegal price discrimination by ensuring that any discriminatory prices were made in a good faith effort to meet the lower price of a competitor.

The Supreme Court rejected this defense, but remanded the case for a new trial and in so doing raised an entirely different issue, the issue of intent in criminal cases.

Chief Justice Burger delivered the opinion of the Court:

> The jury was instructed that if it found interseller verification had the effect of raising, fixing, maintaining, or stabilizing the price of gypsum board, then such verification could be considered as evidence of an agreement to so affect prices. They were further charged, and it is this point which gives rise to our present concern, that "if the effect of the exchanges of pricing information was to raise, fix, maintain, and stabilize prices, then the parties to them are presumed, *as a matter of law,* to have intended that result."
>
> The Government characterizes this charge as entirely consistent with "this Court's long-standing rule that an agreement among sellers to exchange information on current offering prices violates Section 1 of the Sherman Act if it has either the purpose or effect of stabilizing prices.". . .
>
> [A]n effect on prices, without more, will not support a criminal conviction under the Sherman Act. . . . Rather, we hold that a defendant's state of mind or intent is an element of a criminal antitrust offense which must be established by evidence and inferences drawn therefrom and cannot be taken from the trier of fact through reliance on a legal presumption of wrongful intent from proof of an effect on prices. . . . Since the challenged instruction, as we read it, had this prohibited effect, it is disapproved. We are unwilling to construe the Sherman Act as mandating a regime of strict-liability criminal offenses. . . .
>
> The imposition of criminal liability on a corporate official . . . without inquiring into the intent with which [an action] was undertaken, holds out the distinct possibility of overdeterrence; salutary and procompetitive conduct lying close to the borderline of impermissible conduct might be shunned by businessmen who chose to be excessively cautious in the face of uncertainty regarding possible exposure to criminal punishment for even a good-faith error of judgment. . . . The criminal sanctions would be used, not to punish conscious and calculated wrongdoing at odds with statutory proscriptions, but instead simply to *regulate* business practices regardless of the intent with which they were undertaken. . . .

For these reasons, we conclude that the criminal offenses defined by the Sherman Act should be construed as including intent as an element. . . .

Although an effect on prices may well support an inference that the defendant had knowledge of the probability of such a consequence at the time he acted, the jury must remain free to consider additional evidence before accepting or rejecting the inference. Therefore, although it would be correct to instruct the jury that it may infer intent from an effect on prices, ultimately the decision on the issue of intent must be left to the trier of fact alone. . . .

Section 2(a) of the Clayton Act, as amended by the Robinson-Patman Act, . . . embodies a general prohibition of price discrimination between buyers when an injury to competition is the consequence. The primary exception to the Section 2(a) bar is the meeting competition defense which is incorporated as a proviso to the burden-of-proof requirements set out in section 2(b):

> "*Provided, however,* That nothing herein contained shall prevent a seller rebutting the prima facie case thus made by showing that his lower price or the furnishing of services or facilities to any purchaser or purchasers was made in good faith to meet an equally low price of a competitor, or the services or facilities furnished by a competitor."

A good-faith belief, rather than absolute certainty, that a price concession is being offered to meet an equally low price offered by a competitor is sufficient to satisfy the section 2(b) defense. While casual reliance on uncorroborated reports of buyers or sales representatives without further investigation may not, as we noted earlier, be sufficient to make the requisite showing of good faith, nothing in the language of section 2(b) . . . indicates that direct discussions of price between competitors are required. Nor has any court, so far as we are aware, ever imposed such a requirement. . . .

Certainly, evidence that a seller had received reports of similar discounts from other customers, . . . or was threatened with a termination of purchases if the discount were not met . . . would be relevant in this regard. . . .

As an abstract proposition, resort to interseller verification as a means of checking the buyer's reliability seems a possible solution to the seller's plight, but careful examination reveals serious problems with the practice. . . .

[I]f one seller offers a price concession for the purpose of winning over one of his competitor's customers, it is unlikely that the same seller will freely inform its competitor of the details of the concession so that it can be promptly matched and diffused. Instead, such a seller would appear to have at least as great an incentive to misrepresent the existence or size of the discount as would the buyer who received it. . . .

The other variety of interseller verification is, like the conduct charged in the instant case, undertaken pursuant to an agreement, either tacit or express, providing for reciprocity among competitors in the exchange of price information. Such an agreement would make little economic sense, in our view, if its sole purpose were to guarantee all participants the opportunity to match the secret price concessions of other participants under section 2(b). For in such circumstances, each seller would know that his price concession could not be kept from his competitors and no seller participating in the information-exchange arrangement would, therefore, have any incentive for deviating from the prevailing price level in the industry. . . . Regardless of its punitive purpose, the most likely consequence of any such agreement to exchange price information would be the stabilization of industry prices. . . .

We are left, therefore, on the one hand, with doubts about both the need for and efficiency of interseller verification as a means of facilitating compliance with section 2(b), and, on the other, with recognition of the tendency for price discussions between competitors to contribute to the stability of oligopolistic prices and open the way for the growth of prohibited anticompetitive activity. To recognize even a limited "controlling circumstance" exception for interseller verification in such circumstances would be to remove from scrutiny under the Sherman Act conduct falling near its core with no assurance, and indeed with serious doubts, that competing antitrust policies would be served thereby.

The *U.S. Gypsum* decision seemed to break with the Court's previous position concerning intent in price-fixing cases and may have opened up a Pandora's box. Since it is virtually impossible to imagine an agreement that had the *effect* of raising, fixing, or stabilizing prices without having had the *intent* to do so, the decision seems to unnecessarily complicate section 1 cases. Only time will tell whether this precedent has any lasting effect.

In an extremely controversial action, in March 1980, the Justice Department agreed to drop all charges in its second case against the gypsum producers in return for their agreement to pay back-taxes to the Internal Revenue Service. Tying antitrust settlements to IRS policy would seem to set a bad precedent. If this practice becomes common, it could undermine the true objective of the antitrust laws, which is maintaining competition, not collecting taxes.

II OLIGOPOLY

Edward Chamberlin first suggested that in oligopolistic industries firms come to recognize their interdependencies and learn to avoid aggressive price competition *even in the absence* of direct contact with competitors [3]. Since Chamberlin's first analysis, economists have advanced many theories of oligopolistic behavior [4]. Most of these theories come to a similar conclusion: Oligopolists, realizing the futility of aggressive price competition and price wars, avoid aggressive price competition. Furthermore, the theories suggest that oligopolists will prefer to compete through product differentiation and/or advertising, rather than through price.

If these theories are correct, then a lack of price competition would be expected in oligopolistic industries. This presents an extremely difficult problem for antitrust authorities, because oligopolistic behavior that on the surface may appear to be in restraint of trade may represent rational *independent* business behavior aimed at maximizing long-run profits.

One of the earliest oligopoly cases was the 1939 *Interstate Circuit* case. In the *Interstate Circuit* case [*Interstate Circuit v. United States* 306 U.S. 208 (1939)], the Supreme Court suggested that consciously parallel behavior was subject to antitrust attack. Interstate Circuit, a large motion-picture theater chain, combined with another theater chain to send identical letters to eight major motion-picture distributors. In the letters the chains requested that the distributors withhold first-run films from any theater charging less than 25 cents admission or showing first-run films as part of a double feature. There was no evidence suggesting that the eight distributors ever met; however, all eight withdrew their first-run films from the price-chiseling theaters. The Supreme Court ruled that this behavior violated section 1 of the Sherman Act. The next major precedent was handed down seven years later in the 1946 *American Tobacco* case.

American Tobacco Co. v. United States 328 U.S. 781 (1946)   In the *Interstate Circuit* case, the tacit conspiracy's starting point could be traced directly to the eight letters. In the *American Tobacco* case, however, there was no evidence of a particular event that led to a tacit conspiracy.

Recall that the 1911 *American Tobacco* case resulted in the establishment of over a dozen new companies, including Liggett & Myers and R. J. Reynolds. For about a decade the cigarette producers competed aggressively; then, in the early 1920s, price competition suddenly ceased. The tobacco oligopolists must have read Chamberlin's book, because they behaved in classic textbook fashion. The Big 3 (as American Tobacco, Liggett, and Reynolds were known) rigged the tobacco auction markets so that all three purchased tobacco at identical prices. Furthermore, they followed each others' pricing policies in lockstep.

This consciously parallel behavior may have been the natural outgrowth of the oligopolistic structure of the cigarette industry. Nevertheless, relying on strong circumstantial evidence, the Supreme Court ruled for the government. Justice Burton delivered the 7–0 opinion:

The Government introduced evidence showing that, although there was no written or express agreement discovered among American, Liggett and Reynolds, their practices included a clear course of dealing. This evidence convinced the jury of the existence of a combination or conspiracy to fix and control prices and practices as to domestic leaf tobacco, both in restraint of trade as such, and to establish a substantially impregnable defense against any attempted intrusion by potential competitors into these markets.

The Government presented evidence to support its claim that, before the [tobacco] markets opened, the petitioners placed limitations and restrictions on the prices which their buyers were permitted to pay for tobacco. None of the buyers exceeded these price ceilings. . . . There was manipulation of the price of lower grade tobaccos in order to restrict competition from manufacturers of the lower priced cigarettes. . . .

Where one or two of the petitioners secured their percentage of the crop on a certain market or were not interested in the purchase of certain offerings of tobacco, their buyers, nevertheless, would enter the bidding in order to force the other petitioners to bid up to the maximum price. The petitioners were not so much concerned with the prices they paid for the leaf tobacco as that each should pay the same price for the same grade and that none would secure any advantage in purchasing tobacco. . . .

At a time when the manufacturers of lower priced cigarettes were beginning to manufacture them in quantity, the petitioners commenced to make large purchases of the cheaper tobacco leaves used for the manufacture of such lower priced cigarettes. No explanation was offered as to how or where this tobacco was used by petitioners. . . .

The list prices charged and the discounts allowed by petitioners have been practically identical since 1923 and absolutely identical since 1928. Since the latter date, only seven changes have been made by the three companies and those have been identical in amount. The increases were first announced by Reynolds. American and Liggett thereupon increased their list prices in identical amounts.

The following record of price changes is circumstantial evidence of the existence of a conspiracy and of a power and intent to exclude competition coming from cheaper grade cigarettes. During the two years preceding June, 1931, the petitioners produced 90% of the total cigarette production in the United States. In that month tobacco farmers were receiving the lowest prices for their crops since 1905. . . . It was one of the worst years of financial and economic depression in the history of the country. On June 23, 1931, Reynolds, without previous notification or warning to the trade or public, raised the list price of Camel cigarettes, constituting its leading cigarette brand, from $6.40 to $6.85 a thousand. The same day, American increased the list price for Lucky Strike cigarettes, its leading brand, and Liggett the price of Chesterfield cigarettes, its leading brand, to the identical $6.85. . . . [I]n 1932, in the midst of the national depression with the sales of the petitioners' cigarettes falling off greatly in number, the petitioners still were making tremendous profits as a result of the price increase. Their net profits in that year amounted to more than $100,000,000. This was one of the three biggest years in their history. . . .

However, after the above described increase in list prices of the petitioners in 1931, the 10 cent brands made serious inroads upon the sales of the petitioners. These cheaper brands of cigarettes were sold at a list price of $4.75 a thousand and from 1931 to 1932 the sales of these cigarettes multiplied 30 times, rising from 0.28% of the total cigarette sales of the country in June 1931, to 22.78% in November, 1932. In response to this threat of competition from the manufacturers of the 10 cent brands, the petitioners, in January, 1933, cut the list price of their three leading brands from $6.85 to $6 a thousand. In February, they cut again to $5.50 a thousand. . . . Following the first price cut by petitioners, the sales of the 10 cent brands fell off considerably. After the second cut they fell off to a much greater extent. . . . During the period that the list price of $5.50 a thousand was in effect, Camels and Lucky Strikes were being sold at a loss. . . .

Certain methods used by the petitioners to secure a reduction in the retail prices of their cigarettes were in evidence. Reynolds and Liggett required their retailers to price the 10 cent brands at a differential of not more than 3 cents below Camel and Chesterfield cigarettes. . . . In addition to the use of inducements, petitioners also used threats and penalties to enforce compliance with their retail price program, removed dealers from the direct lists, and cancelled arrangements for window advertising, changed credit terms with a resulting handicap to recalcitrant dealers, discontinued cash allowances for advertising, refused to make deals giving free goods, and made use of price cutters to whom they granted advantageous privileges to drive down retail prices where a parity, or price equalization, was not maintained by dealers between brands of petitioners or where the dealers refused to maintain the 3 cent differential between the 10 cent brands and the leading brands of petitioners' cigarettes. . . .

It is not the form of the combination or the particular means used but the result to be achieved that the statute condemns. It is not of importance whether the means used to accomplish the unlawful objective are in themselves lawful or unlawful. Acts done to give effects to the conspiracy may be in themselves wholly innocent acts. . . . No formal agreement is necessary to constitute an unlawful conspiracy. Often crimes are a matter of inference deduced from the acts of the person accused and done in pursuance of a criminal purpose. Where the conspiracy is proved, as here, from the evidence of the action taken in concert by the parties to it, it is all the more convincing proof of an intent to exercise the power of exclusion acquired through that conspiracy. The essential combination or conspiracy in violation of the Sherman Act may be found in a course of dealing or other circumstances as well as in an exchange of words. . . . Where the circumstances are such as to warrant a jury in finding that the conspirators had a unity of purpose or a common design and understanding, the conclusion that a conspiracy is established is justified.

The *American Tobacco* case resulted in total fines of only $255,000 and no structural relief. This raises a serious question regarding the efficiency of remedies in oligopoly cases. If a firm's behavior is the natural result of an oligopolistic market structure, then levying fines is likely to have little, if any, effect on future behavior or economic performance. In fact, behavior in the cigarette industry changed little after the 1946 decision. This suggests that the courts cannot force firms to compete on the basis of price. Competitive pricing behavior usually requires a competitive market structure, and any policy that fails to address the oligopoly structure problem is likely to fail in its attempt to deal with the problem's symptom, a lack of competitive pricing.

The *American Tobacco* case was initially hailed as a major breakthrough in antitrust policy. It was followed in 1948 by several other government victories, including a major case against the five leading motion-picture producers and distributors [*United States v. Paramount Pictures* 334 U.S. 131 (1948)], which resulted in the divestiture of over 65 percent of the majors' movie theaters. In 1954, however, the first major step away from the *American Tobacco* precedent took place in another motion-picture industry case.

***Theatre Enterprises, Inc. v. Paramount Film Distributing Corporation* 346 U.S. 537 (1954)** Following the 1948 *Paramount* decision, Theatre Enterprises built a new theater, the Crest, in suburban Baltimore with the hope of attracting first-run motion pictures. Theatre Enterprises contacted eight major distributors and each refused to supply the Crest with first-run films, despite Theatre Enterprises's offer of substantial financial guarantees. Assuming that the refusals resulted from consciously parallel behavior, which was illegal under the *American Tobacco* and *Paramount* precedents, Theatre Enterprises sued.

In 1954 a 7–1 majority of the Supreme Court ruled against Theatre Enterprises. Justice Clark wrote the opinion:

> Admittedly there is no direct evidence of illegal agreement between the respondents and no conspiracy is charged as to the independent exhibitors in Baltimore, who account for 63% of first-run exhibitions. The various respondents advanced much the same reasons for denying petitioner's offers. Among other reasons, they asserted that day-and-date first-runs are normally granted only to noncompeting theatres. Since the Crest is in "substantial competition" with the downtown theatres, a day-and-date arrangement would be economically unfeasible. And even if respondents wished to grant petitioner such a license, no downtown exhibitor would

waive his clearance rights over the Crest and agree to a simultaneous showing. As a result, if petitioner were to receive first-runs, the license would have to be an exclusive one. However, an exclusive license would be economically unsound because the Crest is a suburban theatre, located in a small shopping center, and served by limited public transportation facilities; and, with a drawing area of less than one-tenth that of a downtown theatre, it cannot compare with those easily accessible theatres in the power to draw patrons. . . .

The crucial question is whether respondents' conduct toward petitioner stemmed from independent decision or from an agreement, tacit or express. . . . [T]his Court has never held that proof of parallel business behavior conclusively establishes agreement or, phrased differently, that such behavior itself constitutes a Sherman Act offense. Circumstantial evidence of consciously parallel behavior may have made heavy inroads into the traditional judicial attitude toward conspiracy; but "conscious parallelism" has not yet read conspiracy out of the Sherman Act entirely. . . . Here each of the respondents had denied the existence of any collaboration and in addition had introduced evidence of the local conditions surrounding the Crest operation which, they contended, precluded it from being a successful first-run house. They also attacked the good faith of the guaranteed offers of the petitioner for first-run pictures and attributed uniform action to individual business judgment motivated by the desire for maximum revenues.

The *Theatre Enterprises* case represented a significant movement away from the *American Tobacco* precedent. The evidence suggested a *reasonable probability* that each distributor was acting independently to maximize profits. Two of the defendant firms, Warner Brothers and Loew's, owned theaters in downtown Baltimore, however, and it is possible that the six other defendants refused to license first-runs to the Crest because they feared retaliation in other cities. If the six other defendant distributors had licensed the Crest, then Warner Brothers and Loew's might have licensed first-runs to suburban theaters in cities where the other defendants owned downtown theaters. If the latter scenario is correct, then the problem stemmed from the continuing vertical integration that existed following the 1948 *Paramount* decision.

United States v. Chas. Pfizer & Co., Inc., American Cyanamid Company and Bristol-Myers Company 426 F.2d 32 (1970) The *Pfizer* case involved the introduction and subsequent marketing of the antibiotic tetracycline. Prior to 1952 three drugs dominated the antibiotic market: Parke, Davis's chloromycetin, American Cyanamid's aureomycin, and Pfizer's terramycin. All three drugs were protected by patents. In 1952 a Pfizer scientist developed tetracycline by dechlorinizing Cyanamid's aureomycin. As a result of publicity surrounding Pfizer's discovery, Cyanamid applied for a product and process patent for tetracycline. There were therefore, two pending patents for tetracycline.

Pfizer believed that its patent had priority, but decided to meet with Cyanamid. In November 1953 Pfizer's chairman met with Cyanamid's chairman. At this meeting, the two companies agreed to recognize the Patent Office as the arbiter of their patent claims and to cross-license the necessary patents to produce tetracycline, regardless of the Patent Office's decision. Ultimately, Cyanamid agreed to withdraw its patent claim, and on January 11, 1955, Pfizer received a patent on tetracycline.

Meanwhile, Bristol-Myers decided to produce tetracycline through a different fermentation process and in 1954 began to sell tetracycline to Squibb and Upjohn, who marketed the Bristol-Myers drug under the Squibb and Upjohn labels. When Pfizer received its patent in 1955, it immediately filed an infringement suit against Bristol-Myers, Squibb, and Upjohn.

Pfizer seemed to have a strong case against Bristol-Myers. In December 1955, however, in an incident totally unrelated to the antibiotic case, John G. Broady, a lawyer-investigator, was convicted of tapping the Bristol-Myers and Squibb telephone lines. Broady had been hired for this illegal activity by Pfizer's general counsel! Pfizer obviously feared the public's reaction to this disclosure, so on December 14 and 15, 1955, the chairmen of Pfizer and Bristol-Myers met along with their patent attorneys.

The government complaint (bill of particulars) charged that at the two December meetings a deal was struck between Pfizer and Bristol-Myers. The government charged that they agreed that Pfizer would license Bristol-Myers to manufacture tetracycline; that Squibb and Upjohn would be denied manufacturing licenses, but would be permitted to market Bristol-Myers's tetracycline; and that tetracycline would be marketed at identical prices by all sellers. The defendants denied that any such illegal deal had been struck, and there was no "smoking gun" evidence that proved an agreement had been reached.

A district court jury trial resulted in a verdict for the government, but in April 1970, by a 2–1 split vote, the Second Circuit Court of Appeals overturned the jury's ruling. Judge Moore wrote the majority opinion:

> Before the openings by counsel, the trial court by way of preliminary instructions had stated to the jury that the conspiracy included "the creation of uniform, non-competitive and unreasonably high prices to the users of broad spectrum antibiotics." In its opening the government had stressed "enormous" profits by comparing factory cost and selling price and gave as an illustration of Cyanamid's 1954 cost a figure of $2.55 production cost for

100 capsules, a 1956 cost of $1.76 and a 1958 cost of $1.59 against a selling price to the druggist of $30.60 and $51 to the consumer. . . .

The government devoted much of its summation to the profits obtained by the respective defendants from their particular drugs. . . .

Instead of charging that the government had relied . . . on specific dates and specified individuals, the court charged that:

> "While the prosecution alleges approximate dates for the commencement of the conspiracy, and charges that the conspiracy continued up to the date of the indictment in August 1961, it is not necessary that the precise dates or extension of the conspiracy throughout the period be proved in order to establish charges."

Along the same lines were the instructions that:

> "This central requirement of an 'agreement' does not mean, however, that in order to create an unlawful combination or conspiracy, the parties must meet together at all. Nor does it mean that their undertaking must be embodied in express or formal contractual statements, or express words of any kind."

A review of the entire charge leaves the definite impression that although the circumstantial evidence and "unreasonably high profits" aspects of the case were stressed, the key issue as to the formation of the conspiracy as particularized by the government was not given proper attention and the importance of establishing a conspiracy as charged so minimized that there can be no assurance that the jury was not misled to defendants' serious prejudice. . . .

[T]hree-quarters of the charge did not relate to the key issue, namely, the formation of the conspiracy as specified in the bill of particulars. Except for mentioning the November 1953 and December 1955 dates, there was nothing in the charge which focused the jury's attention on the primary issue which they were to resolve, namely, did the participants at those meetings conspire to carry out the program as alleged by the government? . . .

Towards the end of the charge, ten pages were expended on the relation of allegedly unreasonably high prices. The court charged that " . . . uniform prices, maintained at a constant level over long periods of time — if such prices are artificial and unrelated to supply and demand or to other variations or changes in the pertinent economic factors — may be considered by you as some evidence from which an agreement or restraint of trade may be inferred." . . .

Quite apart from their relevance, these so-called means and methods could well have so prejudiced the jury that it either failed to resolve the primary issue or subordinated it to the issues stressed. Because of this real possibility, defendants Pfizer, Bristol and Cyanamid are entitled to a new trial. . . .

Defendants also seek reversal because the court, after receiving evidence of the marketing practices and policies of Parke, Davis (not a defendant) which was concededly not engaged in the alleged conspiracy, improperly placed restrictions on them by refusing to permit them to argue to the jury the effect of this evidence upon their innocence or guilt. . . .

Parke, Davis during the critical years of the alleged conspiracy manufactured and sold the antibiotic, chloromycetin. It was the second largest in the antibiotic field, accounting for some 24% of all sales. In the years preceding the alleged conspiracy, its prices paralleled those of the other companies. . . . Naturally defendants sought to capitalize on the fact that Parke, Davis, as a non-conspirator, engaged in the same marketing practices which the government charged created a beyond-reasonable-doubt inference of conspiracy on their part. . . .

Had defendants been allowed to argue without restriction the full effect of the Parke, Davis marketing policies and procedures, defendants could have stressed that Parke, Davis quite independently of any conspiracy had paralleled defendants in its pricing and licensing practices both before and after the commencement of the alleged November 1953 conspiracy. . . .

The restrictions placed upon defendants with respect to Parke, Davis proof and the failure to present to the jury the substance of the defendants' requests to charge constitute sufficient prejudice as to require a new trial.

In 1972 the Supreme Court, by a 3–3 split vote, upheld the court of appeals ruling. Upon remand District Judge Cannella ruled in 1973 that the government had failed to prove its case beyond a reasonable doubt [367 F. Supp. 91 (1973)]. Thus twelve years after it began, the *Pfizer* case finally ended.

The message in the *Pfizer* decision is quite different from the message in the 1946 *American Tobacco* decision. Under the *Pfizer* precedent it appears that conscious parallelism alone is not enough to warrant a conviction under the Sherman Act. Under the present court interpretation a government victory requires additional acts, such as the publication of price lists or the practice of policies that discourage price-cutting.

Even under the present interpretation, however, oligopolists may be subject to antitrust attack if their behavior *strongly* suggests a common attempt to fix or maintain prices. Such a situation arose in the electric turbine industry between 1964 and 1976.

United States v. General Electric Co. Civil No. 28, 228 E.D. Pennsylvania (December 1976) Throughout the 1950s it had been common practice in the electrical equipment industry to fix prices through direct price-fixing agreements. In 1960, however, the entire industry was caught red-handed, and the formal agreements fell apart as firms were fined and executives were sent to prison. Furthermore, through a series of consent decrees the defendants were enjoined from entering into any further attempts to fix prices. One of the consent decrees, signed on October 1, 1960, required General Electric, Westinghouse, and Allis-Chalmers (the only three American producers of turbine generators) to set prices independently and to announce their turbine generator prices publicly. As a result of the uncovering of the conspiracy and of the consent decree, price competition developed in the turbine market between 1960 and 1963. In fact, low prices and large discounts forced Allis-Chalmers out of the market in December 1962. This left only two domestic producers, General Electric and Westinghouse.

In May 1963 GE announced a new turbine pricing policy. First, GE announced its intention of maintaining its book prices and eliminating all discounts. Second, GE published a revised price book that simplified the procedure for determining prices. To determine prices under the new system, buyers simply multiplied GE's book prices by a published multiplier. If GE announced a multiplier of 0.80, actual prices equaled 80 percent of book prices. Third, GE announced a price-protection clause, whereby GE guaranteed that if it lowered any product's price to *any* buyer below its list price, it would retroactively grant the lower price to any company that had purchased that product during the previous six months. Furthermore, to guarantee against secret price reductions, GE opened its books for public inspection. The Justice Department contended that internal GE documents suggested that the purpose of the policy was to signal Westinghouse that GE intended to stabilize prices.

Within days of learning about GE's new price policy, Westinghouse withdrew its own list-price book and began using the GE system, *including the GE price book*. Nine months later, Westinghouse introduced its own price book, but continued to follow the GE pricing policy, including the same multiplier. As a result of these changes, after August 1964 the two firms charged identical prices on all turbine orders.

GE and Westinghouse argued that their pricing policies were simply a form of conscious parallelism, which was legal under the antitrust laws. Furthermore, they contended that this type of behavior would be expected in a duopoly market structure. The Justice Department, however, argued that their conduct went beyond simple conscious parallelism or price leadership. Furthermore, the Justice Department argued that internal documents suggested that both companies *intended* for the policy to stabilize prices, and it decided to file a suit.

In 1976 the two defendants agreed to a consent decree. The decree was aimed at preventing the indirect communication of price information between GE and Westinghouse. There were four major methods used to eliminate indirect price communication. First, the defendants were enjoined from making public statements regarding price that would signal their desire to eliminate price competition. Second, they were prohibited from using the price-protection plan, and they were enjoined from publishing their current-price quotations. Third, the decree banned the publication of price-related information "from which a general pricing policy or strategy can be inferred." Finally, the decree prohibited each firm from indirectly examining its competitor's books by obtaining information from buyers.

The *GE-Westinghouse* consent decree suggests that in a few extreme cases the government may still be able to attack oligopolistic behavior. A more important economic question, however, is whether such an attack will have any significant impact on conduct or performance. Given the highly concentrated nature of the electric turbine market, for example, most economists would expect that price competition would naturally be limited in the long run, probably through some form of tacit understanding. It is doubtful that any behavior-oriented consent decree will have a significant impact on economic performance.

III   TRADE ASSOCIATIONS

Trade associations present another unique set of problems for antitrust enforcement. Trade association practices have varied widely, from innocent information gathering and dissemination to sophisticated attempts to force compliance with list prices. In highly competitive industries it is doubtful that even aggressive attempts to fix prices by associations will be successful. In concentrated markets, however, trade associations may provide a successful vehicle for price-fixing.

As precedents have developed, a Rule of Reason has evolved in trade association cases. Simple information gathering and dissemination has come to be viewed as reasonable, but attempts to *impose* prices directly or indirectly have come to be viewed as unreasonable.

American Column and Lumber Company v. United States 257 U.S. 377 (1921)   In December 1918 the American Hardwood Manufacturers Association was formed. The association's 400 members operated only 5 percent of the total hardwood lumber mills in the United States, but produced 33 percent of total output. Of the 400 members, 365 agreed to a plan for reporting prices to the association.

The plan required *daily* reports on all sales, including buyer and seller identification; kind, grade, and quality specifications; and prices. The reports were gathered and distributed by the manager of statistics, F. R. Gadd, to all plan members, who were subject to association audit. Furthermore, the reports were supplemented by monthly regional meetings to discuss prices. Under the plan prices increased sharply in 1919. The defense attributed these increases to the wartime pent-up demand for lumber and to poor weather conditions.

By a 6–3 split, the Supreme Court ruled that the plan went too far. Justice Clark wrote the opinion:

> After stating that the purpose was not to restrict competition or to control prices but to "furnish information to enable each member to intelligently make prices and to intelligently govern his production," the [plan's] committee [stated the following]:
>
> > . . . By making prices known to each other [prices] will gradually tend toward a standard *in harmony with market conditions,* a situation advantageous to both buyer and seller. . . .
> > *Knowledge regarding prices actually made is all that is necessary to keep prices at reasonably stable and normal levels.* . . .
>
> By keeping all members fully and quickly informed of what the others have done, the work of the plan results in *a certain uniformity of trade practice.* There is no agreement to follow the practice of others, *although members do naturally follow their most intelligent competitors,* if they know what these competitors have been actually doing. . . .
> It is plain that the only element lacking in this scheme to make it a familiar type of the competition suppressing organization is a definite agreement as to production and prices. But this is supplied: by the disposition of men "to follow their most intelligent competitors," especially when powerful; by the inherent disposition to make all the money possible, joined with the steady cultivation of the value of "harmony" of action; and by the system of reports, which makes the discovery of price reductions inevitable and immediate. The sanctions of the plan obviously are, financial interest, intimate personal contact, and business honor, all operating under the restraint of exposure of what would be deemed bad faith and of trade punishment by powerful rivals. . . .
> Genuine competitors do not make daily, weekly and monthly reports of the minutest details of their business to their rivals, as the defendants did; they do not contract, as was done here, to submit their books to the discretionary audit and their stocks to the discretionary inspection of their rivals for the purpose of successfully competing with them; and they do not submit the details of their business to the analysis of an expert, jointly employed, and obtain from him a "harmonized" estimate of the market as it is and as, in his specially and confidentially informed judgment, it promises to be. This is not the conduct of competitors but is so clearly that of men united in an agreement, express or implied, to act together and pursue a common purpose under a common guide.

The plan probably had at best a limited effect on prices because 9,000 independent lumber producers remained outside the association, but since this type of reporting scheme could be used as the basis for an effective price-fixing arrangement, the decision set a good precedent. In 1925, however, the Court appeared to back away from this precedent in the *Maple Flooring* case.

Maple Flooring Manufacturers Association v. United States 268 U.S. 563 (1925)

In 1922 the Maple Flooring Manufacturers Association was organized by twenty-two producers of maple, beech, and birch flooring. Association members produced 70 percent of total national output. Fifty-eight other manufacturers of flooring in the United States remained outside the association.

The government complaint centered on the association's policy of publishing members' average production costs *plus* a booklet showing freight rates from Cadillac, Michigan, to over 5,000 cities. According to the complaint the average-cost figures could easily be combined with freight-rate figures to fix delivered prices throughout the country. This was especially true since previous Maple Flooring Associations, which had been organized as early as 1913, had incorporated suggested minimum prices in their freight-rate books by using just such a formula.

The Supreme Court, by 6–3, ruled in favor of the Maple Flooring Association. Justice Stone delivered the majority opinion:

> Before considering these phases of the activities of the Association, it should be pointed out that it is neither alleged nor proved that there was any agreement among the members of the Association either affecting production, fixing prices or for price maintenance. Both by the articles of association and in actual practice members have been left free to sell their product at any price they choose and to conduct their business as they please.
>
> It cannot, we think, be questioned that data as to the average cost of flooring circulated among the members of the Association when combined with a calculated freight rate which is either exactly or approximately the freight rate from the point of shipment, plus an arbitrary percentage of profit, could be made the basis for fixing prices or for an agreement for price maintenance, which, if found to exist, would under the decisions of this Court, constitute a violation of the Sherman Act. But, . . . the record is barren of evidence that the published list of costs and freight-rate book have been used by the present Association. . . .
>
> It is the consensus of opinion of economists and of many of the most important agencies of Government that the public interest is served by the gathering and dissemination, in the widest possible manner, of information with respect to the production and distribution, cost and prices in actual sales, of market commodities, because the making available of such information tends to stabilize trade and industry, to produce fairer price levels and to avoid the waste which inevitably attends the unintelligent conduct of economic enterprise. . . . Restraint upon free competition begins when

improper use is made of that information through any concerted action which operates to restrain the freedom of action of those who buy and sell. . . .

Persons who unite in gathering and disseminating information in trade journals and statistical reports on industry; who gather and publish statistics as to the amount of production of commodities in interstate commerce; and who report market prices, are not engaged in unlawful conspiracies in restraint of trade merely because the ultimate result of their efforts may be to stabilize prices or limit production through a better understanding of economic laws and a more general ability to conform to them, for the simple reason that the Sherman Law neither repeals economic laws nor prohibits the gathering and dissemination of information.

Justice Stone's position implies that the *public* reporting of price information, in the absence of any overt attempt to fix prices, is legal. A major distinction between the two cases was the fact that the Maple Flooring Association offered its price information to buyers and sellers, whereas the American Column & Lumber Association made its information available only to sellers. In theory, the latter practice should be more restrictive than the former. In reality, however, if the members of the association have a significant amount of market power, either practice can be used as a basis for stabilizing prices.

***Sugar Institute, Inc. v. United States* 297 U.S. 553 (1936)**   The Sugar Institute consisted of fifteen manufacturers, who produced more than 80 percent of the refined cane sugar in the United States. The institute established a code of ethics that distinguished ethical from unethical types of behavior. The code of ethics required far more than the simple announcement of prices. Institute members agreed to refuse to deal with water carriers who refused to announce freight rates or who granted price concessions to any sugar refiner, wholesalers who granted *any* price concessions, and any trucker, broker, or warehouseman who granted secret rebates. The institute actually forced brokers to pledge, under oath, to adhere to the code of ethics. Members were also prohibited from granting quantity price discounts, even if they were justified by lower costs. Finally, f.o.b. (free on board) pricing, whereby buyers paid the mill price plus *actual* freight costs, was prohibited.

By 7–0, the Supreme Court condemned this behavior. Chief Justice Hughes wrote

The *"basic agreement."* — The "Code of Ethics" provided as follows:

"All discriminations between customers should be abolished. To that end, sugar should be sold only upon open prices and terms publicly announced."

The distinctive feature of the "basic agreement" was not the advance announcement of prices, or a concert to maintain any particular basis price for any period, but a requirement of adherence, without deviation, to the prices and terms publicly announced. Prior to the [formation of the] Institute, the list prices which many of the "unethical" refiners announced, "were merely nominal quotations and bore no relation to the actual 'selling bases' at which their sugar was sold. . . . The Institute sought to prevent such departures." . . .

Under the Institute, defendants agreed to sell, and in general did sell sugar only upon open prices, terms and conditions publicly announced in advance of sales, and they agreed to adhere and in general did adhere without deviation, to such prices, terms and conditions until they publicly announced changes." . . .

The restrictions imposed by the Sherman Act are not mechanical or artificial. We have repeatedly said that they set up the essential standard of reasonableness. . . .[T]he dissemination of information is normally an aid to commerce. As free competition means a free and open market among both buyers and sellers, competition does not become less free merely because of the distribution of knowledge of the essential factors entering into commercial transactions. . . .

Questions of reasonableness are necessarily questions of relation and degree. In the instant case, a fact of outstanding importance is the relative position of defendants in the sugar industry. We have noted that fifteen refiners, represented in the Institute, refine practically all the imported raw sugar processed in this country. . . .

The unreasonable restraints which defendants imposed lay not in advance announcements, but in the steps taken to secure adherence, without deviation, to prices and terms thus announced.

The Sugar Institute went to great lengths to eliminate price-cutting, and it was this behavior that led to its condemnation. The final Supreme Court decree restrained the defendants from combining in any program affecting "the sale, marketing, shipment, transportation, storage, distribution, or delivery of refined sugar." The Supreme Court, however, diluted the district court decree by permitting a system of systematic price reporting and dissemination.

Tag Manufacturers Institute v. Federal Trade Commission **174 F.2d 452 (1949)** Following the *Sugar Institute* decision, the government won several cases against trade associations that had followed sophisticated price-reporting schemes. In 1949, however, the government lost an attempt to eliminate a less restrictive reporting policy in the tag industry.

The Tag Manufacturers Institute consisted of thirty-one members, who produced over 95 percent of all business tags. The institute adopted rules that required its members to report their prices under the threat of financial penalty. Relying on evidence of continuing price competition and the general availability of information to both buyers and sellers, the Circuit Court of Appeals ruled in favor of the tag manufacturers.

Chief Judge Magruder spoke for the Court of Appeals:

> Article II of the 1940 Agreement requires the subscribers to report to the [institute] the prices, terms and conditions of each sale or contract to sell any tag products covered by the agreement. . . .
>
> [Article II continued,] "Nothing herein shall be construed as a limitation or restriction upon the right of each Subscriber independently to establish such prices, or such terms and conditions of sale, or policies of whatever nature affecting prices or sales, as he may deem expedient. . . .
>
> [Furthermore,] "[a]ll information relating to prices, terms and conditions of sale disseminated to the Subscribers pursuant hereto shall be freely and fully available to public agencies, distributors and consumers of the products, and to any other properly interested persons; and shall be disseminated in the same manner as to Subscribers, to such of them as may apply therefore and arrange for payment of the reasonable cost of such service." . . .
>
> [T]he evidence of the practice of the parties under the agreement [negates] the possibility of an inference that the real agreement of the Subscribers was that they would adhere to their filed list prices. They all made off-list sales, and reported them to [the institute] as required by the agreement. Off-list pricing has occurred without discernible territorial pattern, with no apparent correlation between the frequency of off-list sales and the size of the orders, or the classes of customers. There has been wide variation in the proportion of off-list business of individual manufacturers from week to week. The Commission found, as an over-all average, that approximately 25 percent of the dollar volume of the aggregate total sales of all the subscribing manufacturers has been at off-list prices. . . .
>
> Despite the fact that the Tag Industry Agreements have been in effect for a number of years, the Commission has produced no evidence indicating that the percentage of adherence to list prices has been on the increase, or indeed, that there is now a greater adherence to list prices than was the case prior to the promulgation of the NRA Code. . . . Nor is there evidence of "retaliatory action" by any Subscriber to coerce other Subscribers into adherence to list prices. . . .
>
> In every one of the instances where more than three manufacturers were bidding for the same order, the customer had a choice of different quoted prices. . . . Not a single buyer was called by the Commission as a witness to testify that he tried shopping around on a price basis among two or more manufacturers and was met by uniformity of price quotations. . . .
>
> It is noteworthy that the Commission has failed to produce a single tag buyer to testify that he was unaware of the existence of this information

service, or that he sought information from [the institute] and could not get it, or that he sought to subscribe to the service and was refused. . . . We agree with petitioners that availability "does not mean that the information must be crammed down the throats of buyers who are not interested in seeing it.". . .

We have come to the conclusion that the reporting agreements herein, and the practices of petitioners thereunder, are lawful under the controlling authorities.

These four trade association cases represent fairly well the present state of the law with regard to trade association activities. Price-reporting schemes that do little more than require members to report prices, and that then make this information available to the public, will generally be permitted. Direct attempts to force adherence to list prices, or restrict price-cutting, will bring an association within the reach of section 1.

IV   THE PROFESSIONS

Until the 1970s it was common for professional societies to restrict competition by forbidding advertising and/or price competition. In recent years, however, the courts have greatly limited the scope of their permitted restrictions, and it is now safe to assume that the professions come well within the jurisdiction of the Sherman Act.

***Goldfarb v. Virginia State Bar* 421 U.S. 773 (1975)**   In 1971 the Goldfarbs purchased a home in Fairfax County, Virginia. In order to secure a mortgage, they were required to obtain title insurance. The Goldfarbs consulted thirty-six lawyers and were told by each of them that the fee would be 1 percent of the value of the property. Furthermore, they were told that the Fairfax County Bar Association suggested this 1 percent fee to its members. Believing that the bar association's action violated the Sherman Act, the Goldfarbs decided to sue.

The Supreme Court, by 8–0, supported the Goldfarbs' position. Chief Justice Burger delivered the Court's opinion:

The fee schedule [all] the lawyers referred to is a list of recommended minimum prices for common legal services. Respondent Fairfax County Bar Association published the fee schedule although, as a purely voluntary association of attorneys, the County Bar has no formal power to enforce it. . . . Although the State Bar has never taken formal disciplinary actions to compel adherence to any fee schedule, it has published reports condoning fee schedules, and has issued two ethical opinions indicating that fee schedules cannot be ignored. The most recent opinion states that "evidence that an attorney *habitually* charges less than the suggested minimum fee schedule adopted by his local bar Association, raises a presumption that such lawyer is guilty of misconduct." . . .

The County Bar argues that because the fee schedule is merely advisory, the schedule and its enforcement mechanism do not constitute price fixing. . . .

The record here, however, reveals a situation quite different from what would occur under a purely advisory fee schedule. Here a fixed, rigid price floor arose from respondents' activities: every lawyer who responded to petitioners' inquiries adhered to the fee schedule, and no lawyer asked for additional information in order to set an individualized fee. The price information disseminated did not concern past standards, . . . but rather minimum fees to be charged in future transactions, and those minimum rates were increased over time. The fee schedule was enforced through the prospect of professional discipline from the State Bar, and the desire of attorneys to comply with announced professional norms. . . . [H]ere a naked agreement was clearly shown, and the effect on prices is plain. . . .

On this record respondents' activities constitute a classic illustration of price fixing. . . .

The County Bar argues that Congress never intended to include the learned professions within the terms "trade and commerce" in section 1 of the Sherman Act, and therefore the sale of professional services is exempt from the Act. No explicit exemption or legislative history is provided to support this contention; rather, the existence of state regulation seems to be its primary basis. . . .

We cannot find support for the proposition that Congress intended any such sweeping exclusion. . . . Congress intended to strike as broadly as it could in section 1 of the Sherman Act, and to read into it so wide an exemption as that urged on us would be at odds with that purpose. . . .

In the modern world it cannot be denied that the activities of lawyers play an important part in commercial intercourse, and that anticompetitive activities by lawyers may exert a restraint on commerce.

The *Goldfarb* case restricted the use of fee schedules in the legal profession. Two years later the Supreme Court addressed another issue, advertising.

Bates v. State Bar of Arizona 433 U.S. 350 (1977)   John R. Bates and Van O'Steen were licensed attorneys in Arizona. In 1974 they opened a legal clinic in Phoenix for the purpose of handling simple legal cases for low fees. For two years, Bates and O'Steen abided by a state bar ban on advertising and watched their practice sink to the verge of bankruptcy. In desperation, on February 22, 1976, they placed an advertisement in the *Arizona Republic,* a newspaper. The advertisement helped business, but it also resulted in disciplinary action by the state bar. When Bates and O'Steen were suspended from practicing law by the State Bar of Arizona, they decided to take the bar association to court.

Bates and O'Steen contended that the advertising ban violated the Sherman Act *and* the First Amendment's protection of freedom of speech. The Supreme Court, by a 5–4 margin, ruled that the state bar's rule against advertising did *not* violate the Sherman Act, but it also ruled that the ban was unconstitutional.

Justice Blackman delivered the opinion:

> Appellants concede that the advertisement constituted a clear violation of Disciplinary Rule 2–101 (B), incorporated in Rule 29 (a) of the Supreme Court of Arizona. . . . The disciplinary rule provides in part:
>
>> "(B) A lawyer shall not publicize himself or his partner, or associate, or any other lawyer affiliated with him or his firm as a lawyer through newspaper or magazine advertisements, radio or television announcements, display advertisements in the city or telephone directories, nor shall he authorize or permit others to do so in his behalf."
>
> In *Parker v. Brown,* 317 U.S. 341 (1943), this Court held that the Sherman Act was not intended to apply against certain state actions. . . . In *Parker* a raisin producer challeng[ed] a state program designed to restrict competition among growers and thereby to maintain prices in the raisin market. The Court held that the State "as sovereign, imposed the restraint as an act of government which the Sherman Act did not undertake to prohibit." Appellee argues, and the Arizona Supreme Court held, that the PARKER exemption also bars the instant Sherman Act claim. We agree. . . .
>
> In the instant case, . . . the challenged restraint is the affirmative command of the Arizona Supreme Court under its Rules 27 (a) and 29 (a) and its Disciplinary Rule 2–101 (B). That court is the ultimate body wielding the State's power over the practice of law, . . . and, thus, the restraint is "compelled by direction of the State acting as a sovereign." . . .
>
> The heart of the [remaining] dispute before us today is whether lawyers . . . may [under the First Amendment] constitutionally advertise the *prices* at which certain routine services will be performed. Numerous justifications are proffered for the restriction of such price advertising. We consider each in turn:
>
> 1. *The Adverse Effect on Professionalism.* . . . It is claimed that price advertising will bring about commercialization, which will undermine the attorney's sense of dignity and self-worth. . . .
>
> [W]e find the postulated connection between advertising and the erosion of true professionalism to be severely strained. At its core, the argument presumes that attorneys must conceal from themselves and from their clients the real-life fact that lawyers earn their livelihood at the bar. . . .

2. *The Inherently Misleading Nature of Attorney Advertising.* It is argued that advertising of legal services inevitably will be misleading. . . .

We are not persuaded that restrained professional advertising by lawyers inevitably will be misleading. . . . The argument that legal services are so unique that fixed rates cannot meaningfully be established is refuted by the record in this case: The appellee State Bar itself sponsors a Legal Services Program in which the participating attorneys agree to perform services like those advertised by the appellants at standardized rates. . . .

[I]t seems peculiar to deny the consumer, on the ground that the information is incomplete, at least some of the relevant information needed to reach an informed decision. The alternative — the prohibition of advertising — serves only to restrict the information that flows to consumers. Moreover, the argument assumes that the public is not sophisticated enough to realize the limitations of advertising, and that the public is better kept in ignorance than trusted with correct but incomplete information. We suspect the argument rests on an underestimation of the public. . . .

3. *The Adverse Effect on the Administration of Justice.* . . . Advertising, it is argued, serves to encourage the assertion of legal rights in the courts, thereby undesirably unsettling societal repose. . . . Although advertising might increase the use of the judicial machinery, we cannot accept the notion that it is always better for a person to suffer a wrong silently than to redress it by legal action. . . .

4. *The Undesirable Economic Effects of Advertising.* It is claimed that advertising will increase the overhead costs of the profession, and that these costs then will be passed along to consumers in the form of increased fees. . . .

Although it is true that the effect of advertising on the price of services has not been demonstrated, there is revealing evidence with regard to products; where consumers have the benefit of price advertising, retail prices often are dramatically lower than they would be without advertising. It is entirely possible that advertising will serve to reduce, not advance, the cost of legal services to the consumer. . . .

5. *The Adverse Effect of Advertising on the Quality of Service.* It is argued that the attorney may advertise a given "package" of service at a set price, and will be inclined to provide, by indiscriminate use, the standard package regardless of whether it fits the client's needs.

Restraints on advertising, however, are an ineffective way of deterring shoddy work. An attorney who is inclined to cut quality will do so regardless of the rule on advertising. . . .

In sum, we are not persuaded that any of the proffered justifications rise to the level of an acceptable reason for the suppression of all advertising by attorneys. . . .

In holding that advertising by attorneys may not be subject to a blanket suppression, and that the advertisement at issue is protected, we, of course, do not hold that advertising by attorneys may not be regulated in

any way. We mention some of the clearly permissible limitations on advertising not foreclosed by our holding.

Advertising that is false, deceptive, or misleading of course is subject to
restraint. . . .

Advertising concerning transactions that are themselves illegal
obviously may be suppressed. . . .

The constitutional issue in this case is only whether the State may
prevent the publication in a newspaper of appellants' truthful advertisement
concerning the availability and terms of routine legal services. We rule
simply that the flow of such information may not be restrained, and we
therefore hold the present application of the disciplinary rule against appellants to be violative of the First Amendment.

Since *price* advertising provides information to consumers, it
generally is procompetitive. As a result of this ruling, price competition
has undoubtedly increased in several professions, including law, op-
tometry, and dentistry. If just one justice, however, had changed his
position, it would have prevented consumers from obtaining the benefits associated with this increased price competition.

National Society of Professional Engineers v. United States **98
S.Ct. 1355 (1978)**   In July 1964 the National Society of Professional
Engineers adopted a code of ethics that prohibited competitive bidding.
Under the code, engineers were prohibited from discussing fees until
after a client had selected an engineer for a project. If a client demanded
an advance discussion of fees, the engineer was required to withdraw
from the project.

The society argued that such a restriction was necessary to protect
the public health, safety, and welfare. According to this defense, competitive bidding would result in low-quality engineering work, which
would result in collapsed buildings and bridges. Of course, given what
would happen to an engineering firm's reputation if one of its buildings
collapsed, it is difficult to place much faith in this argument.

The Supreme Court did not accept the society's position. Justice
Stevens delivered the Court's opinion:

This claim does not . . . involve any claim that the National Society has
tried to fix specific fees, or even a specific method of calculating fees. It
involves a charge that the members of the Society have unlawfully agreed
to refuse to negotiate or even to discuss the question of fees until after a
prospective client has selected the engineer for a particular project. . . .

In this case we are presented with an agreement among competitors to
refuse to discuss prices with potential customers until after negotiations
have resulted in the initial selection of an engineer. While this is not price
fixing as such, no elaborate industry analysis is required to demonstrate the

anticompetitive character of such an agreement. It operates as an absolute ban on competitive bidding, applying with equal force to both complicated and simple projects and to both inexperienced and sophisticated customers. . . . On its face, this agreement restrains trade within the meaning of section 1 of the Sherman Act. . . .

The Sherman Act reflects a legislative judgment that ultimately competition will produce not only lower prices, but also better goods and services. . . . The assumption that competition is the best method of allocating resources in a free market recognizes that all elements of a bargain — quality, service, safety, and durability — and not just the immediate cost, are favorably affected by the free opportunity to select among alternative offers. . . .

The fact that engineers are often involved in large-scale projects significantly affecting the public safety does not alter our analysis. Exceptions to the Sherman Act for potentially dangerous goods and services would be tantamount to a repeal of the statute. In our complex economy the number of items that may cause serious harm is almost endless — automobiles, drugs, foods, aircraft components, heavy equipment, and countless others, cause serious harm to individuals or to the public at large if defectively made. The judiciary cannot indirectly protect the public against this harm by conferring monopoly privileges on the manufacturers. . . .

In sum, the Rule of Reason does not support a defense based on the assumption that competition itself is unreasonable. Such a view of the Rule would create the "sea of doubt" on which Judge Taft refused to embark in *Addyston,* . . . and which this Court has firmly avoided ever since.

These three cases suggest that professional organizations generally cannot restrict price or advertising competition. The professions represented one of the few major new areas of antitrust action in the 1970s, and the fairly strict interpretation adopted by a fairly conservative Supreme Court suggests that no court is likely to significantly change the strict restrictions against agreements that affect price. This remains the clearest and strongest area in antitrust law: Direct agreements among competitors that affect price are illegal *per se.*

V SUMMARY

The Court's tough stand against direct price-fixing agreements makes economic sense. There are so few cases of economically justified price-fixing that a *per se* ban, by avoiding long, complicated, and costly arguments over reasonableness, represents an optimal policy.

With regard to oligopolistic behavior, the issues are far more complex. The way the antitrust laws are worded, and the way they have been interpreted, there is little chance of a major tightening of the existing laws in this area. Consciously parallel behavior is likely to remain outside the reach of the current set of antitrust statutes. Furthermore, in the absence of structural remedies, it is doubtful that convictions and fines will have much impact on oligopolistic behavior. Oligopolists follow consciously parallel behavior because it is rational. It is highly unlikely that fines can force oligopolists to behave irrationally. Unless the courts dramatically change their current position and order structural remedies in oligopoly cases, any long-run change in policy may require new legislation. Such legislation has been periodically proposed, but it has never gotten very far in Congress, and it is impossible to imagine such legislation in the near future. For the near future, therefore, oligopolistic parallel behavior will be beyond the reach of the antitrust laws in all but the most extreme cases.

With regard to trade associations, it has been suggested that the law has been interpreted too leniently [5]. Periodic reporting of price information to competitors can be used to discourage price-cutting because few firms wish to be identified as chiselers by their competitors, who are often also their friends in the association as well as on the golf course. On the other hand, the issue is one of degree. Monthly price reporting would probably have much less of an effect than daily reporting, so some Rule of Reason may be acceptable.

Overall, the antitrust laws have been fairly successful in the area of horizontal agreements. In the absence of the Sherman Act, price-fixing would undoubtedly be far more common, and despite the protestations of a small minority of economists, the economic inefficiencies that would result from permitting collusion would place a significant burden on society [6].

NOTES

1. D. E. Waldman, "Welfare and Collusion: Comment," *American Economic Review,* March 1982, pages 268–271.

2. This view was quite common during the first twenty-five years of this century. See J. M. Clark, *Studies in the Economics of Overhead Costs* (Chicago: University of Chicago Press, 1923), pages 434–450. For a later statement of this position see A. Phillips, *Market Structure, Organization and Performance* (Cambridge, Mass.: Harvard University Press, 1962), pages 221–242. See also F. M. Scherer, *Industrial Market Structure and Economic Performance* (Chicago: Rand-McNally, 1980), pages 218–220.

3. E. H. Chamberlin, *The Theory of Monopolistic Competition* (Cambridge, Mass.: Harvard University Press. 1933).

4. For a survey see Scherer, *Industrial Market Structure and Economic Performance,* Chapters 5 and 6.

5. Ibid., page 524; and D. F. Greer, *Business, Government, and Society* (New York: Macmillan, 1983), page 140.

6. D. Dewey, "Information, Entry, and Welfare: The Case for Collusion," *American Economic Review,* September 1979, page 588. For a rather extreme, and to this author unconvincing, statement of this position, see D. T. Armentano, *Antitrust and Monopoly: Anatomy of a Policy Failure* (New York: Wiley, 1982), Chapter 5.

CHAPTER
SIX

Price
Discrimination

I INTRODUCTION

The Robinson-Patman Act, which amended section 2 of the Clayton Act, is the most controversial of the antitrust statutes. Passed during the Great Depression, its original intention was primarily to prevent large chain store buyers from inducing suppliers to grant price concessions that were unavailable to small retail stores. Ironically, section 2(f), which is the only provision aimed directly at *buyer* behavior, has been ineffective. Instead, the Robinson-Patman Act has been directed almost entirely at *sellers* who grant discriminatory prices.

Sometimes called the Magna Carta for small businesses, the Robinson-Patman Act often appears to turn antitrust policy upside down by protecting small competitors rather than the competitive process. The problem stems from the fact that price discrimination is often pro-competitive, yet the statute does not adequately recognize this fact.

Three economic conditions are necessary for a firm to practice price discrimination successfully. First, a price discriminator must have some market power in the sense that the nondiscriminatory profit-maximizing price is above marginal cost. In the absence of market power the high-priced consumer would simply buy elsewhere. Price discrimination, therefore, cannot exist in perfectly competitive markets, and its observance suggests there are less than perfectly competitive industry structure and performance. Second, the firm must be able to separate its markets according to different elasticities of demand. AT&T separates its long-distance market into an inelastic business segment from 8 A.M. to 5 P.M. on weekdays and a much more elastic segment on evenings and weekends. Third, the product must be non-transferable between consumers; otherwise, a high-priced buyer could simply get a low-priced buyer to purchase the product and then transfer it back to the high-priced buyer. Movie theaters can charge different admission prices for adults and children, but they cannot charge children lower popcorn prices. If they did, most popcorn would be purchased by children and eaten by adults.

The competitive effects of price discrimination vary greatly from case to case. Price discrimination may improve the allocation of resources by bringing price closer to marginal cost and/or improving capacity utilization, thereby lowering average total costs. Consider price discrimination in the airline industry. Suppose a plane is about to take off with only 50 percent of the seats filled. Given that the plane *would* otherwise fly at 50 percent capacity, what is the marginal cost of adding one additional passenger? A little thought suggests that marginal cost approaches zero in this situation. (This ignores the small amount of extra fuel needed to carry a bit more weight and the cost of food served to the extra passenger, which many passengers could live better without anyway.) If the airline offers an additional passenger *any* fare between full fare and zero, allocative efficiency will be improved. Half-priced student stand-by fares, which were common in the 1960s, served just such a purpose. The student stand-by fare covered marginal cost and represented a mutually advantageous economic exchange. Assuming that a full-fare ticket was priced above the student's reservation price, both the student and the airline were better off as a result of the stand-by policy. Furthermore, society was also better off because capacity utilization increased and the average cost per passenger mile decreased.

Another common example of price discrimination that improves efficiency is the case of the small-town doctor who discriminates by income group. Figure 6-1 illustrates this situation. If a small-town doctor faced a demand curve *D* and an average-cost curve AC, then no single fee would enable the doctor to cover average costs, and the town would lose the doctor's services. If, however, the doctor charges a high

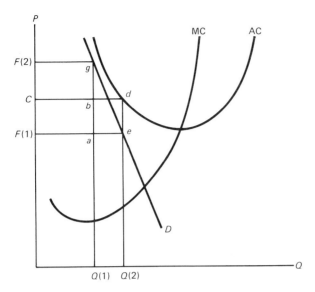

Figure 6-1

fee of $F(2)$ per visit to $Q(1)$ rich patients and a low fee of $F(1)$ to $[Q(2) - Q(1)]$ poor patients, then the doctor can cover costs. Under this discriminatory fee schedule, the physician's average cost for *all* patients would be C, and excess profits (equal to area $F(2)gbC$) earned on rich patients would more than cover the economic loss (equal to area $abde$) sustained on the treatment of the poor. In this case, only through discrimination can the town keep its doctor.

Although most temporary or sporadic price discrimination improves efficiency, some predatory discrimination may be anticompetitive. This predatory discrimination has the specific aim of weakening or driving competitors from the market and then raising prices well above marginal and average costs. Most predatory discrimination is systematic and carried out by dominant firms, and it is only this predatory discrimination that offers any serious threat to the competitive process. Ironically, the Robinson-Patman Act has rarely been successful in attacking predatory discrimination, but it has often been successfully directed at practices that have little, if any, negative effect on competition. Furthermore, at least in theory, true predatory behavior can be attacked under section 2 of the Sherman Act, without reference to the Robinson-Patman Act.

Robinson-Patman Act cases can be grouped into either primary line or secondary line cases according to their effect on competion. *Primary line* cases involve possible injures to the *direct* competitor or competitors. Most primary line injury cases involve geographic price discrimination, where a national firm sells in one submarket at prices significantly below its prices elsewhere. If Sealtest decided to sell its ice cream at a much lower price in Montana than in the rest of the country, this action could cause injury to small local dairies that made ice cream in Montana, even though Sealtest did not manufacture ice cream in Montana. *Secondary line* cases involve possible injuries to the competitor or competitors of a buyer who receives a lower discriminatory price. If Sealtest sold ice cream to the Safeway food chain at a lower price than any other store, it might injure Safeway's competitors, such as A&P.

The Robinson-Patman Act forbids price discrimination "where the effect of such discrimination may be substantially to lessen competition or tend to create a monopoly in any line of commerce or to injure, destroy, or prevent competition with any person who either grants or knowingly receives the benefit of such discrimination, or with customers of either of them." Unlike the other antitrust acts, which require some lessening of competition, the Robinson-Patman Act requires injury *either* to the competitive process *or* to specific competitors. Furthermore, the act requires only that there *may* be a substantial lessening of competition; therefore, any price discrimination that *may* have a negative effect on *any* competitor at *any* level of competition may be subject to Robinson-Patman Act enforcement.

The Robinson-Patman Act provided two major defenses: cost justification and meeting competition. The act, however, left the standards for allowing either defense wide open for judicial interpretation. Most of the major issues in the following cases revolve around the judicial standards for an acceptable defense.

II SECONDARY LINE CASES

Three of the earliest major Robinson-Patman Act cases involved basing-point pricing systems. Under a basing-point system, an industry established one or more geographic locations as basing points, and buyers were charged prices that included standard freight charges from the basing point, even if the seller's manufacturing plant was located far from the basing point. Basing-point systems were most common in industries characterized by high transportation costs relative to value.

The most famous system was the steel industry's *Pittsburgh-Plus* system. During the early part of the twentieth century Pittsburgh was the only basing point in the steel industry, and all steel shipments included a freight charge from Pittsburgh, even if the steel was shipped from Chicago or Birmingham. If a Chicago appliance manufacturer purchased steel from a Chicago steel mill, it paid for freight from Pittsburgh! Since no freight charge actually existed, the Chicago producer was able to pocket this phantom freight. On the other hand, if a Chicago mill sold steel to a Pittsburgh firm, it would be forced to absorb the freight charge.

Basing-point systems have several advantages for oligopolists. First and foremost, since prices are fixed for delivery anywhere in the country, the system is an excellent method for maintaining discipline. Second, all firms do reasonably well under basing-point systems. Firms located at a basing point can compete with producers located far from the basing point, and firms located far from the basing point obtain phantom freight on many shipments to cover their freight absorption on shipments made close to the basing point.

From an efficiency viewpoint, however, basing-point systems create significant problems. First, basing-point systems often result in a significant amount of *cross-hauling,* a situation where shipments pass each other in transit while traveling to buyers located far from manufacturing facilities. Cross-hauling occurs frequently because firms located at a basing point often make shipments to areas that can more efficiently be served by local mills and during recessions in particular, in an attempt to increase capacity utilization, firms located far from a basing point often make shipments to buyers located close to the basing point. Under the Pittsburgh-Plus system it was not uncommon for Pittsburgh-based firms to ship steel to Chicago while Chicago-based mills were shipping steel to Pittsburgh. Such a situation would obviously increase total transportation costs. Under an f.o.b. (free on board) pricing system cross-hauling would be unlikely because locally produced steel would almost always be cheaper than steel produced at a distant mill.

Another efficiency problem was the ease with which a basing-point system could be used as a form of tacit collusion. The system established uniform prices throughout the nation. Furthermore, the system discouraged price chiseling because if chiselers were caught, the other members of the industry would establish a punitive basing point at the chiseler's plant location. Prices would then be established from the punitive basing point at a level that was below the chiseler's average cost. The price chiseler would sustain an economic loss on *every* sale and would eventually be forced to raise prices to industry-wide levels, to leave the market, or to sell out to a competitor. The punitive basing-point system was successful because the price chiseler sustained economic losses on *every* sale. Other firms sustained losses only on the sales into the price chiseler's local market.

Finally, the system created economically inefficient plant-location incentives. Since there was an advantage associated with being located close to a basing point, far too much capacity relative to demand located at designated basing points. In the early part of the century Pittsburgh produced over five times its steel requirements, but Detroit had to import most of its steel for producing automobiles.

Two rather obvious questions may arise: What does the basing-point system have to do with the Robinson-Patman Act? And, why not attack these systems under the Sherman Act? Basing-point systems have been successfully challenged under the Sherman Act, but the two earliest cases were Robinson-Patman Act cases. In these cases the FTC argued that buyers located close to a seller, but far from a basing point, paid higher mill net prices and, therefore, were discriminated against. The first two rulings were handed down on the same day in 1945. Both concerned the basing-point system in the glucose (corn syrup) industry.

Corn Products Refining Company v. Federal Trade Commission **324 U.S. 726 (1945)**   The Corn Products Refining Company was a large glucose manufacturer that operated plants in Chicago and in Kansas City, Missouri. It sold glucose primarily to candy manufacturers, and all sales were made at delivered prices based on the single basing point of Chicago. Candy manufacturers outside Chicago paid a higher price than Chicago buyers, even if they were located in Kansas City and purchased from the Corn Products plant in Kansas City.

In 1939 the Chicago price was $2.09 per hundred pounds, and the Kansas City price was $2.49 ($2.09 + $0.40 phantom freight from Chicago). The FTC argued that the system discriminated against candy manufacturers located in Kansas City because the net price (net price = price − actual freight) in Kansas City was $2.49 compared with only $1.79 ($2.09 − $0.40) on glucose shipped *from* the Kansas City plant to Chicago candy manufacturers. The commission argued that candy manufacturers located in Kansas City were, therefore, injured by this discrimination.

The Supreme Court ruled 8–0 in favor of the FTC. Justice Stone delivered the opinion:

> Petitioners point out that there is no discrimination under their basing point system between buyers at the same points of delivery, and urge that the prohibition of section 2 (a) is directed only at price discrimination between buyers at the same delivery points. There is nothing in the words of the statute to support such a distinction, since the statute is not couched in terms of locality. . . . The purchasers of glucose from petitioners are found to be in competition with each other, even though they are in different localities.
>
> Petitioners further contend that basing point systems were well known prior to the enactment of the Robinson-Patman Act and were considered by Congress to be legal. . . .
>
> When the Robinson-Patman Act was adopted in 1936, there was no settled construction of [section 2] of the Clayton Act in the federal courts contrary to that now urged by the Commission. . . . In fact, in 1924 in the only decision involving the problem, the Federal Trade Commission, after extensive investigation and hearings, ordered the United States Steel Corporation and its subsidiaries to cease and desist from the sales of their

rolled steel products on the "Pittsburgh-Plus" price system. The Commission held that the use of a single basing point at Pittsburgh for steel plants over the country was a violation of section 2 of the Clayton Act, as well as section 5 of the Federal Trade Commission Act, as they then read.

[P]etitioners argue that Congress, by the rejection of a provision of the Robinson-Patman Bill, which would have in effect prohibited all basing point systems has indicated its intention to sanction all such systems. . . .

Such a drastic change in existing pricing systems as would have been effected by the proposed amendment engendered opposition, which finally led to the withdrawal of the provision by the House Committee on the Judiciary. We think this legislative history indicates only that Congress was unwilling to require f.o.b. factory pricing, and thus to make all uniform delivered price systems and all basing point systems illegal *per se*. . . .

Petitioners insist that the Commission's findings, based upon the facts stipulated, do not support its conclusion that petitioners' discriminations have the prescribed effect [on competition]. . . .

Since petitioners' basing point system results in a Chicago delivered price which is always lower than any other, including that at Kansas City, a natural effect of the system is the creation of a favored price zone for the purchasers of glucose in Chicago and vicinity, which does not extend to other points of manufacture and shipment of glucose. Since the cost of glucose, a principal ingredient of low-priced candy, is less at Chicago, candy manufacturers there are in a better position to compete for business, and manufacturers of candy located near other factories producing glucose, distant from the basing point, as Kansas City, are in a less favorable position. . . . The Commission's findings that glucose is a principal ingredient of low priced candy and that differences of small fractions of a cent in the sales price of such candy are enough to divert business from one manufacturer to another, readily admit of the Commission's inference that there is a reasonable probability that the effect of the discriminations may be substantially to lessen competition. . . .

The Commission's conclusions are amply supported by its findings and the evidence, and the judgment is *Affirmed.*

In later sections of the *Corn Products* decision the Court banned two other practices as discriminatory. First, the Corn Products Company had a policy of announcing price increases in advance. It would then give buyers five days to purchase at the old prices and thirty days to take delivery at the old prices. Certain favored customers, however, were permitted longer option periods. The Supreme Court ruled that this practice was an illegal method of indirect price discrimination. Second, the Corn Products Company had spent over $750,000 to advertise Curtiss Candy (makers of Baby Ruth and Butterfingers) as "rich in dextrose." This practice violated section 2(e) of the Robinson-Patman Act, which banned the furnishing of services to one company that were not available "to all purchasers on proportionally equal terms."

On the same day that it handed down the *Corn Products* decision, the Supreme Court handed down a companion ruling in the *Staley* case.

Federal Trade Commission v. A. E. Staley Manufacturing Co. 324 U.S. 746 (1945)

Staley was a glucose producer located in Decatur, Illinois. It competed with the Corn Products Refining Company and also followed a single basing-point system based on Chicago-delivered prices. When Staley entered the industry in 1920, the basing-point system was well established, and Staley argued that its adoption of the system was made in good faith to meet competition. The Court of Appeals upheld Staley's position. The Supreme Court, however, reversed that decision.

Justice Stone again delivered the opinion:

[T]he conclusion of the Commission that the price discriminations involved are prohibited by section 2 (a) [is] challenged here. But, for the reasons we have given in our opinion in the *Corn Products Refining Company* case, the challenge must fail. The sole question we find it necessary to discuss here is whether respondents have succeeded in justifying the discriminations by an adequate showing that the discriminations were made "in good faith" to meet equally low prices of competitors. . . .

[I]t appears that in 1920, when repondents began the manufacture of glucose or corn syrup, they found that syrup manufactured by their competitors "was being sold at delivered prices in the various markets of the United States"; that in Chicago two large factories were manufacturing syrup and delivering it in Chicago at prices lower than prices then prevailing in any other market; and that delivered price in such other markets was generally equal to the Chicago price plus the published freight rate from Chicago to the point of delivery. Respondents thus found in operation a pricing system which, if followed, would produce exact identity in prices of glucose of the several producers when sold in any city in the United States. . . . When respondents soon found that their product would command the same market price as that of their competitors, they "adopted the practice of selling at the same delivered prices as [their] competitors, whatever they might be." . . .

If respondents' argument is sound, it would seem to follow that even if the competitor's pricing system were wholly in violation of section 2 of the Clayton Act, respondents could adopt and follow it with impunity. . . .

We think the conclusion is inadmissible, in view of the clear Congressional purpose not to sanction by section 2 (b) the excuse that the person charged with a violation of the law was merely adopting a similarly unlawful practice of another . . .

Respondents have never attempted to establish their own non-discriminatory price system, and then reduced their price when necessary to meet competition. Instead they have slavishly followed in the first instance a pricing policy which, in their case, resulted in systematic discriminations, by charging their customers upon shipments from Decatur, the Chicago base price plus their competitors' actual costs of delivery from Chicago. Moreover, there is no showing that if respondents had charged non-discriminatory prices, they would be higher in all cases than those now prevailing under their basing point system. Hence it cannot be said that respondents' price discriminations have resulted in "lower" prices to meet equally low prices of a competitor. . . .

The Commission's conclusion seems inescapable that respondents' discriminations, such as those between purchasers in Chicago and Decatur, were established not to meet equally low Chicago prices of competitors there, but in order to establish elsewhere the artificially high prices whose discriminatory effect permeates respondents' entire pricing system. . . .

Section 2 (b) does not require the seller to justify price discriminations by showing that in fact they met a competitive price. But it does place on the seller the burden of showing that the price was made in good faith to meet a competitor's. The good faith of the discrimination must be shown in the face of the fact that the seller is aware that his discrimination is unlawful, unless good faith is shown, and in circumstances which are peculiarly favorable to price discrimination abuses. We agree with the Commission that the statute at least requires the seller, who has knowingly discriminated in price, to show the existence of facts which would lead a reasonable and prudent person to believe that the granting of a lower price would in fact meet the equally low price of a competitor. . . .

The Commission's order will be sustained.

The *Staley* decision established two important precedents. First, the decision established that it was not an acceptable good faith defense to meet a competitor's *illegally* discriminatory price. Second, it established the future standard for judging good faith defenses as the showing "of facts which would lead a reasonable and prudent person to believe that the granting of a lower price would in fact meet the equally low price of a competitor."

The final legal death knell for basing-point systems came just three years later in the *Cement Institute* case.

Federal Trade Commission v. Cement Institute 333 U.S. 683 (1948) The *Cement Institute* case differed from the *Corn Products* and *Staley* cases in several important respects. First, it was filed as a FTC Act and Robinson-Patman Act case. Second, it involved a multiple basing-point system. Under a multiple basing-point system, several different cities were established as basing points for the calculation of delivered prices, and each American city was placed in a different basing-point zone for the purpose of these calculations.

The major FTC charge was that the cement manufacturers had

engaged in an "unfair method of competition" and had "restrained and hindered competition . . . by means of a combination among themselves made effective through mutual understanding or agreement to employ a multiple basing point system of pricing." The Supreme Court decision pointed out many concerted anticompetitive actions, including boycotts, discharging uncooperative employees, opposition to building new plants, establishment of punitive basing points to destroy price chiselers, and supplying freight-rate books for use in calculating actual or phantom freight. On this basis the Court ruled that the Cement Institute had violated the FTC Act. This ruling was consistent with the tough stand taken against conscious parallelism in the 1940s and closely followed the 1946 *American Tobacco* precedent (see Chapter 5).

The second count in the FTC complaint charged a Robinson-Patman Act violation, and Justice Black's opinion made virtually all basing-point systems illegal as violations, not of the FTC Act, but of the Robinson-Patman Act. Justice Black's basic argument was that the combined effect of the *Corn Products* and *Staley* decisions was to ban all basing-point systems. Justice Black wrote

> In the *Corn Products* case the Court, in holding illegal a single basing point system, specifically reserved decision upon the legality under the Clayton Act of a multiple basing point price system but only in view of the "good faith" proviso of section 2 (b), and referred at that point to the companion *Staley* opinion. The latter case held that a seller could not justify the adoption of a competitor's basing point price system under section 2 (b) as a good faith attempt to meet the latter's equally low price. Thus the combined effect of the two cases was to forbid the adoption for sales purposes of any basing point system. It is true that the Commission's complaint in the *Corn Products* and *Staley* cases simply charged the individual respondents with discrimination in price through use of a basing point price system, and did not, as here, allege a conspiracy or combination to use that system. But the holdings in those two cases that section 2 forbids a basing point system are equally controlling here, where the use of such a system is found to have been the result of a combination. . . .
>
> Each of the respondents, whether all its mills were basing points or not, sold some cement at prices determined by the basing point formula and governed by other base mills. Thus, all respondents to this extent adopted a discriminatory pricing system condemned by section 2.

For all pratical purposes the *Cement Institute* case ended legal basing-point systems in the United States. The steel industry, for example, voluntarily abandoned its multiple basing-point system after the handing down of the *Cement Institute* decision, but basing-point systems still occasionally arise. The plywood industry adopted a basing-point system well into the 1970s [see In the Matter of Boise Cascade

Corp. F.T.C. Docket 8958 (1978)]. Under the plywood industry's system, Southern plywood mills charged Southern buyers prices that included freight charges from Portland, Oregon. It has been estimated that the system resulted in $600 million a year in phantom freight [1]. In 1982 several defendants agreed to pay over $165 million in damages to put an end to a private class-action suit that had been filed against the plywood manufacturers in 1972.

A *per se* ban on industry-wide systematic basing-point systems is justified. Basing-point systems distort market prices and costs. Furthermore, by encouraging firms to enter basing-point industries with stable price structures, the systems may encourage excessive entry and a great deal of excess capacity [2]. Individual producers may, from time to time, be forced to adopt a delivered pricing system to match local competition, but this can be just as easily accomplished under a uniform f.o.b. pricing system with freight absorption to meet a competitor's lower price. At the very least, buyers should have the option of f.o.b. pricing with buyer pickup at the mill. Although some economists might disagree, the elimination of most basing-point systems has probably been the most significant positive economic effect of the Robinson-Patman Act.

***Federal Trade Commission v. Morton Salt Company* 334 U.S. 37 (1948)**   One week after handing down the *Cement Institute* decision, the Supreme Court handed down its first major precedent in a quantity-based system case. Morton Salt was the nation's leading producer of table salt. Morton followed a strict quantity-based system of price discrimination. Prices were determined as shown in Table 6–1. Only five large chains, American Stores, National Tea, Kroger, Safeway, and A&P, received the top discount. As a result, these five chains could sell at a retail price below the price that many independent wholesalers paid Morton for salt. Morton argued that the discounts were available to all purchasers and, therefore, were not discriminatory.

The Supreme Court ruled 7–2 against Morton. Justice Black delivered the majority opinion:

> Respondent's basic contention, which it argues this case hinges upon, is that its "standard quantity discounts, available to all on equal terms, as contrasted, for example, to hidden or special rebates, allowances, prices or discounts, are not discriminatory within the meaning of the Robinson-Patman Act." Theoretically, these discounts are equally available to all, but functionally they are not. For as the record indicates (if reference to it on this point were necessary) no single independent retail grocery store, and probably no single wholesaler, bought as many as 50,000 cases or as much as $50,000 worth of table salt in one year. . . . The legislative history of the Robinson-Patman Act makes it abundantly clear that Congress consid-

Table 6–1   MORTON SALTS PRICES FOR DIFFERENT QUANTITIES

Quantity	Price per Case
Less than carload	$1.60
Carload	$1.50
5,000 carloads/year	$1.40
50,000 carloads/year	$1.35

ered it to be an evil that a large buyer could secure a competitive advantage over a small buyer solely because of the large buyer's quantity purchasing ability. The Robinson-Patman Act was passed to deprive a large buyer of such advantages except to the extent that a lower price could be justified by reason of a seller's diminished costs due to quantity manufacture, delivery or sale, or by reason of the seller's good faith effort to meet a competitor's equally low price. . . .

It is argued that the findings fail to show that respondent's discriminatory discounts had in fact caused injury to competition. . . . The statute requries no more than that the effect of the prohibited price discriminations "may be substantially to lessen competition . . . or to injure, destroy, or prevent competition." After a careful consideration of this provision of the Robinson-Patman Act, we have said that "the statute does not require that the discriminations must in fact have harmed competition, but only that there is a reasonable possibility that they 'may' have such an effect." Here the Commission found what would appear to be obvious, that the competitive opportunities of certain merchants were injured when they had to pay respondent substantially more for their goods than their competitors had to pay. The findings are adequate. . . .

[Morton Salt] suggested that in considering the adequacy of the evidence to show injury to competition respondent's carload discounts and its other quantity discounts should not be treated alike. The argument is that there is an obvious saving to a seller who delivers goods in carload lots. . . . Since Congress has not seen fit to give carload discounts any favored classification we cannot do so. Such discounts, like all others, can be justified by a seller who proves that the full amount of the discount is based on his actual savings in cost. The trouble with this phase of respondent's case is that it has thus far failed to make such proof.

It is also argued that respondent's less-than-carload sales are very small in comparison with the total volume of its business and for that reason we should reject the Commission's finding that the effect of the carload discrimination may substantially lessen competition and may injure competition between purchasers who are granted and those who are denied this discriminatory discount. To support this argument, reference is made to the fact that salt is a small item in most wholesale and retail businesses and in consumers' budgets. For several reasons we cannot accept this contention.

There are many articles in a grocery store that, considered separately, are comparatively small parts of a merchant's stock. Congress intended to protect a merchant from competitive injury attributable to discriminatory prices on any or all goods sold in interstate commerce, whether the particular goods constituted a major or minor portion of his stock. Since a grocery store consists of many comparatively small articles, there is no possible way effectively to protect a grocer from discriminatory prices except by applying the prohibitions of the Act to each individual article in the store.

Furthermore, in enacting the Robinson-Patman Act, Congress was especially concerned with protecting small businesses which were unable to buy in quantities, such as the merchants here who purchased in less-than-carload lots. To this end it undertook to strengthen this very phase of the old Clayton Act. . . .

Apprehension is expressed in this Court that enforcement of the Commission's order against respondent's continued violations of the Robinson-Patman Act might lead respondent to raise table salt prices to its carload purchasers. Such a conceivable, though, we think, highly improbable, contingency, could afford us no reason for upsetting the Commission's findings and declining to direct compliance with a statute passed by Congress.

Two important precedents emerged from the *Morton Salt* case. First, only a reasonable *possibility* of injury to competition or competitors was required by the majority. This considerably reduced the burden of proof in Robinson-Patman Act cases since it is almost always possible to find a reasonable *possibility* that either competition or a competitor will be injured by price discrimination. Second, the *Morton Salt* case established that pure quantity-based discounts had to be *fully* cost justified.

The *Morton Salt* decision is certainly subject to criticism on economic grounds. In fact, the decision suggests the basic economic conflict that arises in so many Robinson-Patman Act cases. If all price discrimination is eliminated, a firm's output is likely to decline, and average costs are almost certain to rise. Ultimately, as a result, consumer prices may also rise. Furthermore, in the long run the banning of all quantity discounts may not even help small retailers. If the banning of discounts on salt encouraged the large chains to produce their own salt (i.e., backward vertical integration), then Morton's output would decline, its average costs might increase, and, as a result, Morton might increase its price to *small* retailers that are unable to produce their own salt. Under such circumstances, the difference between what large and small retailers pay for salt might increase. In addition, society's average cost of producing salt would likely rise, so long as some economies of scale in salt production exist for *either* Morton *or* the large chains. In any event, the decision clearly represented an attempt to protect small retailers from large chains, regardless of the effect on efficiency.

Standard Oil Company of Indiana v. Federal Trade Commission **340 U.S. 231 (1951) and *Federal Trade Commission v. Standard Oil Company of Indiana* 355 U.S. 396 (1958)** The next major secondary line case dealt with the other major defense established in the Robinson-Patman Act, the good faith meeting of competition. The *Standard Oil* case reached the Supreme Court twice before finally being settled in 1958. Standard Oil had followed a policy of charging four large Detroit jobber-retailers prices 1.5 cents per gallon less than its service station customers. Each of the four jobbers sold some of its gasoline at retail, and two of the four jobbers charged lower retail prices than generally prevailed for Standard Oil's gasoline. Each of the four took deliveries in tank-car quantities of 8,000–12,000 gallons, rather than the typical tank-wagon quantities of 700–800 gallons that were delivered to service stations. There were some cost savings associated with these large-quantity purchases; however, the *entire* 1.5 cent differential could not be cost justified.

Once its cost justification failed, Standard Oil argued that the reductions were made in a good faith effort to meet competition. The commission, however, ruled that meeting competition was not an *absolute* defense under section 2(b). The FTC's argument was a technical one, based on the fact that section 2(a) seemed to make only cost justification an absolute defense. The meeting of competition defense was relegated to section 2(b), which dealt primarily with the burden of proof in Robinson-Patman Act cases (see Chapter 2). A careful reading of the act suggests that the commission may have had a point. The Supreme Court, however, by 5-3, ruled that a good faith meeting of competition establishes an *absolute* defense under the Robinson-Patman Act. Justice Burton delivered the majority opinion:

> Petitioner placed its reliance upon evidence offered to show that its lower price to each jobber was made in order to retain that jobber as a customer and in good faith to meet an equally low price offered by one or more competitors. The Commission, however, treated such evidence as not relevant. . . .
>
> The trial examiner made findings on the point but the Commission declined to do so saying:
>
>> "Based on the record in this case the Commission concludes as a matter of law that it is not material whether the discriminations in price granted by the respondent to the said four dealers were made to meet equally low prices of competitors. . . . [E]ven though the lower prices in

question may have been made by respondents in good faith to meet the lower prices of competitors, this does not constitute a defense in the face of affirmative proof that the effect of the discrimination was to injure, destroy and prevent competition with the retail stations operated by the said named dealers and with stations operated by their retailer-customers."

The court below affirmed the Commission's position. . . .

[T]here has been widespread understanding that, under the Robinson-Patman Act, it is a complete defense to a charge of price discrimination for the seller to show that its price differential had been made in good faith to meet a lawful and equally low price of a competitor. . . .

The heart of our national economic policy long has been faith in the value of competition. In the Sherman and Clayton Acts, as well as in the Robinson-Patman Act, "Congress was dealing with competition, which it sought to protect, and monopoly, which is sought to prevent." . . . It is enough to say that Congress did not seek by the Robinson-Patman Act either to abolish competition or so radically to curtail it that a seller would have no substantial right of self-defense against a price raid by a competitor. For example, if a large customer requests his seller to meet a temptingly lower price offered to him by one of his seller's competitors, the seller may well find it essential as a matter of business survival, to meet that price rather than to lose the customer. It might be that this customer is the seller's only available market for the major portion of the seller's product, and that the loss of this customer would result in forcing a much higher unit cost and higher sales price upon the seller's other customers. There is nothing to show a congressional purpose, in such a situation, to compel the seller to choose only between ruinously cutting its prices to all its customers to match the price offered to one, or refusing to meet the competition and then ruinously raising its prices to its remaining customers to cover increased unit costs. There is, on the other hand, plain language and established practice which permits a seller, through section 2 (b), to retain a customer by realistically meeting in good faith the price offered to that customer, without necessarily changing the seller's price to its other customers.

In a case where a seller sustains the burden of proof placed upon it to establish its defense under section 2 (b), we find no reason to destroy that defense indirectly, merely because it also appears that the beneficiaries of the seller's price reductions may derive a competitive advantage from them or may, in a natural course of events, reduce their own resale prices to their customers. It must have been obvious to Congress that any price reduction to any dealer may always affect competition at that dealer's level as well as at the dealer's resale level, whether or not the reduction to the dealer is discriminatory. . . . The proviso in section 2 (b), as interpreted by the Commission, would not be available when there was or might be an injury to competition at a resale level. So interpreted, the proviso would have such little, if any, applicability as to be practically meaningless. We may, therefore, conclude that Congress meant to permit the natural consequences to follow the seller's action in meeting in good faith a lawful and equally low price of its competitor.

The case was remanded to the FTC for reconsideration of Standard Oil's meeting of competition defense. The commission ruled that Standard Oil had not acted in good faith, but instead was following a simple pricing system, where purchasers of over 2 million gallons a year received a lower price. The case was then appealed once more to the Supreme Court.

By the narrowest of margins, 5–4, the Supreme Court found for Standard Oil. Seventeen years after the case began, Justice Clark delivered the majority opinion:

> The Commission . . . seemingly does not contest the fact that Standard's deductions were made to meet the equally low prices of its competitors. However, Standard was held not to have acted in good faith, and the section 2 (b) defense precluded, because of the Commission's determination that Standard's reduced prices were made pursuant to a price system rather than being "the result of departures from a nondiscriminatory price scale." The Court of Appeals found no basis in the record for such a finding and vacated the order of the Commission. . . .
>
> The sole question then is one of fact: were Standard's reduced prices to four "jobber" buyers — Citrin-Kolb, Stikeman, Wayne, and Ned's — made pursuant to a pricing system rather than to meet individual competitive situations? . . .
>
> The findings show that both major and local suppliers made numerous attempts in the 1936–1941 period to lure these "jobbers" away from Standard with cut rate prices, often-times much lower than the-one-and-one-half-cent reduction Standard was giving them. It is uncontradicted, as pointed out in one of the Commission dissents, that Standard lost three of its seven "jobbers" by not meeting competitors' pirating offers in 1933–1934. All of this occurred in the context of a major gasoline price war in the Detroit area, created by an extreme overabundance of supply — a setting most unlikely to lend itself to general pricing policies. . . .
>
> After a prolonged period of haggling, during which Ned's pressured Standard with information as to numerous more attractive price offers made by other suppliers, Standard responded to an ultimatum from Ned's in 1936 with a half-cent-per-gallon reduction from the tank-wagon price. The Commission concedes that this first reduction occurred at a time when Ned's did not meet the criteria normally insisted upon by Standard before giving any reduction. Two years later, after a still further period of haggling and another Ned's ultimatum, Standard gave a second reduction of still another cent. . . .

Standard's use here of two prices, the lower of which could be obtained under the spur of threats to switch to pirating competitors, is a competitive deterrent far short of the discriminatory pricing of *Staley* [and] *Cement*, . . . and one which we believe within the sanction of section 2 (b) of the Robinson-Patman Act.

Justice Douglas spoke for the four dissenting justices:

The Court today cripples the enforcement of the Robinson-Patman Act . . . in an important area. . . .

Standard admitted that it gave reduced prices to some retailers and refused those reduced prices to other retailers. Before granting these retailers the reduced prices Standard classified them as "jobbers." Standard's definition of a "jobber" took into account the volume of sales of the "jobber," his bulk storage facilities, his delivery equipment, and his credit rating. If Standard's tests were met, the "retailer" became a "jobber" even though he continued to sell at retail. Moreover, Standard's test of who was a "jobber" did not take into account the cost to Standard of making these sales. . . . It comes down to this: a big retailer gets one price; a small retailer gets another price. . . .

The mere fact that a competitor offered the lower price does not mean that Standard can lawfully meet it. . . .

It is only a *lawful* lower price that may be met. Were it otherwise then the law to govern is not the Robinson-Patman Act but the law of the jungle. . . .

If this proviso were construed to permit showing of a competing offer as an absolute bar to liability for discrimination, then it would nullify the act entirely at the very inception of its enforcement, for in nearly every case mass buyers receive similar discriminations from competing sellers of the same product. . . . A discrimination in violation of this bill is in practical effect a commercial bribe to lure the business of the favored customer away from the competitor, and if one bribe were permitted to justify another the bill would be futile to achieve its plainly intended purposes.

Justice Douglas's dissent points out a major problem in this case and with the act in general. Suppose Gulf offered a discriminatory price to one of Standard Oil's jobbers; should Standard Oil be permitted to cut Gulf's price? Under the *Staley* precedent one would think not; however, under the *Standard Oil* precedent it would appear legitimate to match even an illegal price. Furthermore, once Standard Oil was permitted to cut Gulf's price, shouldn't Texaco be permitted to cut Standard Oil's price, and then Shell be permitted to cut Texaco's price? In other words, once one price cut in good faith is permitted, shouldn't every subsequent price cut be permitted? In which case the act would become almost worthless. This is not just a hypothetical question. During the litigation period of the *Standard Oil* case, the FTC had similar suits pending against Gulf, Texaco, and Shell. On the other hand, if good faith defenses were not permitted in such cases, it would tend to make prices more rigid in some oligopolies. This suggests another of the many dilemmas raised by Robinson-Patman Act enforcement.

The most important precedent coming out of the two *Standard Oil* decisions was the establishment of the good faith meeting of competition as an absolute defense in Robinson-Patman Act cases.

United States v. Borden Company **370 U.S. 460 (1962)** The 1962 *Borden* case concerned the pricing practices of two major distributors of milk in Chicago, Borden and Bowman Dairy. Both firms charged independent stores prices that included volume discounts based on daily purchases. In June 1954, for example, Borden established the price schedule shown in Table 6–2. Furthermore, Borden granted two large chains, A&P and Jewel, a flat 8.5 percent discount. A few large independents also received a 5.5 percent discount.

Bowman's discount schedule was similar, but more complex. It placed firms in one of seventeen discount groups, with discounts ranging from 3 percent to 8 percent. Furthermore, Bowman offered A&P and Kroger an 11 percent discount.

These pricing policies placed independents into one group, which had its prices determined by a volume-based discount schedule, and two large chains into an entirely separate group. Both firms used a cost justification defense, and each introduced a large volume of statistical evidence to support its claims; however, by 7–1, the Supreme Court rejected the defenses.

Justice Clark delivered the majority opinion:

> In defense the appellees each introduced voluminous cost studies in justification of their pricing systems. . . . There was no dispute as to the existence of price discrimination; the sole question was whether the differences in price reflected permissible allowances for variances in cost. . . .

Table 6–2   BORDEN'S VOLUME DISCOUNTS (JUNE 1954)

Average Converted Units per Day	Discount
0–24	0 percent
25–74	2 percent
75–149	3 percent
150 or more	4 percent

The Borden pricing system produced two classes of customers. The two chains, A&P and Jewel, with their combined total of 254 stores constituted one class. The 1,322 independent stores, grouped in four brackets based on the volume of their purchases, made up the other. Borden's cost justification was built on comparisons of its average cost per $100 of sales to the chains in relation to the average cost of similar sales to each of the four groups of independents. The costs considered were personnel (including routemen, clerical and sales employees), truck expenses, and losses on bad debts and returned milk. Various methods of cost allocation were utilized: Drivers' time spent at each store was charged directly to that store; certain clerical expenses were allocated between the two general classes; costs not susceptible of either of the foregoing were charged to the various stores on a per stop, per store, or volume basis.

Bowman's cost justification was based on differences in volume and methods of delivery. It relied heavily upon a study of the cost per minute of its routemen's time. It determined that substantial portions of this time were devoted to three operations, none of which were ever performed for the 163 stores operated by its two major chain customers. These added work steps arose from the method of collection, i.e., cash on delivery and the delayed collections connected therewith, and the performance of "optional customer services." . . . In essence, the Bowman justification was merely a comparison of the cost of these services in relation to the disparity between the chain and independent prices. Although it was shown that the five sample independents in the Government's prima facie case received the added services, it was not shown or found that all 2,500 independents supplied by Bowman partook of them. On the basis of its studies Bowman estimated that about two-thirds of the independent stores received the "optional customer services" on a daily basis and that "most store customers pay the driver in cash daily."

We believe it was erroneous for the trial court to permit cost justifications based upon such classifications. . . .

High on the list of "musts" in the use of the average cost of customer groupings under the proviso of section 2 (a) is a close resemblance of the individual members of each group on the essential point or points which determine the costs considered.

In this regard we do not find the classifications submitted by the appellees to have been shown to be of sufficient homogeneity. . . . Turning first to Borden's justification, we note that it not only failed to show that the economies relied upon were isolated within the favored class but affirmatively revealed that members of the classes utilized were substantially unlike in the cost saving aspects considered. For instance, the favorable cost comparisons between the chains and the larger independents were for the greater part controlled by the higher average volume of the chain stores in comparison to the average volume of the 80 member class to which these independents were relegated. . . . [S]uch a grouping for cost justification purposes, composed as it is of some independents having volumes comparable to, and in some cases larger than, that of the chain stores, created artificial disparities between the larger independents and the chain stores. It is like averaging one horse and one rabbit. As the Federal Trade Commission said in *In the Matter of Champion Spark Plug Co.,* 50 F.T.C. 30, 43 (1953): "A cost justification based on the difference between an estimated average cost of selling to one or two large customers and an average cost of selling to all other customers cannot be accepted as a defense to a charge of price discrimination." . . .

Likewise the details of Bowman's cost study show a failure in classification. Only one additional point need be made. Its justification emphasized its costs for "optional customer service" and daily cash collection with the resulting "delay to collect." As shown by its study these elements were crucial to Bowman's cost justification. In the study the experts charged all independents and no chain store with these costs. Yet, it was not shown that all independents received these services daily or even on some lesser basis. . . . Under such circumstances the use of these cost factors across the board in calculating independent store costs is not permissible justification, for it possibly allocates costs to some independents whose mode of purchasing does not give rise to them. . . .

In sum, the record here shows that price discriminations have been permitted on the basis of cost differences between broad customer groupings, apparently based on the nature of ownership but in any event not shown to be so homogeneous as to permit the joining together of these purchasers for cost allocation purposes. If this is the only justification for appellees' pricing schemes, they are illegal.

Borden and Bowman each attempted to use detailed statistical studies to justify their price discrimination; however, the Supreme Court ruled that their groupings were too broad for cost-averaging purposes. The decision suggests several reasons why firms have great difficulty establishing a valid cost justification defense. First, price discrimination must be *fully* cost justified, penny for penny. If prices differ by $1.00 and a firm justifies a 75 cent, or even 90 cent, cost difference, the defense is likely to fail. Furthermore, cost estimates must be based on average-cost estimates *not* marginal-cost estimates. Since the average cost, including an allocation for overhead, of servicing a large buyer is likely to be much higher than the marginal cost, this sets a very stringent standard for the legitimate use of the cost justification defense. The standard makes sense *if* the objective of policy is to prevent discounts to large buyers because under a marginal-cost rule almost all discrimination could be justified (a problem to be addressed later), but it makes for an almost "anything goes" standard because there is no generally accepted method for allocating fixed and joint production costs. Because the cost justification defense is extremely difficult to establish, there were only *two* cost justification defenses accepted in court between 1936 and 1954 [3].

American Oil Company v. Federal Trade Commission 325 F.2d 101 (1963) The *Morton Salt* precedent required only a reasonable *possibility* of injury to competition under the Robinson-Patman Act. In the 1963 *American Oil* case the Seventh Circuit Court of Appeals appeared to loosen up a bit on this standard. American Oil successfully argued that its lower prices to four dealers during a 1958 price war in Smyrna, Georgia, had not had a substantial effect on competition.

Smyrna is located fifteen miles northwest of Atlanta. On October 10, 1958, a Shell station in Smyrna lowered its price to meet the price of a Paraland service station selling unbranded gasoline. Other major-brand stations (Texaco, Sinclair, and Gulf) followed the Shell station's price reduction. As a result, American Oil's four Smyrna dealers requested and received a lower price in the form of an increased *competitive price allowance* (CPA). Over the next seventeen days, American Oil offered an increased CPA that varied between 3.5 and 11.5 cents per gallon. Six other American Oil dealers located in Marietta, Georgia, just north of Smyrna, received no CPAs. The price war ended on October 28, when the major-brand stations all increased their prices to their former high levels. The FTC argued that American Oil's price discrimination had injured the six American Oil dealers in Marietta.

The Seventh Circuit Court of Appeals held, however, that American Oil's price discrimination had not caused a substantial injury to competition. Judge Castle wrote

> The gasoline price war in the Smyrna area attracted patrons from the Marietta area. There is testimony that there was a preference on the part of some motorists for American gasolines, but only "if the price differential was not too great." And with respect to all major brands of gasoline the retail price differential between the two communities during the period here involved was such that it strains credulity to expect that customer loyalty and brand preference would have retained for American's Marietta dealers all of their patrons and their usual volume of business during the seventeen days of price cutting in the adjoining area. . . .
>
> Anderson, one of the six unfavored Marietta American dealers, operated a combined grocery store and service station on State route 3. . . . There is evidence which supports a conclusion that the reduction in the volume of Anderson's gasoline sales during the period of the Smyrna price war represented a loss of gross profit to him of as much as $150.00. . . . Marietta dealer Hitt, who was located about five miles from Hicks [a favored American Oil dealer], further north on route 3, testified that although "he might have lost some" business during the Smyrna price war period he "never complained about it." . . .

Morris was located approximately one and one-half miles north of Seagraves [another favored American Oil dealer]. He testified that most of his business was transient but that the "locals" complained that his price was "higher than other people who had the same gasoline down the road". His sales dropped approximately 1,000 gallons during October 1958. This would represent a loss of about fifty dollars gross profit. . . .

Thus, whatever injury to ability to compete, whether actual or probable, as is shown by the record, was not only minimal but there is no substantial evidence to show that it was the result of American's price reductions to its Smyrna dealers rather than for the most part attributable to the fact that the major brands of gasoline were being sold in the Smyrna area for substantially less than in the Marietta area. American's dealer assistance in the Smyrna area in the form of increased "CPA's", higher than those extended to its Marietta area dealers, was the result of such condition not the cause of it. . . .

[T]here must be something more than an essentially temporary minimal impact on competition and probative analysis must reveal a causal relation between the price discrimination and an actual or reasonably probable injury to competition in the context of the factual situation involved.

The standard set in the *American Oil* case makes a good deal of economic sense. The FTC's interpretation would have protected competitors (American Oil's Marietta dealers) at the expense of the competitive process. Furthermore, the type of temporary and unsystematic price discrimination exhibited by American Oil can only have a positive effect on competition.

Perkins v. Standard Oil Company of California 395 U.S. 642 (1969)   Clyde A. Perkins entered the oil and gasoline business in 1928 as the operator of one service station. By the mid-1950s Perkins was one of the largest independent wholesaler-retailers of gasoline and oil in the states of Washington and Oregon. From 1945 until 1957 Perkins purchased virtually all of his gasoline from Standard Oil of California. Beginning in 1955 Standard Oil charged Perkins a higher price for gasoline than it charged either its own branded dealers or Signal Oil & Gas Co., a wholesaler that sold to Perkins's competitors. Perkins argued that because of this discrimination he was forced to sell out to Union Oil in 1957.

Perkins filed suit, and in 1963 a jury awarded Perkins $1,298,213.71 in treble damages and attorney's fees. The court of appeals sustained the damages that resulted from Standard Oil's price discrimination in favor of its own branded dealers. With regard to Signal's purchases, the court of appeals ordered a new trial because Signal had sold this gasoline to Western Hyway (a wholesaler), which then sold it to Regal Stations (a retailer). According to the court of appeals, Regal Stations, as Perkins's retail competitor, was too far removed in the distribution chain from Standard Oil for Standard Oil to be held liable for damages without further proof of Regal Stations' independent share of the responsibility for Perkins's demise.

By 6–2, the Supreme Court overturned the court of appeals and ruled that even fourth-level competitive effects were subject to Robinson-Patman Act enforcement. Justice Black delivered the opinion:

> We disagree with the Court of Appeals conclusion. . . . Here, Perkins' injuries resulted in part from impaired competition with a customer (Regal) of a customer (Western Hyway) of the favored purchaser (Signal). The Court of Appeals termed these injuries "fourth level" and held that they were not protected by the Robinson-Patman Act. We conclude that this limitation is wholly an artificial one and is completely unwarranted by the language or purpose of the Act. . . .
>
> [T]o read "customer" more narrowly in this section . . . would allow price discriminators to avoid the sanctions of the Act by the simple expedient of adding an additional link to the distribution chain. Here, for example, Standard supplied gasoline and oil to Signal. Signal, allegedly because it furnished Standard with part of its vital supply of crude petroleum, was able to insist upon a discriminatorily lower price. Had Signal then sold its gas directly to the Regal stations, giving Regal stations a competitive advantage, there would be no question, even under the decision of the Court of Appeals in this case, that a clear violation of the Robinson-Patman Act had been committed. Instead of selling directly to the retailer Regal, however, Signal transferred the gasoline first to its subsidiary, Western Hyway, which in turn supplied the Regal stations. Signal owned 60% of the stock of Western Hyway; Western in turn owned 55% of the stock of the Regal stations. We find no basis in the language or purpose of the Act for immunizing Standard's price discriminations simply because the product in question passed through an additional formal exchange before reaching the level of Perkins' actual competitor. . . . Here Standard discriminated in price between Perkins and Signal, and there was evidence from which the jury could conclude that Perkins was harmed competitively when Signal's price advantage was passed on to Perkins' retail competitor Regal. . . .
>
> Furthermore, there was evidence that Perkins repeatedly complained to Standard officials that the discriminatory price advantage given Signal was being passed down to Regal and evidence that Standard officials were aware that Perkins' business was in danger of being destroyed by Standard's discriminatory practices. This evidence is sufficient to sustain the jury's award of damages under the Robinson-Patman Act.

The *Perkins* case ends our analysis of secondary line cases. In secondary line cases the Courts have taken a tough stand against price discrimination. There are few acceptable defenses, and this explains why most cases have ended with FTC cease and desist orders rather than in court. Primary line cases, however, present a different picture.

III   PRIMARY LINE CASES

Federal Trade Commission v. Anheuser-Busch, Inc. **363 U.S. 536 (1960) and** *Anheuser-Busch, Inc. v. Federal Trade Commission* **289 F.2d 835 (1961)**   The 1960 *Anheuser-Busch* case dealt with a court of appeals ruling that, if upheld, would have essentially made the Robinson-Patman Act useless in cases of geographic price discrimination. In 1954 Anheuser-Busch lowered the price of Budweiser beer in St. Louis considerably below the price it charged elsewhere. The FTC ruled that this behavior violated the Robinson-Patman Act, but the Seventh Circuit Court of Appeals held that "the threshold statutory element of price discrimination had not been established." The circuit court argued that since Anheuser-Busch charged the same price to all purchasers in St. Louis, no price discrimination had occurred.

The Supreme Court unanimously overturned the court of appeals. Chief Justice Warren delivered the opinion:

> The limited nature of our inquiry can be fully appreciated only in the light of the correspondingly narrow decision of the Court of Appeals, which rested entirely upon the holding that the threshold statutory element of price discrimination had not been established. Thus the Court of Appeals did not consider whether the record supported a finding of the requisite competitive injury, whether respondent's good faith defense was valid, or whether the Commission's order was unduly broad. We have concluded that the Court of Appeals erred in its construction of section 2 (a) and that the evidence fully warranted the Commission's finding of price discrimination. . . .
>
> A discussion of the import of the section 2 (a) phrase "discriminate in price," in the context of this case, must begin with a consideration of the purpose of the statute with respect to primary-line competition. The Court of Appeals expressed some doubt that section 2 (a) was designed to protect this competition at all. . . . While "precision of expression is not an outstanding characteristic of the Robinson-Patman Act," it is certain at least that section 2 (a) is violated where there is a price discrimination which deals the requisite injury to primary-line competition, even though secondary-line and tertiary-line competition are unaffected. . . .
>
> The legislative history of section 2 (a) is equally plain. The section, when originally enacted as part of the Clayton Act in 1914, was born of a desire by Congress to curb the use by financially powerful corporations of localized price-cutting tactics which had gravely impaired the competitive position of other sellers. . . .

Respondent concedes that a competitive relationship among purchasers is not a prerequisite of price discrimination, but maintains that at least there must be "proof that the lower price is below cost or unreasonably low for the purpose or design to eliminate competition and thereby obtain a monopoly." Since such a finding is lacking here, respondent argues that it cannot be said that there was price discrimination. . . .

Respondent also urges that its view is grounded upon the statutory scheme of section 2 (a), which penalized sellers only if an anticompetitive effect stems from a *discriminatory* pricing pattern, not if it results merely from a low price. Thus, the argument goes, unless there is proof that high prices in one area have subsidized low prices in another, the price differential does not fall within the compass of the section. . . . Finally, respondent argues that, unless its position is accepted, the law will impose rigid price uniformity upon the business world, contrary to sound economics and the policy of the antitrust laws.

The trouble with respondent's arguments is not that they are necessarily irrelevant in a section 2 (a) proceeding, but that they are misdirected when the issue under consideration is solely whether there has been a price discrimination. . . . Rather, a price discrimination within the meaning of the provision is merely a price difference. . . .

These assumptions, we now conclude, were firmly rooted in the structure of the statute, for it is only by equating price discrimination with price differentiation that section 2 (a) can be administered as Congress intended. . . .

What we have said makes it quite evident, we believe, that our decision does not raise the specter of a flat prohibition of price differentials, inasmuch as price differences constitute but one element of a section 2 (a) violation. In fact, as we have indicated, respondent has vigorously contested this very case on the entirely separate grounds of insufficient injury to competition and good faith lowering of price to meet competition. . . . Our interest is solely with this case, and at this stage of the litigation that interest is confined exclusively to identifying and keeping distinct the various statutory standards which are part of the section 2 (a) complex.

The judgment of the Court of Appeals is reversed and the case is remanded to that court for further proceedings not inconsistent with this opinion.

Having established that geographic discrimination came within the jurisdiction of the Robinson-Patman Act, the Court sent the case back to the court of appeals. The facts were straightforward. Before its first price decrease Anheuser-Busch controlled 12.5 percent of the St. Louis beer market. Griesedieck Western, Falstaff, and Griesedieck Brothers controlled 38.9, 29.4, and 14.4 percent, respectively. Following two price cuts, which lowered Budweiser's prices to its competitors' levels, Budweiser's market share increased to 39.3 percent; Griesedieck

Western's share fell to 23.1 percent; Griesedieck Brothers' share declined to just 4.8 percent; and Falstaff's share declined minimally to 29.1 percent. The price reductions lifted Budweiser from fourth place (last among the majors) to first place in the St. Louis market. When Anheuser-Busch increased its prices in March 1955, Budweiser's market share declined to only 17.5 percent.

The circuit court dismissed the case for a second time, ruling that Anheuser-Busch's price discrimination had not caused any injury to competition. Judge Schackenberg wrote the opinion:

> In the fall of 1953 after an increase in costs due to a new wage contract, AB [Anheuser-Busch] increased the price of Budweiser 15 cents a case in all markets except those in Missouri and Wisconsin. In many areas this small increase was multiplied by wholesalers' and retailers' markups to $1.20 a case at the retail level.
>
> Despite similar cost increases due to the same new wage contracts, a number of brewers, including Falstaff and AB's other St. Louis competitors, chose to absorb the increased costs, and did not raise prices in any market in which they did business. Their right to do so is not challenged. However, as a consequence, there was a spread between the price of Budweiser and the price of other beers. . . . As a result, in November and December 1953, AB began to suffer severe sales losses in the Midwest sales area, supplied by its St. Louis brewery — losses as high as 73% in Nebraska, 53% in Oklahoma, 58% in Texas, etc. In some states AB's sales were down as much as 83% below the previous year; and while industry sales were down only 8%, AB's sales were more than 35% below the previous year. . . .
>
> AB tried to roll back its price increase in one area, Ohio — but found, as it had anticipated, that the retailers and wholesalers were unwilling to give up their total additional markup of $1.20 per case merely because AB reduced its price 15 cents per case.
>
> The first price reduction in St. Louis went into effect on January 4, 1954 and amounted to 25 cents per case. This still left the price of Budweiser 33 cents higher than the prices of its three principal competitors in St. Louis. . . .
>
> Then, on June 21, 1954, the second price reduction of Budweiser in St. Louis was made, the new price being the same as its three competitors had been, and were then, charging for their beers. . . .
>
> While it is true that AB's sales increased in St. Louis during the period of the price reductions, . . . nevertheless AB's competitors still controlled more than three-fourths of the market sales in the twelve months after the price of Budweiser was voluntarily increased in St. Louis in March, 1955. While Budweiser and other premium beers were selling at the same price in St. Louis, buyers had a greater freedom of choice at the same price level and thus the contest for beer sales was intensified. . . .
>
> Whatever position AB obtained was temporary, by 1956 its sales had receded to 17.5% of the market, whereas Falstaff at that time had

increased to 43% of the market from the 29.4% it had enjoyed before the price reductions.

The examiner expressly found that there was no proof that AB used income or profit from the rest of its business to stabilize losses in St. Louis, or indeed that there were any losses by AB in St. Louis during the period of the price reductions.

AB's two price reductions were parts of an experimental program of sales promotion in the St. Louis market and the reductions were temporary and made necessary by competitive conditions. A primary result of AB's price reductions was that the consumers of beer in St. Louis enjoyed a lower price on Budweiser, since the price reductions were passed on to them by the retailers. . . .

From these undisputed facts we find that the commission failed to prove that AB's price reductions in 1954 caused any present, actual injury to competition.

The circuit court recognized correctly that the effect of Anheuser-Busch's price reductions was to improve efficiency by bringing price closer to marginal cost and giving consumers a wider choice of lower-priced beers. Furthermore, the court implicitly recognized that market competition on a *local* rather than national level determined prices in the beer industry. Prices would be expected to vary significantly from one regional market to another. Anheuser-Busch's behavior was not predatory, and the circuit court decision correctly protected the competitive process rather than the market positions of Budweiser's competitors.

The *Anheuser-Busch* case was not appealed to the Supreme Court, however, the 1967 *Utah Pie* Supreme Court decision suggests that the FTC may have won such an appeal under the Warren court.

Utah Pie Company v. Continental Baking Company 386 U.S. 685 (1967)   The *Utah Pie* decision is one of the most controversial antitrust decisions. Utah Pie was a small company that had been baking pies for thirty years when it entered the frozen pie market in 1957. Utah Pie must have made great pies because it quickly captured 66.5 percent of the Salt Lake City market. Three large national firms, Pet Milk, Continental, and Carnation, also sold frozen pies in Utah. The case centered on the response of the three national firms to Utah Pie's domination of the Salt Lake City market.

Pet Milk produced frozen pies in California and Pennsylvania. Prior to 1960 Pet sold pies in Utah under it own Pet-Ritz label and also under a private label to Safeway Foods. The court of appeals found that despite a 30–35 cent per dozen freight charge, Pet sold its Pet-Ritz brand in seven of forty-four months at prices that were lower in Salt Lake City than in California. Furthermore, in August 1960 Pet introduced a new pie to the Utah market under the Swiss Miss label at prices ranging between $3.25 and $3.30 per dozen. The same Swiss Miss pies were selling at higher prices in markets located closer to Pet's manufacturing plant in California.

Continental sold frozen pies under its Morton label. Its market share in Utah was small throughout the period 1958–1960, averaging about 2 percent. In June 1961, however, Continental offered its large apple pies in Utah at $2.85 per dozen, a price well below its apple pie prices in other markets. Evidence suggested that the $2.85 price may have been below "its direct cost plus an allocation for overhead." As a result of this price reduction, Continental's market share increased to 8.3 percent, and Utah Pie was forced to cut its apple pie prices to $2.75 per dozen.

Carnation held a 10.3 percent share of the Utah frozen pie market in 1958. In 1959 its share declined to 8.6 percent. Carnation then cut its price by 60 cents per dozen in Utah. The Supreme Court concluded that at this price Carnation was selling pies at prices below average total cost and well below its competitors' prices in Salt Lake City.

The evidence suggested that each of the defendants attempted at one time or another to cut into Utah Pie's market share. As a result, Utah Pie's share declined from 66.5 percent in 1958 to 34.3 percent in 1959, 45.5 percent in 1960, and 45.3 percent in 1961. It remained the leading seller in every year except 1959, when Pet Milk barely edged it out, 35.5 percent to 34.3 percent. Furthermore, it remained a profitable company throughout the four-year period.

The circuit court of appeals dismissed the case, holding that the evidence failed to support a finding of injury to competition. The Supreme Court, however, by 6–2, overturned the court of appeals. Justice White wrote the opinion:

> The major competitive weapon in the Utah market was price. The location of [Utah Pie's] plant gave it natural advantages in the Salt Lake City marketing area and it entered the market at a price below the then going prices for respondents' comparable pies. . . . Utah Pie, which entered the market at a price of $4.15 per dozen at the beginning of the relevant period, was selling "Utah" and "Frost 'N' Flame" pies for $2.75 per dozen when the instant suit was filed some 44 months later. . . .
>
> We deal first with petitioner's case against the Pet Milk Company. . . .
>
> [T]here was evidence from which the jury could have found considerably more price discrimination by Pet with respect to "Pet-Ritz" and "Swiss Miss" pies than was considered by the Court of Appeals. In addition to the seven months during which Pet's prices in Salt Lake were lower than prices in the California markets, there was evidence from which the jury could reasonably have found that in 10 additional months the Salt Lake City prices for "Pet-Ritz" pies were discriminatory as compared with sales in western markets other than California. . . .

Second, with respect to Pet's Safeway business, the burden of proving cost justification was on Pet and, in our view, reasonable men could have found that Pet's lower priced, "Bel-air" sales to Safeway were not cost justified in their entirety. Pet introduced cost data for 1961 indicating a cost saving on the Safeway business greater than the price advantage extended to that customer. These statistics were not particularized for the Salt Lake market, but assuming that they were adequate to justify the 1961 sales, they related to only 24% of the Safeway sales over the relevant period. The evidence concerning the remaining 76% was at best incomplete and inferential. . . .

Third, the Court of Appeals almost entirely ignored other evidence which provides material support for the jury's conclusion that Pet's behavior satisfied the statutory test regarding competitive injury. This evidence bore on the issue of Pet's predatory intent to injure Utah Pie. . . . Pet's own management, as early as 1959, identified Utah Pie as an "unfavorable factor," one which "d[u]g holes in our operation" and posed a constant "check" on Pet's performance in the Salt Lake City market. Moreover, Pet candidly admitted that during the period when it was establishing its relationship with Safeway, it sent into Utah Pie's plant an industrial spy to seek information that would be of use to Pet in convincing Safeway that Utah Pie was not worthy of its custom. . . .

It seems clear to us that the jury heard adequate evidence from which it could have concluded that Pet had engaged in predatory tactics in waging competitive warfare in the Salt Lake City market. . . .

Petitioner's case against Continental is not complicated. . . .

We again differ with the Court of Appeals. Its opinion that Utah was not damaged [by Continental] as a competitive force apparently rested on the fact that Utah's sales volume continued to climb in 1961 and on the court's own factual conclusion that Utah was not deprived of any pie business which it otherwise might have had. But this retrospective assessment fails to note that Continental's discriminatory below-cost price caused Utah Pie to reduce its price to $2.75. . . . Safeway, which had been buying Utah brand pies, immediately reacted and purchased a five-week supply of frozen pies from Continental, thereby temporarily foreclosing the proprietary brands of Utah and other firms from the Salt Lake City Safeway market. . . . [The jury] could also have reasonably concluded that a competitor who is forced to reduce his price to a new all-time low in a market of declining prices will in time feel the financial pinch and will be a less effective competitive force. . . .

After Carnation's temporary setback in 1959 it instituted a new pricing policy to regain business in the Salt Lake City market. . . . [I]n all but August 1961 the Salt Lake City delivered price was 20 cents to 50 cents lower than the prices charged in distant San Francisco. The Court of Appeals held that only the early 1960 prices could be found to have been below cost. That holding, however, simply overlooks evidence from which the jury could have concluded that throughout 1961 Carnation maintained a below-cost price structure and that Carnation's discriminatory pricing, no less than that of Pet and Continental, had an important effect on the Salt Lake City market. . . .

This case concerns the sellers' market. In this context, the Court of Appeals placed heavy emphasis on the fact that Utah Pie constantly increased its sales volume and continued to make a profit. But we disagree with its apparent view that there is no reasonably possible injury to competition as long as the volume of sales in a particular market is expanding and at least some of the competitors in the market continue to operate at a profit. Nor do we think that the Act only comes into play to regulate the conduct of price discriminators when their discriminatory prices consistently undercut other competitors. . . . Courts and commentators alike have noted that the existence of predatory intent might bear on the likelihood of injury to competition. In this case there was some evidence of predatory intent with respect to each of these respondents. There was also other evidence upon which the jury could rationally find the requisite injury to competition. . . . We believe that the Act reaches price discrimination that erodes competition as much as it does price discrimination that is intended to have immediate destructive impact. In this case, the evidence shows a drastically declining price structure which the jury could rationally attribute to continued or sporadic price discrimination.

Justice Stewart presented the dissenting opinion:

In 1958 Utah Pie had a quasi-monopoly 66.5% of the market. In 1961 — after the alleged predations of the respondents — Utah Pie still had a commanding 45.3%. . . . Unless we disregard the lessons so laboriously learned in scores of Sherman and Clayton Act cases, the 1961 situation had to be considered more competitive than that of 1958. Thus, if we assume that the price discrimination proven against the respondents had any effect on competition, that effect must have been beneficent. . . .

[L]ower prices are the hallmark of intensified competition.

The Court of Appeals squarely identified the fallacy which the Court today embraces:

". . . a contention that Utah Pie was entitled to hold the extraordinary market share percentage of 66.5, attained in 1958, falls of its own dead weight. To approve such a contention would be to hold that Utah Pie was entitled to maintain a position which approached, if it did not in fact amount to a monopoly, and could not exist in the face of proper and healthy competition."

I cannot hold that Utah Pie's monopolistic position was protected by the federal antitrust laws from effective price competition, and therefore respectfully dissent.

It is easy to understand why the *Utah Pie* decision created so much controversy. The case concerned the basically unsuccessful attempt of three competitors to break a firm's domination (66.5 percent market share) of a local market by cutting prices in a temporary and rather sporadic manner. Without question, the effect of these price reductions on consumers and short-run welfare was positive, with prices reduced to levels closer to marginal cost.

There is another side to the case however. Each of the three national firms showed some evidence of predatory intent. Pet Milk went so far as to send an industrial spy into Utah Pie's plant. Furthermore, although prices always covered marginal costs, there was serious doubt that they always covered average total costs. Finally, there is no doubt that below-cost pricing *can* be used by large national firms in local markets to attempt to destroy local competition. If this behavior were always permitted, it might result in long-run problems since a few large national firms could come to dominate many markets.

The *Utah Pie* decision resulted in a good deal of criticism from economists and was a major impetus for an article by Areeda and Turner in which they argued that only prices below marginal cost should be considered predatory [4]. Furthermore, since marginal costs are so difficult to estimate, Areeda and Turner suggested average *variable* cost as a proxy. Areeda and Turner's position was in turn criticized by many economists [5]. In this author's opinion, the Areeda and Turner position is far too extreme. In fact, carried to its logical conclusion (i.e., only prices below average *variable* cost are predatory), their position implies that only prices below a firm's *short-run shut-down price* are predatory! Such a strict standard may occasionally be breached by some crazy competitor *obsessed with* the elimination of another competitor, but virtually all price discrimination takes place at prices well above average variable costs.

The Areeda and Turner position has already had a significant impact on some court decisions. In *International Air Industries v. American Excelsior* the Fifth Circuit Court of Appeals came close to adopting their exact position.

International Air Industries Inc. and Vebco, Inc. v. American Excelsior Company 517 F.2d 714 (1975)

International Air Industries controlled a subsidiary, Vebco, which was primarily a distributor of air-conditioning and heating equipment in El Paso, Texas. American Excelsior (AMXCO) was the world's largest manufacturer of evaporative cooler pads for air conditioners. AMXCO's manufacturing operation was located in Arlington, Texas. Beginning in 1953 and continuing throughout 1969, the only cooler pads distributed by Vebco were produced by AMXCO.

Prior to 1969 AMXCO had favored its El Paso distributors over its Arizona distributors by absorbing the freight costs of shipments from its El Paso distributors to their Arizona customers; however, AMXCO did not pay freight costs for its Arizona distributors' shipments to their El

Paso customers. In 1969 AMXCO decided to eliminate this discrimination in favor of its El Paso distributors by eliminting all freight payments. As a result, Vebco decided to hand-manufacture and distribute its own cooler pads. When AMXCO learned of Vebco's manufacturing plans, it terminated its relationship with Vebco, but took no price action against Vebco even though it was losing sales in El Paso.

At the same time, Southwest Industries was formed and began machine-manufacturing and marketing cooler pads in El Paso. Because of its concern about the emergence of Southwest Industries, Vebco reached an agreement with AMXCO in 1970 whereby it purchased cooler pads specially packaged under a Vebco label. On March 1, 1971, however, Vebco failed to verify an order for three carloads of AMXCO pads that it had previously ordered. As a result, AMXCO concluded that Vebco would now compete against AMXCO by selling its own make of pads, and AMXCO decided to compete directly against Vebco.

Using estimates based on the previous public bids of Vebco and Southwest, and customer information, AMXCO offered a 25 percent discount in El Paso, which placed its El Paso prices considerably below its prices in other markets. AMXCO, however, made no sales at the 25 percent discount because Vebco matched the price. Furthermore, one customer reported to AMXCO that Vebco was offering up to a 50 percent discount. AMXCO then cut prices to a 32.5 percent discount, but Vebco once again matched the AMXCO price.

Ultimately, Vebco had trouble profitably maintaining a 32.5 percent discount, and so on March 29, 1971, it reduced its discount to 25 percent. AMXCO was then able to make one sale to K-Mart at a 39 percent discount. On May 28, 1971, Vebco filed a suit against AMXCO under the Robinson-Patman Act, and it later filed a Sherman Act claim as well. As soon as the suit was filed, AMXCO reduced its discounts to between 19 percent and 25 percent for the entire 1972 season.

Evidence indicated that Vebco's sales had increased every year since 1968 and that its percentage of the El Paso market had increased in 1971. Its markup on cooler pads, however, had declined in 1971.

Vebco's case relied on evidence of lost profits and predatory intent. According to Vebco, intent was suggested by a March 17, 1971, memo written by Carl Gillespie, AMXCO's division manager, which stated

[I]f we are committed to a program of stunting the possible growth of Vebco and keeping our foot in this quite sizable cooler pad market, then the real question we have here is just what price do we need to determine as our lowest price level.

A jury found in favor of AMXCO, and Vebco appealed. The Fifth Circuit Court of Appeals, relying heavily on the Areeda and Turner doctrine, supported AMXCO. Judge Morgan wrote

Since the allegedly harmful actions in this case involve pricing, we must examine the relationship between AMXCO's prices and costs in order to determine whether their price behavior was predatory. . . . When a firm sets its price equal to its average cost, its total revenues cover total costs, including normal returns on investment. If a monopolist is selling at a price at or above average cost, but could earn higher profits at a higher price, it may be attempting to deter entry into the field. . . . In either case, we believe that a price above average cost is a fairly competitive price for it is profitable to the monopolist if not to its rivals; in effect, the price excludes only less efficient firms.

In the case before us the entry of Vebco and Southwest created excess manufacturing capacity in the cooler pad market. Therefore, AMXCO's marginal cost was almost certainly below its average cost. In such a situation we do not believe that the monopolist's pricing behavior could be deemed anti-competitive unless the monopolist set a price below its own marginal cost — since any sale at or above marginal cost does not decrease short-run net returns. . . . [E]stablishing a price floor above marginal cost would permit the survival of far less efficient firms. Certainly, forcing a monopolist to charge a price higher than marginal cost could reduce industry output and waste economic resources in the short-run.

It is frequently quite difficult to calculate the incremental cost of making and selling the last unit (i.e., marginal cost) from a conventional business account. Consequently, the firm's average variable cost may be effectively substituted for marginal cost in predatory pricing analysis. Thus, a firm's pricing behavior can be considered anti-competitive when it sells at a price below its average variable cost. . . .

Evidence of AMXCO's costs was not cogently presented at trial, apparently because neither side considered it important. . . . AMXCO's largest discount of 39.25% (at which only one sale was made) produced a profit to the sales division of nearly 15 cents a pad. Thus, not only was the manufacturing division operating at a profit, but the sales division had a gross margin of around 33%. It would appear that AMXCO was selling its cooler pad at a price far above even its average cost.

Finally, we note that, in addition to believing the evidence rebutting Vebco's prima facie case, the jury could reasonably have found that AMXCO established one of the statute's affirmative defenses. The statute provides that even where price discrimination occurs, a discriminator may not be held liable for a violation of the Act if "his lower price . . . was made in good faith to meet an equally low price of a competitor." . . . AMXCO need not have shown that its prices were in fact equal to those of Vebco, "but must only [have shown] facts which would lead a 'reasonable and prudent person' to believe that the granting of the lower prices would in fact meet the equally low price of a competitor."

The facts of this case would enable a jury to believe that AMXCO set its price as a reasonable and prudent firm would, to meet Vebco's lower price.

The facts in the *AMXCO* case were very similar to those in the *Utah Pie* case; however, the decision relied on the Areeda and Turner doctrine, instead of the *Utah Pie* precedent. Under this doctrine, Utah Pie would almost certainly have lost its case because its competitors' prices were always above marginal cost and average variable cost. Unfortunately, the *AMXCO* case was never appealed to the Supreme Court, so a Supreme Court precedent on the Areeda and Turner doctrine has yet to be established.

In 1977 the Tenth Circuit Court of Appeals relied heavily on the *AMXCO* precedent in *Pacific Engineering & Production v. Kerr-McGee* [551 F.2d 790 (1977)]. For long periods of time Kerr-McGee had charged prices for ammonium perchlorate that were well below average total cost but above average variable cost. Kerr-McGee had also followed a series of aggressive practices that could easily have been used as evidence of predatory intent. The court of appeals, however, ruled in favor of Kerr-McGee, in part because "sales were always at prices above average variable cost and 'contributed to the company's cash flow.' "

The *AMXCO* decision can be defended on efficiency grounds. The evidence suggested that Vebco was at least as responsible as AMXCO for the price decline. Nevertheless, the widespread adoption of the average *variable* cost test may result in significant problems in the future since even the most aggressive predatory behavior could be justified. Such a position could have its greatest impact on monopolization cases. Even the 1911 *Standard Oil* and *American Tobacco* decisions could possibly have been overturned based on strict adherence to the Areeda and Turner doctrine.

Federal Trade Commission v. Borden Company 383 U.S. 637 (1966) and **Borden Company v. Federal Trade Commission 381 F.2d 175 (1967)** The 1966 and 1967 *Borden* decisions concerned the issue of private-label pricing. Since 1938 Borden had sold its evaporated milk under its Borden (Elsie the Cow) brand label and also under private labels, such as A&P. Despite the fact that the milk was identical in physical content, Borden charged a higher price for the Borden brand.

Borden began selling private-label evaporated milk in Tennessee and South Carolina in 1956. This private-label milk was produced in Borden's Southern plants. As a result of Borden's entry, business was diverted from some small private-label manufacturers that were located in the Midwest but sold in the South. The FTC complained that the practice violated the Robinson-Patman Act. The Fifth Circuit Court of Appeals put aside the commission's cease and desist order, which argued that private-label milk "as a matter of law" was not of the same grade and quality as branded milk. The Supreme Court, by 7–2, overturned the circuit court. Justice White delivered the majority opinion:

> The position of Borden and of the Court of Appeals is that the determination of like grade and quality, which is a threshold finding essential to the applicability of section 2 (a), may not be based solely on the physical properties of the products without regard to the brand names they bear and the relative public acceptance these brands enjoy — "consideration should be given to all commercially significant distinctions which affect market value, whether they be physical or promotional." Here, because the milk bearing the Borden brand regularly sold at a higher price than did the milk with a buyer's label, the court considered the products to be "commercially" different and hence of different "grade" for the purposes of section 2 (a), even though they were physically identical and of equal quality. . . .
>
> We reject this construction of section 2 (a) as did both the examiner and the Commission in this case. The Commission's view is that labels do not differentiate products for the purpose of determining grade or quality, even though the one label may have more customer appeal and command a higher price in the marketplace from a substantial segment of the public. . . .
>
> Obviously there is nothing in the language of the statute indicating that grade, as distinguished from quality, is not to be determined by the characteristics of the product itself, but by consumer preferences, brand acceptability or what customers think of it and are willing to pay for it. . . .
>
> Because it was feared that the Act would require the elimination of such price differentials, . . . it was suggested that the proposed section 2 (a) be amended so as to apply only to sales of commodities of "like grade, quality and *brand*." [Emphasis added by the Court.] There was strong objection to the amendment and it was not adopted by the Committee. . . .
>
> The Commission will determine, subject to judicial review, whether the differential under attack is discrimination within the meaning of the Act, whether competition may be injured, and whether the differential is cost-justified or is defensible as a good-faith effort to meet the price of a competitor. . . .
>
> The judgment of the Court of Appeals is reversed and the case is remanded for further proceedings consistent with this opinion.

Justice Stewart wrote the dissenting opinion:

> By pursuing product comparison only so far as the result of laboratory analysis, the Court ignores a most relevant aspect of the inquiry into the question of "like grade and quality" under section 2 (a): Whether the products are different in the eyes of the consumer. . . .
>
> The product purchased by a consumer includes not only the chemical

components that any competent laboratory can itemize, but also a host of commercial intangibles that distinguish the product in the marketplace. . . . Contrary to the Court's suggestion, this consumer expectation cannot accurately be characterized as a misapprehension. Borden took extensive precautions to insure that a flawed product [with Borden's own label on it] did not reach the consumer. None of these precautions was taken for the private brand milk packed by Borden. . . . "[C]ommercially the 'advertised' brands had come in the minds of the public to mean a different grade of milk. The public may have been wrong; . . . it may have been right. . . . But right or wrong, that is what it believed and its belief was the important thing." . . .

The caprice of the Commission's present distinction thus invites Borden to incorporate slight tangible variations in its private label products, in order to bring itself within the Commission's current practice of considering market preferences in such cases. . . .

In the guise of protecting producers and purchasers from discriminatory price competition, the Court ignores legitimate market preferences and endows the Federal Trade Commission with authority to disrupt price relationships between products whose identity has been measured in the laboratory but rejected in the marketplace.

This decision could have revolutionized the private-label industry, but upon remand the circuit court ruled that Borden's private-label business had not injured competition. Judge Hutcheson delivered the opinion:

Seven Midwestern canners, competitors of Borden, testified in support of the complaint with respect to competitive injury to the primary line. Marketing only private label milk, they sell on a local basis without advertising. . . . The record discloses that sales constituting about 7% of their production, or roughly 240,000 cases, had been diverted to Borden. In essence, this business was attracted to Borden because it was selling private label milk cheaper than were these competitors. There is disagreement as to the reason for Borden's lower prices. The examiner was of the opinion that the primary reason for Borden's lower prices was that by using an f.o.b. plant method, Borden was able to take advantage of its obviously more favorable plant locations. . . . The examiner concluded that 86% of the sales were diverted to Borden because of its advantageous locations and consequent freight advantage.

The Commission disagreed that freight advantage was the foremost reason for the diversion of business, declaring that the lower prices of Borden's private label milk, as compared to the Borden brand milk, was another important element; it also stressed Borden's size in relation to the smaller competitors. . . . Indeed, there is evidence that Borden itself had lost private label sales in the Northeast to other competitors (Pet and Carnation) whose more favorable plant locations in that area had given them a similar advantage in freight over Borden. . . .

Borden's share of the market [in question] increased only from 9.9% in 1955 to 10.7% in 1957. During the same period, the total market share of the competitors increased in about the same proportion, from 6.3% to 6.8%.

We conclude for two reasons that the record does not contain substantial evidence to support a finding that there may be a substantial injury to competition at the seller's level. The first is that we think it significant that the testifying competitors have experienced an increase in absolute sales volume and have bettered their market position in approximately the same proportion as has Borden. . . .

The second reason is the absence of the necessary causal relationship between the difference in prices and the alleged competitive injury. . . . [N]one of the evidence adduced by the testifying competitors relates to the price difference between the milks marketed by Borden; instead it relates to the price difference between their own private label milk and Borden's private label milk. The competitors actually assert only that Borden was able to sell private label milk for a lower price than they could, and regarding that assertion, the price of Borden brand milk is immaterial in this case. In short, the evidence simply does not support the precise price discrimination alleged in the complaint. . . .

We are of the firm view that where a price differential between a premium and non premium brand reflects no more than a consumer preference for the premium brand, the price difference creates no competitive advantage to the recipient of the cheaper private brand product on which injury could be predicated. "[R]ather it represents merely a rough equivalent of the benefit by way of the seller's national advertising and promotion which the purchaser of the more expensive branded product enjoys."

The circuit court opinion clearly is at odds with parts of the Supreme Court decision. In fact, the last paragraph in the above excerpt basically says to the Supreme Court: "We do not agree with your opinion, so we shall ignore it." The decision of the court of appeals suggests that lower courts often have the de facto power to overturn higher courts.

From an economic perspective, the circuit court decision makes a good deal more sense than the Supreme Court position because brand products and private-label products must be considered to be different from the consumers' perspective, or else their prices would be equal. Furthermore, as Justice Stewart pointed out, the Supreme Court position raises the possibility of some strange behavior. Under the Supreme Court ruling Borden could have *reduced* the quality of the private-label milk (perhaps by adding rodent hairs) and then have *legally* sold it for a lower price! Fortunately, the circuit court ruling saved the public from the possible negative implications of the Supreme Court decision.

IV   ILLEGALLY INDUCED PRICE DISCRIMINATION

Recall from Chapter 2 that the Robinson-Patman Act was initially passed in large part to prevent major chain stores with *monopsony* power from inducing lower prices from suppliers. Section 2(f) was aimed directly at this type of behavior; however, there have been very few successful cases filed under section 2(f). One major reason for this lack of success can be traced back to the 1953 *Automatic Canteen* precedent.

Automatic Canteen Company of America v. Federal Trade Commission **346 U.S. 61 (1953)**   Automatic Canteen operated over 230,000 candy vending machines, so it purchased a great deal of candy. It constantly requested lower prices from its candy suppliers under the threat of cutting off its purchases. Furthermore, Automatic Canteen would often estimate *its suppliers'* cost savings on large-quantity sales to Automatic Canteen and then inform its suppliers of the prices it would find acceptable.

Evidence suggested that this was a classic attempt on the part a large buyer to induce price concessions from suppliers. In other words, it was precisely the problem Congress apparently had in mind when it passed the Robinson-Patman Act. By 6–3, however, the Supreme Court ruled in favor of Automatic Canteen. Justice Frankfurter delivered the majority opinion:

> Section 2 (f) does not reach all cases of buyer receipt of a prohibited discrimination in prices. It limits itself to cases of knowing receipt of such prices. The Commission seems to argue, in part, that the substantive violation occurs if the buyer knows only that the prices are lower than those offered other buyers. Such a reading not only distorts the language but would leave the word "knowingly" almost entirely without significance in section 2 (f). A buyer with no knowledge whatsoever of facts indicating the possibility that price differences were not based on cost differences would be liable if in fact they were not. . . .
>
> While we need not decide whether systematic receipt of prices in itself could ever be sufficient to give the buyer the requisite knowledge, we think, as the argument itself recognizes, that the inquiry must be into the buyer's knowledge of illegality. . . .
>
> For section 2 (f) was explained in Congress as a provision under which a seller, by informing the buyer that a proposed discount was unlawful under the Act, could discourage undue pressure from the buyer. Of course, such devices for private enforcement of the Act through fear of prosecution could equally well have been achieved by providing that the buyer would be liable if, through the seller or otherwise, he learned that the price he sought or received was lower than that accorded competitors, but we are unable, in the light of congressional policy as expressed in other antitrust legislation,

to read this ambiguous language as putting the buyer at his peril whenever he engages in price bargaining. Such a reading must be rejected in view of the effect it might have on that sturdy bargining between buyer and seller for which scope was presumably left in the areas of our economy not otherwise regulated. . . .

We therefore conclude that a buyer is not liable under section 2 (f) if the lower prices he induces are either within one of the seller's defenses such as the cost justification or not known by him to be within one of those defenses. . . .

By placing a very heavy burden of proof on the commission in section 2(f) cases, the Supreme Court made successful prosecution very difficult. After the *Automatic Canteen* decision, there was little chance of an FTC victory in a section 2(f) case, unless a seller informed a buyer that the buyer was requesting an illegally discriminatory price. The Supreme Court reinforced this position as recently as 1979, in the *A&P* case.

Great Atlantic & Pacific Tea Company v. Federal Trade Commission 440 U.S. 69 (1979)   In 1965 A&P solicited a bid from Borden to supply A&P's 200 Chicago stores with private-label milk. Borden offered a plan that would have saved A&P $410,000 a year, but A&P was dissatisfied with the offer and solicited a competitive bid from Bowman Dairy. Bowman made a bid that would have saved A&P $737,000 a year. A&P's Chicago buyer then informed Borden, "I have a bid in my pocket. You [Borden] people are so far out of line it is not even funny. You are not even in the ballpark." A&P's buyer also told Borden that a $50,000 further reduction "would not be a drop in the bucket." Because Borden had just built a new $5 million dairy in Illinois, it could not afford to lose A&P's business, so it then offered an $820,000 a year discount. When it made this offer, Borden emphasized that it was only attempting to meet Bowman's offer.

The FTC ruled that because A&P knew that it was the beneficiary of an illegally low price, it had violated Section 2(f). The Second Circuit Court of Appeals affirmed the FTC order.

The Supreme Court, however, ruled 6–2 in favor of A&P. Justice Stewart delivered the majority opinion:

As finally enacted, section 2 (f) provides:

"That it shall be unlawful for any person engaged in commerce, in the course of such commerce, knowingly to induce or receive a discrimination in price *which is prohibited by this section.*" [Emphasis added by the Court.]

. . . Under the plain meaning of section 2 (f), therefore, a buyer cannot be liable if a prima facie case could not be established against a seller or if the seller has an affirmative defense. In either situation, there is no price discrimination "prohibited by this section." . . .

The [commission] . . . argues that the petitioner may be liable even assuming that Borden had such a defense. . . . Since A&P knew for a fact that the final Borden bid beat the Bowman bid, it was not entitled to assert the meeting-competition defense even though Borden may have honestly believed that it was simply meeting competition. . . .

The short answer to these contentions of the [commission] is that Congress did not provide in section 2 (f) that a buyer can be liable even if the seller has a valid defense. . . .

In a competitive market, uncertainty among sellers will cause them to compete for business by offering buyers lower prices. . . . Under the view advanced by the respondent, however, a buyer, to avoid liability, must either refuse a seller's bid or at least inform him that his bid has beaten competition. Such a duty of affirmative disclosure would almost inevitably frustrate competitive bidding and, by reducing uncertainty, lead to price matching and anticompetitive cooperation among sellers. . . .

The test for determining when a seller has a valid meeting-competition defense is whether a seller can "show the existence of facts which would lead a reasonable and prudent person to believe that the granting of a lower price would in fact meet the equally low price of a competitor." . . .

Under the circumstances of this case, Borden did act reasonably and in good faith when it made its second bid. . . .

Borden was informed by the petitioner that it was in danger of losing its A&P business in the Chicago area unless it came up with a better offer. It was told that its first offer was "not even in the ball park" and that a $50,000 improvement "would not be a drop in the bucket." . . .

Borden was unable to ascertain the details of the Bowman bid. It requested more information about the bid from the petitioner, but this request was refused. It could not then attempt to verify the existence and terms of the competing offer from Bowman without risking Sherman Act liability. . . . Under these circumstances, the conclusion is virtually inescapable that in making that offer Borden acted in a reasonable and good-faith effort to meet its competition, and therefore was entitled to a meeting-competition defense.

Since Borden had a meeting-competition defense and thus could not be liable under section 2 (b), the petitioner who did no more than accept that offer cannot be liable under section 2 (f). . . .

Justice Marshall dissented:

Neither the language nor the sparse legislative history of section 2 (f) justifies this enervating standard for the determination of buyer liability. To the contrary, the Court's construction disregards the congressional purpose to curtail the coercive practices of chainstores and other large buyers. . . .

I would hold that under section 2 (f), the Robinson-Patman Act defenses must be available to buyers on the same basic terms as they are to sellers. . . . In my view, a buyer should be able to claim [a meeting-competition] . . . defense — independently of the seller — if he acted in good faith to induce the seller to meet a competitor's price, regardless of whether the seller's price happens to beat the competitor's. But a buyer who induces the lower bid by misrepresentation should not escape Robinson-Patman liability. . . .

In my judgment, the numerous ambiguities in the record dictate that this case be remanded to the Commission. The Court, however, avoids a remand by concluding in the first instance that A&P's seller necessarily had a meeting-competition defense. In so doing, the Court usurps the factfinding function best performed by the Commission.

One of the greatest ironies of the Robinson-Patman Act is the minuscule number of cases filed under section 2(f). Between 1936 and 1966, only 30 out of 1,100 Robinson-Patman Act cases, or 0.03 percent of all cases, were section 2(f) cases [6]. One of the major congressional concerns at the time the law was passed, therefore, has not been addressed successfully by enforcement.

V SUMMARY

The Robinson-Patman Act has come under increasing criticism in recent years. Some of this criticism is highly justified, but it may have resulted in too strong a bias in favor of dominant firms that use price discrimination to discipline rivals. The widespread adoption of the Areeda and Turner doctrine, in particular, could cause problems in the future. Before jumping to any conclusions, however, one should at least wait for a test of this doctrine in the Supreme Court.

One major result of the criticism of the Robinson-Patman Act has already been observed. The FTC is filing far fewer cases in recent years. The FTC filed 219 Robinson-Patman complaints in 1963, but only 2 in 1975 [7]. If this trend continues the act may essentially wither away. Despite the government's reluctance to file cases, private suits still abound and are likely to continue. Legislative action to abolish or change the law could still have a significant impact.

The Robinson-Patman Act has not been entirely without its bright moments. The elimination of basing-point systems alone was a major accomplishment. Furthermore, it should always be remembered that there is nothing in the act that prevents a firm from lowering its prices across the board to *all* buyers in response to a competitor's price reduction. In many such cases an across the board price reduction would result in large increases in consumer welfare. It is certainly true, however, that the costs of enforcement have been high, and the act has resulted in far too many costly legal battles over the right of competitors to compete aggressively through the use of lower prices.

Before recommending the repeal of the Robinson-Patman Act, it might be useful to imagine an economy without any restrictions on price discrimination. Such an economy would almost certainly be more concentrated since large firms would routinely maintain or increase their market shares by granting quantity discounts to large buyers that were not based on cost differences. Furthermore, geographic price discrimination might prevent the growth of local firms that one day might rise to compete with large dominant firms.

A pragmatic approach might be to leave the present act on the books, but to limit its use to the relatively few cases of truly anticompetitive price discrimination, particularly the use of price discrimination by dominant firms to discipline rivals. Perhaps the recent reduction in FTC activity indicates a movement in this direction.

NOTES

1. W. G. Shepherd and C. Wilcox, *Public Policies Toward Business* (Homewood, Ill.: Irwin, 1979), page 218.

2. D. E. Waldman, "Welfare and Collusion: Comment," *American Economic Review,* March 1982, pages 268–271.

3. F. M. Scherer, *Industrial Market Structure and Economic Performance* (Chicago: Rand-McNally, 1980), page 578.

4. P. Areeda and D. Turner, "Predatory Pricing and Related Practices Under Section 2 of the Sherman Act," *Harvard Law Review,* 1975, pages 697–733.

5. See F. M. Scherer, "Predatory Pricing and the Sherman Act: Comment," *Harvard Law Review,* 1976, pages 869–903; O. Williamson, "Predatory Pricing: A Strategic and Welfare Analysis," *Yale Law Journal,* 1977, pages 284–340; and R. H. Koller II, "When Is Pricing Predatory?" *Antitrust Bulletin,* 1979, pages 283–306.

6. Scherer, *Industrial Market Structure and Economic Performance,* page 574.

7. D. F. Greer, *Business, Government, and Society* (New York: Macmillan, 1983), page 203.

CHAPTER
SEVEN

Patents

A United States patent is a seventeen-year legal monopoly grant that is awarded to inventors in exchange for their agreement to disclose their inventions to the public. A valid patent gives an inventor monopoly power to decide on the use, transfer, or withholding of an invention. Although the awarding of a patent has an admirable objective, the dissemination of technological knowledge that might otherwise be kept secret, the patent grant may be abused and come directly in conflict with one of the major goals of antitrust policy, a reduction in monopoly power. This chapter examines the real and potential conflicts that may arise between the monopoly patent grant and the antitrust laws.

I THE ECONOMICS OF THE PATENT SYSTEM

Patents exist for one economic purpose — to increase the rate of technological advance. Without question, there are some major technological breakthroughs that would never have been developed, or would have been developed much later, in the absence of patent protection. Economic theory suggests, however, that patent protection may not always increase the rate of technological advance. In fact, economic theory suggests that in some cases patent protection *decreases* the rate of technological advance [1].

To more easily understand the potential dilemma associated with the current system, consider the following three possible patent scenarios.

Scenario 1 Suppose a weekend garage inventor, hypothetically named Mr. Tinker, is driven to invent, not by money, but by a fairly common character trait — curiosity. One day Mr. Tinker discovers a new method for cheaply harnessing solar energy. Although Mr. Tinker never gave any thought to the patent system as he worked on his invention every weekend, upon realizing the importance of his discovery, he runs to a patent attorney and a few years later receives a patent. He then turns the patent over to a large firm, hypothetically called International Money Machines (IMM), and on the basis of Mr. Tinker's patent IMM develops a solar energy device, which it prices well above marginal and average cost. Over the next decade other firms spend millions of dollars in an unsuccessful attempt to invent around the IMM patent. Finally, after seventeen years, the IMM patent is made public, but by then IMM is a virtual monopolist in the solar energy business. Furthermore, during the period of patent protection, IMM patented a number of minor technological advances based on Mr. Tinker's original patent, so that by the time the original patent expires, IMM is firmly entrenched as the leader in the solar energy field, and few firms will consider attempting to challenge IMM's dominance. Mr. Tinker, IMM's management, and IMM's stockholders have all made large fortunes, but the solar energy industry has performed in a very inefficient manner in terms of *static* efficiency. Furthermore, in order to protect its investment in Tinker's original device, IMM withheld using some of its improvement patents for several years; therefore, IMM slowed the rate of technological advance on improvements to the Tinker patent. In scenario 1, society has benefited from Mr. Ticker's device, but has also paid a price in the form of reduced static efficiency and a slow rate of technological improvement on the basic patent.

Scenario 2 Now consider an alternative scenario to the Mr. Tinker story, one without patent protection. Mr. Tinker develops the same solar energy device and takes the device to IMM. A member of the IMM development department likes the idea, and IMM decides to proceed with development. Because of a lack of patent protection, IMM decides to introduce the device as quickly as possible, before its competitors learn about the existence of the invention (perhaps rumors of the device have already begun to circulate). IMM is first into the market, and initially charges a high profit-maximizing price. Within twelve to twenty-four months, IMM and Mr. Tinker have made a very substantial profit, and the first copies of Mr. Tinker's invention appear on the market. After another twenty-four months there are many copies on the market, but to keep one step ahead of the competition, IMM and some of its competitors have already marketed more advanced devices based on the Tinker device. Within five years, the basic Tinker device is obsolete, and many companies are competing for a share of the solar energy market. Some firms make a profit, others sustain an economic loss and leave the market, but on the *average* the industry is earning normal economic profits. Prices approximate marginal and average cost, and the industry is performing efficiently from a *static* standpoint. In this scenario, the lack of patent protection has actually increased the rate of technological advance, and the outcome is preferable to the first scenario's outcome from *both* a static and a dynamic perspective.

Scenario 3   Now consider another possible scenario in the absence of patent protection. Mr. Tinker develops the same solar energy device and approaches the development department at IMM. After careful consideration the development department concludes that although the device is technologically sound, development would be too expensive, and without patent protection IMM could not expect to earn a profit. Mr. Tinker then approaches a dozen other large high-technology firms, but each responds in the same negative manner. Finally, completely discouraged, Mr. Tinker gives up, and the device never becomes a commercial reality. Because of a lack of patent protection, society has lost the potential benefits associated with Mr. Tinker's device.

Economic uncertainty surrounding the patent system exists because it is impossible to determine how often the first scenario occurs, as opposed to how often the second or third scenario *would* occur in the absence of patent protection. The second scenario, without patent protection, is clearly preferable to the first scenario, with patent protection. The first scenario, with patent protection, however, is clearly preferable to the third scenario, without patent protection.

Another way to consider this dilemma is to recognize the *fact* that some inventions and innovations are *patent dependent* but others are *not patent dependent;* that is, some technology would become available only if a patent system exists, but other technology would become available just as quickly, or even more quickly, without a patent system. Like so many other economic issues, therefore, the patent system involves a system of trade-offs. Some inventions and innovations that are not patent dependent are protected in order to ensure that society receives the benefits of *all patent-dependent* inventions and innovations. Since the system clearly involves social costs as well as social benefits, public policy should be cautious and not simply grant patent holders *unrestricted* rights and privileges.

II   ANTITRUST POLICY TOWARD PATENTS

Antitrust policy has attempted to limit the most obvious patent abuses while still permitting patent holders to obtain the basic monopoly benefits associated with the system. The first major issue addressed under the antitrust laws was the use of price-fixing clauses in patent licensing agreements.

Section 1 of the Sherman Act forbids all restraints in trade, and the courts interpreted this as a *per se* ban on *all* direct price-fixing agreements (see Chapter 5). The Constitution, however, explicitly grants a patentee the "exclusive right to make, use, and vend the invention or discovery." Although there is no explicit constitutional right to fix prices, the exclusive-right provision can be interpreted as ensuring that a patent holder has the right to fix the sale price on a patented item even if it is produced under license by another manufacturer. The basic precedent on this issue was set in the 1926 *General Electric* case.

United States v. General Electric Company **272 U.S. 476 (1926)**   General Electric owned the three basic patents for the use of tungsten filaments in light bulbs. Without these patents it was virtually impossible to compete successfully in the light bulb market, and GE could have maintained a monopoly on light bulbs by simply refusing to license its patents. GE, however, granted Westinghouse a license on March 1, 1912. Under the terms of the license, Westinghouse agreed to follow GE's pricing and distribution policy. The licensing agreement explicitly forbad Westinghouse from underpricing GE. In the absence of patent protection such an agreement would clearly have been in violation of the antitrust laws. The licensing plan enabled General Electric to maintain a 69 percent market share, while Westinghouse held a 16 percent share, other licensed manufacturers held an 8 percent share, and nonlicensed manufacturers of inferior bulbs held a 7 percent share. GE set the price on 93 percent of the light bulbs produced in the United States.

The case presented a classic dilemma in patent antitrust law. If the courts prevented GE from fixing bulb prices, GE could have adopted a nonlicensing policy and produced all tungsten filament bulbs itself. On the one hand, if the courts permitted price-fixing on the patented bulbs, it would eliminate some of the incentive for GE's competitors to create improved bulbs because GE and the licensees would all lose if aggressive competition erupted after the development of a new light bulb. By permitting price-fixing and encouraging more licensing, the courts might reduce GE's short-run monopoly power a bit, but they would create an environment that would be less conducive to technological change in the future. On the other hand, by strictly enforcing the ban on price-fixing, the courts might create an even stronger short-run monopoly for GE, but such a ruling would create an increased incentive for Westinghouse and others to invent around the tungsten filament patents. There are pros and cons involved with both possible outcomes, but the issue basically boiled down to a choice between (1) the *possibility* of a bit more monopoly power today in exchange for the *possibility* of a more rapid rate of technological advance in the future and (2) the *possibility* of a bit less monopoly power today, along with the *possibility* of a slower rate of technological advance in the future.

The Supreme Court decided in favor of a bit less monopoly power today and ruled in favor of General Electric. Justice Taft delivered the unanimous opinion of the Court:

> Had the Electric Company, as owner of the patents entirely controlling the manufacture, use and sale of the tungsten incandescent lamps, in its license to the Westinghouse Company, the right to impose the condition that its sales should be at prices fixed by the licensor subject to change according to its discretion? . . .
>
> The owner of a patent may assign it to another and convey, (1) the exclusive right to make, use and vend the invention throughout the United States, or, (2) an undivided part or share of that exclusive right, or (3) the exclusive right under the patent within and through a specific part of the United States. . . . Conveying less than title to the patent, or part of it, the patentee may grant a license to make, use and vend articles under the specifications of his patent for any royalty or upon any condition the performance of which is reasonably within the reward which the patentee by the grant of the patent is entitled to secure. It is well settled, as already said, that where a patentee makes the patented article and sells it, he can exercise no future control over what the purchaser may wish to do with the article after his purchase. It has passed beyond the scope of the patentee's rights. . . . But the question is a different one which arises when we consider what a patentee who grants a license to one to make and vend the patented article may do in limiting the licensee in the exercise of the right to sell. The patentee may make and grant a license to another to make and use the patented articles, but withhold his right to sell them. The licensee in such a case acquires an interest in the articles made. He owns the material of them and may use them. But if he sells them, he infringes the right of the patentee, and may be held for damages and enjoined. If the patentee goes further, and licenses the selling of the articles, may he limit the selling by limiting the method of sale and the price? We think he may do so, provided the conditions of sale are normally and reasonably adapted to secure pecuniary reward for the patentee's monopoly. One of the valuable ele-

ments of the exclusive right of a patentee is to acquire profit by the price at which the article is sold. The higher the price, the greater the profit, unless it is prohibitory. When the patentee licenses another to make and vend, and retains the right to continue to make and vend on his own account, the price at which his licensee will sell will necessarily affect the price at which he can sell his own patented goods. It would seem entirely reasonable that he should say to the licensee, "Yes, you may make and sell articles under my patent, but not so as to destroy the profit that I wish to obtain by making them and selling them myself."

The basic *General Electric* precedent has never been overturned. If a license contains an agreement to abide by the patentee's price, the courts will generally uphold the price-fixing agreement. This ruling can be defended on economic grounds, but it can also be attacked on economic grounds. Since a patentee usually holds a significant cost advantage over any licensee (by virtue of the licensee's royalty payments), a patent holder should be able to compete with its licensees without benefit of a price-fixing clause. In fact, if a licensee elects to charge a lower price than a patentee, the patentee should be able to *at least* match the lower price, *unless* the licensee is a more efficient producer. If the licensee is a more efficient producer, there is little economic justification for protecting the *inefficient* patentee. In other words, in those rare cases where a licensee can produce a good at a lower social cost than a patentee, it would seem to make economic sense to prevent price-fixing and encourage the efficient licensee to charge a lower price. Of course, the licensee would still have to pay royalties to the patentee.

The *General Electric* precedent provided a sound defense in straightforward cases where *one* patentee licensed *one* patent to a few firms, but it quickly became clear that the courts would not permit a group of firms to pool a large number of patents in an obvious attempt to use patent protection to avoid the antitrust laws. The *Hartford-Empire* case presented the classic example of such an attempt to monopolize an industry through the use of a *patent-pooling* arrangement.

Hartford-Empire Company v. United States 323 U.S. 386 (1945) The *Hartford-Empire* case involved one of the most extensive patent pools in United States history. At the turn of the century, glass was still made primarily by hand. In 1904, however, Owens-Illinois developed the first fully automated suction process machine for producing glass containers. When Owens-Illinois refused to license its revolutionary machine, many glass container manufacturers were threatened with extinction. Unfortunately for Owens-Illinois, a competing machine was developed that used the suspended gob feeding process. Hartford-Fairmont (the predecessor of Hartford-Empire) acquired the basic gob process patents and then improved them. At the same time, the

Empire Machine Company, which was controlled by Corning Glass, owned certain gob process patent applications that interfered with Hartford-Fairmont's patents. In 1916 Hartford-Fairmont and Empire granted each other exclusive cross-licenses on their gob process patents. Further negotiations led to the consolidation of the two firms as the Hartford-Empire Company on October 6, 1922.

Throughout this period, Owens-Illinois also held gob process patents that were in conflict with Hartford-Empire's patent claims. On April 9, 1924, Owens-Illinois and Hartford-Empire settled their conflicting patent claims. Under the agreement Owens-Illinois granted Hartford-Empire an exclusive license on its gob process patents, and Hartford-Empire granted Owens-Illinois a *nonexclusive* license to make machines under Hartford-Empire's patents; Owens-Illinois received one-half of all of Hartford-Empire's royalties over $600,000 per year; and Owens-Illinois received a veto over any attempt by Hartford-Empire to grant a license to any company that used any of Owens-Illinois's patents. The agreement also prevented Owens-Illinois from entering the pressed and blown glass field, which was reserved for Corning Glass, and left Owens-Illinois in complete control of its original suction process patents.

After reaching this settlement with Owens-Illinois, Hartford-Empire attempted to purchase all of the existing patents on gob feeder equipment. By 1938 Hartford-Empire had acquired over 600 glass manufacturing patents. These included over a hundred assigned by Corning Glass, over sixty assigned by Owens-Illinois, and over seventy assigned by Hazel-Atlas. Once its control was complete, Hartford-Empire allocated each glass manufacturer a strict production quota on each specific type of glass container. Furthermore, Hartford-Empire often refused to license its patents to potential entrants, as well as to established glass manufacturers. In 1938, as a result of these complex agreements, 94 percent of all glass containers were produced on machines using one or more of Hartford-Empire's patents, and the Justice Department charged Hartford-Empire with conspiring to monopolize the glass container industry.

The district court ruled that Hartford-Empire's behavior went beyond the legitimate use of the patent privilege. The remedies adopted by the district court were quite severe. The court ordered Hartford-Empire to license all existing patents royalty free, to license *all future* patents at reasonable royalties to *any* applicant requesting a license, and to supply any applicant with the necessary know-how to use the patents. Basically, the district court confiscated most of Hartford-Empire's present and future patent rights.

The Supreme Court upheld the judgment against Hartford-Empire, but it substantially watered down the remedy. Justice Roberts spoke for the Court, which ruled 6–0 against Hartford-Empire. Two justices, however, dissented in part and argued that the district court's remedies should have been upheld. Justice Roberts wrote

It is clear that, by cooperative arrangements and binding agreements, the appellant corporations, over a period of years, regulated and suppressed competition in the use of glassmaking machinery and employed their joint patent position to allocate fields of manufacture and to maintain prices of unpatented glassware.

The [defenses] offered by the appelants are unconvincing. It is said, on behalf of Hartford, that its business, in its inception, was lawful and within the patent laws; and that, in order to protect its legitimate interests as holder of patents for automatic glass machinery, it was justified in buying up and fencing off improvement patents. . . .

The explanation fails to account for the offensive and defensive alliance of patent owners with its concomitant stifling of initiative, invention, and competition. . . .

The Government sought the dissolution of Hartford. The court, however, decided that a continuance of certain of Hartford's activities would be of advantage to the glass industry and denied, for the time being that form of relief. The court was of [the] opinion, however, that the long series of transactions and the persistent manifestations of a purpose to violate the antitrust statutes required the entry of a decree which would preclude the resumption of unlawful practices. . . .

The present suit is . . . [a civil suit] and we may not impose penalties in the guise of preventing future violations. This is not to say that a decree need deal only with the exact type of acts found to have been committed or that the court should not, in framing its decree, resolve all doubts in favor of the Government, or may not prohibit acts which in another setting would be unobjectionable. But, even so, the court may not create, as to the defendants, new duties, prescription of which is the function of Congress, or place the defendants, for the future, "in a different class than other people," as the Government has suggested. The decree must not be "so vague as to put the whole conduct of the defendants' business at the peril of a summons for contempt"; enjoin "all possible breaches of the law"; or cause the defendants hereafter not "to be under the protection of the law of the land." With these principles in mind we proceed to examine the terms of the decree entered. . . .

[T]he decree as entered requires that each of the defendants must hereafter forever abstain from leasing a patented machine, no matter what the date of the invention, and compels each of them if he desires to distribute patented machinery to sell the machine which embodies the patent to every one who applies, at a price to be fixed by the court. The injunction as drawn is not directed at any combination, agreement, or conspiracy. It binds every defendant forever irrespective of his connection with any other or of the independence of his action.

[The decree] enjoins each of the corporate and individual appellants from engaging in the distribution of machinery used in glass manufacture or in the distribution of glassware in interstate commerce unless each files with the court an agreement (a) to license, without royalty or charge of any kind, and for the life of all patents, any applicant to make, to have made for it, and to use any number of machines and methods embodied in inventions covered by any patent or patent application now owned or controlled by such defendant; (b) to license, at a reasonable royalty (to be fixed by the court, in case of dispute) any applicant to make, have made for it, and to use any number of machines and methods in the manufacture of glassware embodying inventions covered by patents hereafter applied for or owned or controlled by any defendants; (c) to make available to any licensee, under "(a)" and "(b)" at cost, plus a reasonable profit, all drawings and patterns "relating to the machinery or methods used in the manufacture of glassware" embodied in the licensed inventions (with immaterial exceptions).

Since the provisions of [the decree] . . . in effect confiscate considerable portions of the appellants' property, we think they go beyond what is required to dissolve the combination and prevent future combinations of like character. It is to be borne in mind that the Government has not in this litigation attacked the validity of any patent or the priority ascribed to any by the Patent Office, nor has it attacked, as excessive or unreasonable, the standard royalties heretofore exacted by Hartford. Hartford has reduced all of its royalties to a uniform scale and has waived and abolished and agreed to waive and abolish all restrictions and limitations in its outstanding leases so that every licensee shall be at liberty to use the machinery for the manufacture of any kind or quantity of glassware comprehended within the decree. . . .

[I]f, as we must assume on this record, a defendant owns valid patents, it is difficult to say that, however much in the past such defendant has abused the rights thereby conferred, it must now dedicate them to the public.

That a patent is property, protected against appropriation both by individuals and by government, has long been settled. . . .

Legislative history is also enlightening upon this point. Repeatedly since 1908 legislation has been proposed in Congress to give the courts power to cancel a patent which has been used as an instrument to violate antitrust laws. Congress has not adopted such legislation. The temporary National Economic Committee recommended imposition of such a penalty for violation of antitrust laws. But its recommendation was not adopted by Congress. . . .

Congress was asked as early as 1877, and frequently since to adopt a system of compulsory licensing of patents. It has failed to enact these proposals into law. It has also rejected the proposal that a patentee found guilty of violation of the antitrust laws should be compelled, as a penalty, to license all his future inventions at reasonable royalties. . . .

[T]he decree should be modified to permit the reservation of reasonable royalties and its provisions should be restricted to feeders, formers, stackers and lehrs and patents covering these or improvements of them, or methods or processes used in connection with them. . . .

For example, if Ball or Thatcher should procure a patent on a bottle-capping machine or for composition of glass, there is no reason to compel a license to Hartford or Hazel or anyone else. . . .

[I]n view of the nature of the conspiracy found, an injunction should go against the further prosecution of all infringement suits, pending at the date this suit was brought. Hartford and the other corporate defendants . . . should be required to lease or license glassmaking machinery of the classes each now manufactures to any who may desire to take licenses . . . at standard royalties and without discrimination or restriction, and if at the time of entry of the decree there are any alleged infringers who are willing to take such licenses they should be released, and the patent owner deprived of all damages and profits which it might have claimed for past infringement. The decree should, however, be without prejudice to the future institution of any suit or suits for asserted infringements against persons refusing to take licenses under any of the presently licensed inventions arising out of their use after the date of the decree. The decree should not forbid any defendant from seeking recovery from infringement, occurring after the date of the final decree, of patents not covering feeders, formers, stackers, lehrs or processes or applicable to any of them. . . .

The [decree] now covers every kind of invention and every patent, present and future, in any field if owned or controlled or distributed by an appellant.

The injunction will stop all inventions or acquirement of patents in any field by any appellant unless for its own use in its business, for it sets such limitations upon the reward of a patent as to make it practically worthless except for use by the owner. It is unlimited in time. It is not limited to any joint action or conspiracy violative of the antitrust laws; it covers inventions in every conceivable field. . . .

A patent owner is not in the position of a quasi-trustee for the public or under any obligation to see that the public acquires the free right to use the invention. He has no obligation either to use it or to grant its use to others. If he discloses the invention in his application so that it will come into the public domain at the end of the 17-year period of exclusive right he has fulfilled the only obligation imposed by the statute. . . .

[T]he decree entered is vacated and the cause is remanded for further proceedings in conformity to this opinion.

The major glass container manufacturers initially feared Hartford-Empire's potential domination of the industry. This fear gradually shifted to acceptance as the major producers realized that they could use Hartford-Empire's patent control to form a cartel, in effect, in the industry. Over the years the major producers benefited greatly from Hartford-Empire's refusal to license patents to potential entrants and its continual filing of false-infringement suits against potential competitors. Under Hartford-Empire's protective wings, major manufacturers such as Owens-Illinois, Anchor-Hocking, and Hazel-Atlas were able to earn reasonable profits and were relatively free from major competitive threats. Since Hartford-Empire's policies served to entrench the major firms' positions, it is not surprising that the major producers chose to join, rather than fight, Hartford-Empire.

Despite the 1945 decision against Hartford-Empire, the glass container industry remained highly oligopolistic. Twenty-five years of patent control enabled the leading firms to maintain their market shares well into the future [2]. In fact, in 1955 Owens-Illinois still held over a third of the market for glass containers, and the four-firm concentration ratio remained high at 63 percent. The case, therefore, suggests that market power built upon patent control is likely to continue long after the patents expire. In this case, even the remedy of forced licensing had only a limited effect on market structure.

United States v. United States Gypsum Company 333 U.S. 364 (1948) The *U.S. Gypsum* case presents another classic example of patent abuse. Since its organization in 1901 U.S. Gypsum had been the dominant firm in the gypsum products market. In 1939 U.S. Gypsum controlled 55 percent of the wallboard market, and the eight-firm concentration ratio was over 90 percent. U.S. Gypsum's control was built primarily on one patent, the Utzman patent for producing wallboard with closed edges. Until 1912 wallboard had been produced by sandwiching a gypsum core between two pieces of paper. Utzman's idea was to enclose the edges of the gypsum core with a paper cover so that the edges would be much less likely to crumble. Essentially, Utzman received a patent for the idea of covering the entire gypsum core (including the edges) with paper instead of enclosing just the two sides. It is hard to believe that such a minor technological advance could result in U.S. Gypsum's domination of an entire industry for a quarter century, but it did.

Between 1917 and 1929 U.S. Gypsum had followed an agressive policy of filing an infringement suit against any firm that came close to infringing on the Utzman patent. The circuit court of appeals had upheld one of these infringement suits in 1921, and shortly thereafter, U.S. Gypsum began settling suits out of court by licensing competitors to produce wallboard under the Utzman patent at prices fixed by U.S. Gypsum. In this manner, by 1929 virtually all wallboard with closed edges was produced under the Utzman patent.

If U.S. Gypsum had simply licensed the Utzman patent to competitors with a price-fixing clause, it probably would have been beyond the reach of the Sherman Act under the *General Electric* precedent. U.S. Gypsum, however, carried its policies far beyond the mere licensing of one patent with a price-fixing clause. When the Utzman patent expired in 1929, U.S. Gypsum met with each of its licensees to work out a new set of patent agreements based on a new U.S. Gypsum patent for producing bubble board, a new type of gypsum wallboard produced by introducing a soap foam into the gypsum wallboard mixture. Bubble board was supposedly a lighter and lower-cost product, which would increase the industry's profits. On June 6, 1929, two months before the Utzman patent expired, U.S. Gypsum and its licensees met in Chicago to discuss a new licensing agreement. What eventually emerged was an agreement signed on August 6, 1929, the *exact day* the Utzman patent expired, that extended U.S. Gypsum's patent control. Each licensee agreed to pay a royalty on "all plaster board and gypsum wallboard of every kind" whether or not made by patented processes or embodying product claims. The agreement covered fifty patents and seven patent applications and was to run until the most junior patent expired. As it turned out, two bubble board patents were granted in 1937, so the agreements were to run until 1954. As in the earlier agreement, U.S. Gypsum was to fix the minimum price on *all* wallboard products.

Technically, the agreement gave U.S. Gypsum only the right to fix *minimum* prices on gypsum products, but in reality the agreement gave U.S. Gypsum control of actual prices. U.S. Gypsum issued a series of bulletins that detailed both prices and terms of sale for gypsum board. Furthermore, the bulletins adopted a basing-point method of pricing gypsum board. Each licensee was required to quote a mill net price from the nearest basing point and then add freight from the basing point on all shipments. To prevent competition through product differentiation, U.S. Gypsum also specified standard wallboard sizes and shapes. Furthermore, the licenses prohibited the granting of long-term credit, consignment sales, and the delivery of wallboard directly to building sites. Finally, in order to prevent chiseling, U.S. Gypsum set up a subsidiary called Board Survey, Inc., to check on complaints that a licensee had violated the agreement.

Evidence suggested that the agreement resulted in increased gypsum board prices after 1929, and letters written by the licensees to U.S. Gypsum indicated that the major objective of the agreement was to raise and stabilize wallboard prices.

By 8–0, the Supreme Court condemned the 1929 agreements. Justice Reed delivered the Court opinion:

> We think that the industry-wide license agreements, entered into with knowledge on the part of licensor and licensees of the adherence of others, with the control over prices and methods of distribution through the agreements and the bulletins were sufficient to establish a *prima facie* case of

conspiracy. Each licensee, as is shown by the uncontradicted references to the meetings and discussion that were preliminary to execution of the licenses, could not have failed to be aware of the intention of United States Gypsum and the other licensees to make the arrangements for licenses industry-wide. The license agreements themselves, on their face, showed this purpose. The licensor was to fix minimum prices binding both on itself and its licensees; the royalty was to be measured by a percentage of the value of all gypsum products, patented or unpatented; the license could not be transferred without the licensor's consent; the licensee opened its books of accounts to the licensor; the licensee was protected against competition with more favorable licenses and there was a cancellation clause for failure to live up to the arrangements. . . . Certainly they are overwhelming evidence of a plan of the licensor and licensees to fix prices and regulate operations in the gypsum board industry. . . .

These licenses and bulletins show plainly a conspiracy to violate the Sherman Act. Price fixing of this type offends. It is well settled that price fixing, without authorizing statutes, is illegal *per se* . . . Patents grant no privilege to their owners of organizing the use of those patents to monopolize an industry through price control, through royalties for the patents drawn from patent-free industry products and through regulation of distribution. Here patents have been put to such uses as to collide with the Sherman Act's protection of the public from evil consequences. . . . The defendants did undertake to control prices and distribution in gypsum board. They did utilize an agency, Board Survey, Inc., to make this control effective. . . . Such facts, together with the other indicia of intent to monopolize the gypsum board industry, hereinbefore detailed as to the agreements, bulletins and declarations, convince us that the defendants violated the Sherman Act.

The *General Electric* case affords no cloak for the course of conduct revealed in the voluminous record in this case. That case gives no support for a patentee, acting in concert with all members of an industry, to issue substantially identical licenses to all members of the industry under the terms of which the industry is completely regimented, the production of competitive unpatented products suppressed, a class of distributors squeezed out, and prices on unpatented products stabilized. We apply the "rule of reason" of *Standard Oil Co. v. United States,* to efforts to monopolize through patents as well as in non-patent fields. . . . That conclusion follows despite the assumed legality of each separate patent license, for it is familiar doctrine that lawful acts may become unlawful when taken in concert.

An analysis of the *Hartford-Empire* and *U.S. Gypsum* cases suggests that patents can be used not only as a spur for technological advance, but also as a spur for collusion. Furthermore, since collusion is likely to reduce the incentive for technological advance, abusive patent behavior of this type almost certainly reduces the rate of technological advance. The *Hartford-Empire* and *U.S. Gypsum* cases represent extreme examples of patent abuse. Other cases, however, present more difficult policy dilemmas.

United States v. Line Material Company 333 U.S. 287 (1948) The *Line Material* case involved the issue of price-fixing in cross-licensing agreements. The products involved were two patented dropout fuse cutouts (circuit breakers) and the housing suitable for use with the cutouts. Line Material held a 1935 patent on the housing that was uncontested by both parties. In March 1939, however, the Southern States Equipment Corporation received a patent on a new fuse cutout that had been developed by George N. Lemmon. On October 17, 1939, Line Material received a patent on a more advanced fuse cutout based on the Lemmon patent and developed by Schultz and Steinmayer. A manufacturer could produce the best possible fuse cutout only by using *both* the Lemmon and the Schultz patents.

Even before the patents were issued in 1939, Line Material and Southern States realized the potential patent conflict, and in May 1938 the two firms agreed to a royalty-free, cross-licensing agreement. Line Material licensed the Schultz patent to Southern States, along with the *exclusive* right to grant sublicenses to others. In return, Line Material received a license for the Lemmon cutout, but without permission to sublicense the Lemmon device. Line Material agreed not to sell cutouts under the Lemmon patent at prices that were below those fixed by Southern States, and Southern States made the same agreement with regard to equipment produced using the Schultz patent. Southern States and Line Material then proceeded to license the Lemmon *and* Schultz patents to ten other manufacturers (including General Electric and Westinghouse). Each license contained a price-fixing clause that prevented the licensee from underpricing Southern States and Line Material.

The district court ruled that the licenses were made in "good faith, . . . to gain a legitimate return to the patentees on the inventions." By 5–3, however, the Supreme Court overturned the district court decision. Justice Reed delivered the opinion:

> [T]he ultimate question for our decision on this appeal may be stated, succinctly and abstractly, to be as to whether in the light of the prohibition of section 1 of the Sherman Act, . . . two or more patentees in the same patent field may legally combine their valid patent monopolies to secure mutual benefits for themselves through contractual agreements, between themselves and other licensees, for control of the sale price of the patented devices. . . .
>
> As the Schultz patent could not be practiced without the Lemmon

[patent], the result of the agreement between Southern and Line for Line's sublicensing of the Lemmon patent was to combine in Line's hands the authority to fix the prices of the commercially successful devices embodying both the Schultz and Lemmon patents. . . .

By the patentees' agreement the dominant Lemmon and the subservient Schultz patents were combined to fix prices. In the absence of patent or other statutory authorization, a contract to fix or maintain prices in interstate commerce has long been recognized as illegal *per se* under the Sherman Act. This is true whether the fixed price is reasonable or unreasonable. It is also true whether it is a price agreement between producers for sale or between producer and distributor for resale.

It is equally well settled that the possession of a valid patent or patents does not give the patentee any exemption from the provisions of the Sherman Act beyond the limits of the patent monopoly. By aggregating patents in one control, the holder of the patents cannot escape the prohibitions of the Sherman Act. . . .

Nothing in the patent statute specifically gives a right to fix the price at which a licensee may vend the patented article. While the *General Electric* case holds that a patentee may, under certain conditions, lawfully control the price the licensee of his several patents may charge for the patented device, no case of this Court has construed the patent and anti-monopoly statutes to permit separate owners of separate patents by cross-licenses or other arrangements to fix the prices to be charged by them and their licensees for their respective products. Where two or more patentees with competitive, non-infringing patents combine them and fix prices on all devices produced under any of the patents, competition is impeded to a greater degree than where a single patentee fixes prices for his licensees. The struggle for profit is less acute. Even when, as here, the devices are not commercially competitive because the subservient patent cannot be practiced without consent of the dominant, the statement holds good. The stimulus to seek competitive inventions is reduced by the mutually advantageous price-fixing arrangement. . . . The merging of the benefits of price fixing under the patents restrains trade in violation of the Sherman Act in the same way as would the fixing of prices between producers of nonpatentable goods.

If the objection is made that a price agreement between a patentee and a licensee equally restrains trade, the answer is not that there is no restraint in such an arrangement but, when the validity of the *General Electric* case is assumed, that reasonable restraint accords with the patent monopoly granted by the patent law. . . .

The argument of respondents is that if a patentee may contract with his licensee to fix prices, it is logical to permit any number of patentees to combine their patents and authorize one patentee to fix prices for any number of licensees. . . . It seems to us, however, that such argument fails to take into account the cumulative effect of such multiple agreements in establishing an intention to restrain. . . . Even where the agreements to fix prices are limited to a small number of patentees, we are of the opinion that it crosses the barrier erected by the Sherman Act against restraint of trade though the restraint is by patentees and their licensees. . . .

The decree of the District Court is reversed and the case is remanded for the entry of an appropriate decree in accordance with this opinion.

Four of the five justices making up the majority in this case called for the complete overturning of the *General Electric* precedent. Justice Douglas wrote the following concurring decision, which was also signed by Justices Black, Murphy, and Rutledge. Justice Douglas stated

My view comes to this — it is part of practical wisdom and good law not to permit *United States v. General Electric Co.,* 272 U.S. 476, to govern this situation, though if its premise be accepted, logic might make its application to this case wholly defensible. But I would be rid of *United States v. General Electric Co.* My reasons for overruling it start with the Constitution itself. . . .

The Constitution grants Congress the power "To promote the Progress of Science and useful Arts, by securing for limited Times to Authors and Inventors the exclusive Right to their respective Writings and Discoveries." . . .

Congress faithful to that standard, has granted patentees only the "exclusive right to make, use, and vend the invention or discovery." . . .

The patent statutes do not sanction price-fixing combinations. They are indeed wholly silent about combinations. . . . There is no grant of power to combine with others to fix the price of patented products. Since the patent statutes are silent on the subject, it would seem that the validity of price-fixing combinations in this field would be governed by law. And since the Sherman Act outlaws price-fixing combinations it would seem logical and in keeping with the public policy expressed in that legislation to apply its prohibitions to patents as well as to other property. The Court made an exception [to the Sherman Act] in the [*General Electric*] case . . . in order to make the patent monopoly a more valuable one to the patentee. . . . It is reasoned that if the patentee could not control the price at which his licensees sold the patented article, they might undersell him; that a price-fixing combination would give him protection against that contingency and therefore was a reasonable device to secure him a pecuniary reward for his invention. Thus the *General Electric* case inverted . . . the Constitution and made the inventor's reward the prime rather than the incidental object of the patent system.

In that manner the Court saddled the economy with a vicious monopoly. In the first place, this form of price fixing underwrites the high-cost producer. . . . It is said in reply that he, the patentee, has that monopoly anyway — that his exclusive right to make, use, and vend would give him the right to exclude others and manufacture the invention and market it at any price he chose. That is true. But what he gets by the price-fixing agreement with his competitors is much more than that. He then gets not a benefit inherent in the right of exclusion but a benefit which flows from suppression of competitors. Then he gets the benefits of the production and marketing facilities of competitors without the risks of price competition. . . . In short, he and his associates get the benefits of a conspiracy or combination in restraint of competition. That is more than an "exclusive right" to an invention; it's an "exclusive right" to form a combination with competitors to fix the prices of the products of invention. . . .

It is not apparent that any such restriction or condition promotes the progress of science and the useful arts. But however that may be, the Constitution places the rewards to inventors in a secondary role. It makes the public interest the primary concern in the patent system. To allow these price-fixing schemes is to reverse the order and place the rewards to inventors first and the public second. This is not the only way a patentee can receive a pecuniary reward for his invention. He can charge a royalty which has no relation to price fixing. Or he can manufacture and sell at such price as he may choose.

Justice Douglas's position was quite logical because as he pointed out there are other ways of receiving a reasonable return on a patent besides price-fixing. Patentees are free to charge reasonable royalties that should guarantee a reasonable return in the absence of price-fixing. Furthermore, as previously noted, royalties present the patentee with a significant cost advantage compared with its licensees; therefore, most patentees should be able to charge lower prices than their licensees. Finally, price-fixing creates certain advantages for the patentee that are absent with royalties. Most important, price-fixing creates a strong interdependence between the patentee and its licensees to maintain industry discipline and stability from both a price and quality standpoint. Price-fixing, therefore, might reduce the level of competition between the patentee and its licensees.

With specific regard to the *Line Material* case, the Supreme Court decision made sense. If price-fixing had been permitted in this case, the two firms would have lost some of their incentive to develop more advanced fuse cutouts because the introduction of a more advanced cutout would have threatened stability. Furthermore, the absence of price-fixing should have created a more competitive environment, one in which more effort would be put forth by *all* competitors to develop new technology. It would appear, therefore, that there is little to be gained, and something to be lost, by permitting price-fixing in cross-licensing agreements.

United States v. Singer Manufacturing Company **374 U.S. 174** **(1963)** Another potential problem with cross-licensing agreements is their use by one group of firms to exclude another firm or firms from the market. In the *Singer* case it was alleged that Singer had conspired with a Swiss firm and an Italian firm to prevent the distribution of Japanese zigzag sewing machines in the United States. Early in 1953 Singer had completed the development of a multiple-cam zigzag sewing machine called the 401. In September 1953, however, Vigorelli, an Italian firm, introduced a machine incorporating most of the major advances in the 401. Singer concluded that Vigorelli already had applications on file for the necessary patents to produce the 401 and sought a cross-licensing agreement with Vigorelli. On November 17, 1955, Singer and Vigorelli concluded a nonexclusive, worldwide, and royalty-free cross-licensing agreement. The two firms also agreed not to bring any infringement actions against each other in any country.

A short time later, much to Singer's chagrin, Singer learned that Gegauf, a Swiss firm, had a similar patent with an effective priority date in Italy of May 31, 1952. This placed both the Singer and the Vigorelli patents in jeopardy. To make matters worse for Singer, in December 1955 Singer learned that Vigorelli and Gegauf had negotiated a cross-licensing agreement covering their zigzag patents. At this point, Singer decided its wisest policy was to approach Gegauf with a cross-licensing offer.

During negotiations with Gegauf it became clear that Gegauf felt secure in the priority of its patent claims over Singer's, but felt insecure about inroads into the United States market by Japanese manufacturers of zigzag machines. Singer used Gegauf's fear of the Japanese to negotiate a cross-licensing agreement. Singer argued that without a cross-licensing agreement Singer and Gegauf would spend so much time and money fighting each other that the Japanese would come to dominate the American market.

Approximately one week after the Gegauf-Singer agreement had been concluded, Vigorelli suggested that the three firms should act in concert to contest the Japanese patent claims in the United States. Singer immediately rejected this idea and argued that each firm should advance its own patent claims, but Singer suggested to Vigorelli that Singer could best represent the interests of *all three firms* in the United States and that it might be advantageous for Singer to hold the American patent rights for all three companies. Vigorelli then approached Gegauf with the idea of transferring Gegauf's American patents to Singer. Initially, Gegauf demanded $250,000 for its patent rights from Singer, and negotiations broke down. Continued fear of the Japanese, however, made Gegauf reconsider, and eventually it assigned its American patents to Singer for $90,000. Under the agreement Gegauf provided Singer with a nonexclusive, royalty-free license, and Singer guaranteed Gegauf that it would not make a slavish copy of the Gegauf machine.

After receiving the Gegauf patent Singer instituted two infringement suits against Brother, the largest importer of Japanese sewing machines. Furthermore, Singer brought an action before the United States Tariff Commission seeking to exclude *all* imported machines coming within the claims of the Gegauf patent.

The Supreme Court, by 8–1, ruled that Singer's actions went beyond the legitimate use of patents and violated sections 1 and 2 of the Sherman Act. Justice Clark delivered the majority opinion:

> What is claimed here is that Singer engaged in a series of transactions with Gegauf and Vigorelli for an illegal purpose, i.e., to rid itself and Gegauf, together, perhaps, with Vigorelli, of infringements by their common competitors, the Japanese manufacturers. . . .
>
> [B]y entwining itself with Gegauf and Vigorelli in such a program Singer went far beyond its claimed purpose of merely protecting its own 401 machine — it was protecting Gegauf and Vigorelli, the sole licensees under the patent at the time, under the same umbrella. This the Sherman Act will not permit. . . . [T]he conspiracy arises implicitly from the course of dealing of the parties, here resulting in Singer's obligation to enforce the patent to the benefit of all three parties. While there is no contract so stipulating, the facts as found by the trial court indicate a common purpose to suppress the Japanese machine competition in the United States through the use of the patent, which was secured by Singer on the assurances to Gegauf and its colicensee, Vigorelli, that such would certainly be the result. . . .
>
> Moreover this overriding common design to exclude the Japanese machines in the United States is clearly illustrated by Singer's action before the United States Tariff Commission. Less than eight months after the patent was issued it started this effort to bar infringers in one sweep. . . .
>
> It is strongly urged upon us that application of the antitrust laws in this case will have a significantly deleterious effect on Singer's position as the sole remaining domestic producer of zigzag sewing machines for household use, the market for which has been increasingly preempted by foreign manufacturers. Whether economic consequences of this character warrant relaxation of the scope of enforcement of the antitrust laws, however, is a policy matter committed to congressional or executive resolution. . . . [I]t "is equally well settled that the possession of a valid patent or patents does not give the patentee any exemption from the provisions of the Sherman Act beyond the limits of the patent monopoly. By aggregating patents in one control, the holder of the patents cannot escape the prohibitions of the Sherman Act." . . .
>
> The judgment of the District Court is reversed and the case is remanded for the entry of an appropriate decree in accordance with this opinion.

The *Singer* case further restricted the rights of patent holders. Singer had never attempted to restrict Vigorelli or Gegauf from competing in the American market, and the three firms had not attempted to fix prices. There was, however, an implied conspiracy in their actions that was sufficient for the Court to conclude that a violation of the Sherman Act had occurred.

Royal Industries v. St. Regis Paper Company 1970 Trade Cases Paragraph 73,076 The *Royal Industries* case raised several other interesting legal questions with regard to the *General Electric* doctrine. In April 1963 Royal Industries obtained a patent for producing plastic-bag tie strips from one Gerald C. Bower, the owner of Plas-Ties Corporation. Shortly thereafter, Royal acquired 80 percent of the stock in Plas-Ties. Plas-Ties remained a separate subsidiary, however, with Bower retaining 20 percent stock ownership. In May 1963 Plas-Ties and Pollack Paper Company, a division of St. Regis Paper, signed a written licensing agreement. The license contained all of the usual provisions, plus one further stipulation. It contained the following price-reduction formula: "If Royal reduces its selling prices below those set forth in the attached Exhibit A, said 10% royalty shall be reduced one percentage point for each 5% reduction in the selling prices, provided however that the royalty shall not be reduced below 5%." Exhibit A was simply a list of Plas-Ties's selling prices. There was, however, no explicit price-fixing clause in the *written* agreement.

From May 1963 until February 1966 St. Regis and Plas-Ties maintained identical prices. In February 1966, however, St. Regis lowered its prices. The next month, Plas-Ties matched St. Regis's lower prices. In June 1966 St. Regis lowered its prices again, and Royal, but not Plas-Ties, complained. A conference was held, and this conference became a major point of dispute during the trial. Royal contended that a price-fixing agreement had been reached at the conference; St. Regis denied that any price-fixing agreement had been consummated. In any event, after the June conference, St. Regis raised its prices a bit, but they remained below Plas-Ties's prices. Then in May 1967 St. Regis again reduced its prices. This proved to be the last straw for Royal. In a letter dated June 8, 1967, Royal threatened that unless St. Regis raised its prices to match Plas-Ties's prices, its license would be terminated. When St. Regis refused to raise its prices, Royal terminated the license. St. Regis ignored the termination notice, and Royal then filed an infringement suit against St. Regis.

Judge Whelan wrote the district court decision in favor of St. Regis:

> Even were it possible for plaintiff to prove what it claims was an oral price fixing agreement made during the course of negotiations . . . such oral price fixing agreement could have no legal effect since it violates the Sherman and Clayton Acts' prohibition against agreements in restraint of trade in that it would require defendant to sell its products made under the

patented process at the price fixed by Plas-Ties Corporation, an entirely separate corporation from [Royal]. Plaintiff's assertion that such an agreement is valid under the doctrine of the *General Electric* case is not sound. In [that] case the patentee entered into an agreement with its licensee that required the licensee to sell products made under the patent in question at a price no lower than that at which the patentee sold the same products. In the instant case, however, the oral agreement contended for by plaintiff would require defendant not to sell at the prices fixed by plaintiff but rather at the prices fixed by its competitor, to wit, Plas-Ties Corporation also holding a license from plaintiff to manufacture under the patent. . . .

This Court is of the opinion that the patent-antitrust exception allowed by the *General Electric* case is a very limited one. . . . Thus, the question presents itself, where the patent owner does not compete with the licensee with respect to the patented product, is a price fixing agreement such as the one sought to be introduced in this case "normally and reasonably adapted to secured pecuniary reward for the patentee's monopoly." We think not. . . .

Plaintiff's reliance upon an oral price fixing agreement made in June 1966, some two and one-half years after plaintiff had granted a patent license to defendant, is completely without merit. The limited exception given by the *General Electric* doctrine to a price fixing agreement is that the price fixing agreement is one of the conditions under which the patent license is given. Such doctrine could under no circumstances by extended to protect a patentee who, after he has divested himself of his patent monopoly by granting a license, attempts to require the licensee to conform to prices fixed by either the patentee or as in this case by another corporation, Plas-Ties Corporation. It is the opinion of this Court that such a subsequent price fixing agreement would be as clear a violation of the antitrust laws as exists in any price fixing agreement where no patent was involved. The patent monopoly having been relinquished, there would be no shield behind which to hide the presumptively illegal price fixing agreement. The *General Electric* doctrine merely permits a patentee to require price confirmation as a condition under which a patentee licenses another to use the patented process. The patentee is not given any exception from the provisions of the Sherman Act beyond the limits of the patent monopoly.

In 1969 the Ninth Circuit Court of Appeals upheld the district court ruling [420 F.2d 449 (1969)], but the circuit court ruling was much more limited than the district court decision. Instead of ruling on the antitrust implications of the case, the circuit court dismissed the case on the legal technicality that Royal could not terminate the licensing agreement without the consent of Plas-Ties as a coplaintiff. Since Plas-Ties, not Royal, was supplying the patent and the know-how to St. Regis, the court ruled that it was necessary for Plas-Ties to join Royal in any suit against St. Regis. The circuit court, therefore, decided in favor of St.

Regis on a legal technicality, without overturning the district court decision.

The *Royal Industries* ruling further restricted the *General Electric* doctrine by bringing into question several practices. The decision suggested that any price-fixing agreement made *after* an initial patent licensing agreement is likely to be viewed with deep suspicion by the courts. Furthermore, by resticting Royal to act only in concert with Plas-Ties, the circuit court added a further restiction to the patent holder's rights.

III SUMMARY

Each of the last five cases suggests that the *General Electric* doctrine has been significantly watered down since 1926. Nevertheless, a patentee's basic right to set the price of a patented item has never been explicitly overturned, and in straightforward cases it is still safe for a patentee to set the price of a patented device. Any attempt to extend the power of one patent into other areas such as through a patent-pooling agreement or a conspiracy directed against one or more competitors, however, is on shaky ground.

The primary issues examined in this chapter have been price-fixing and conspiracy. Although a strong case can be made for preventing all price-fixing agreements in patent licensing agreements, it is important to realize that in the absence of the right to fix prices many patents would be underworked because the patentee would simply refuse to grant *any* licenses. Such a refusal to license policy is perfectly legal and raises one of the more important economic questions regarding patents: Should patentees have the right to refuse to license a patent, or should *all* patents be mandatorily licensed at reasonable royalties?

Antitrust policy has helped to eliminate some of the more blatant abuses of the patent system; however, the major issues with regard to the patent system are much broader than those addressed in this chapter. The most important issues are whether the patent system creates net benefits or net costs and, assuming the system creates net benefits, whether seventeen years is the optimal length of time for patent protection. Many economists would argue that seventeen years is far too long a period for patent protection and that all patents should be licensed at reasonable royalties. A full examination, of these issues, however, goes far beyond the scope of this book [3].

NOTES

1. See W. G. Shepherd and C. Wilcox, *Public Policies Toward Business* (Homewood, Ill.: Irwin, 1979) pages 506–508; F. M. Scherer, *Industrial Market Structure and*

Economic Performance (Chicago: Rand-McNally, 1980), Chapter 16, especially pages 443–450; C. T. Taylor and Z. A. Silberston, *The Economic Impact of the Patent System* (Cambridge, England: Cambridge University Press, 1973); and W. D. Nordhaus, *Invention, Growth, and Welfare* (Cambridge, Mass.: M.I.T. Press, 1969).

2. D. E. Waldman, *Antitrust Action and Market Structure* (Lexington, Mass.: Heath, 1978), pages 110–111.

3. See Taylor and Silberston, *The Economic Impact of the Patent System;* and F. M. Scherer, *The Economic Effects of Compulsory Patent Licensing* (New York: New York University Graduate School of Business Administration, 1977).

CHAPTER

EIGHT

Vertical Restraints of Trade and Group Boycotts

In previous chapters most of our concern has been *horizontal* restraints of trade, such as collusion and price discrimination, or single-firm monopoly power. In this chapter we consider attempts by manufacturers to extend their market power forward into the wholesale or retail market. These *vertical* restrictions may entail benefits not only for manufacturers, but for wholesalers and retailers as well, particularly if the retailers are able to use vertical restrictions to promote collusion. In fact, the impetus for these restrictions sometimes comes, not from the manufacturer, but from the retailer.

Before examining vertical restraints, it is useful to recall the discussion of vertical integration in Chapter 4. Every one of the restrictions analyzed in this chapter can be considered as an alternative to increased vertical integration. The economic arguments against these practices are the same as the arguments against increased vertical integration. Specifically, these vertical constraints can either increase the capital barrier to entry or facilitate collusion (see Chapter 4).

This chapter examines five types of restrictions: tying arrangements, exclusive-dealing agreements, territorial and customer restrictions, resale-price maintenance, and group boycotts.

I TYING ARRANGEMENTS

If a firm has market power over good X, it may require that its buyers purchase another good, good Y, in order to obtain good X. If, for example, a film distributor has exclusive rights over a new, popular film, hypothetically entitled "Rocky X," and it also controls a less popular film, hypothetically entitled "The Grasshopper That Ate Cleveland," then the distributor could require every theater that exhibited "Rocky X" to show "The Grasshopper That Ate Cleveland" also. Such a requirement has been termed a *tying agreement*, where "Rocky X" is the *tying product* and "The Grasshopper That Ate Cleveland" is the *tied product*.

The economic impact of tying has been debated extensively over the past two decades. Opinions vary widely, from those who believe that tying is *never* anticompetitive to those who believe that under certain circumstances tying can be an effective method of increasing monopoly power and monopoly profits [1]. Conventional wisdom today rejects the extreme position, which argues that tying is never anticompetitive, but most economists accept the argument that tying agreements usually have few anticompetitive effects.

The possible anticompetitive impact of tying can be illustrated by examining Kodak's tying of film and film processing. Prior to 1956 Kodak sold photographic film with the condition that the buyer had to have the film processed by Kodak. Since Kodak produced superior, patented film, this was an effective method of extending its power from film to film processing. Kodak's practice had several anticompetitive effects. First, since Kodak controlled 90 percent of the processed film market, it was extremely difficult for independent film processors to find any film to process. The tying arrangement thus foreclosed a huge share of the processing market, making entry into processing (the tied-product market) very difficult. Second, because Kodak's policy foreclosed 90 percent of the market, just about the only way to enter the film processing market was to follow Kodak's lead and produce film as well as processing services. This greatly increased the capital barrier to entry because entrants were virtually forced to enter two markets, film and film processing, instead of one. This required not only more capital, but large research and development expenditures to produce noninfringing film capable of competing with Kodak's film. It is not surprising, therefore, that no competitor threatened Kodak's processing market share *until* 1956, when Kodak agreed to a consent decree ending the tie. Shortly thereafter, the processing market became highly competitive [2].

A number of arguments have been advanced by defendants in an effort to justify tying arrangements. First, it has been argued that tying is necessary for technological reasons. Sometimes this argument makes sense, as in the *Jerrold* case below. More often, this argument seems almost frivolous, as when International Salt contended that only its salt would prevent its salt dispensing machines from clogging up [3]. Second, franchisors such as Chicken Delight and Dunkin' Donuts have argued that it is necessary to tie ingredients together in order to maintain the high quality associated with their trademarks [4]. This argument has met with some success in the courts.

Prior to the passage of the Clayton Act, in 1914, the courts had taken a fairly lenient attitude toward tying arrangements, particularly the tying of unpatented supplies to patented machinery. Since the passage of the Clayton Act, however, the courts have generally taken a tough position toward tying arrangements. An analysis of the following cases, however, will demonstrate that tying arrangements are not illegal *per se*.

International Business Machines v. United States 298 U.S. 131 (1936)

One of the government's earliest tying victories was in the 1936 *IBM* case. IBM refused to lease its tabulating machines unless the lessee agreed to purchase its entire requirements of tabulating cards from IBM. IBM had significant market power in the tabulating machine market, and under this plan IBM was able to control over 80 percent of the market for both machines and cards. Remington Rand, the only other producer of tabulating machines, followed the same policy of tying its cards to its machines.

IBM argued that the tie was necessary to protect its tabulating machines from damage caused by the use of "inferior" cards. Its argument was considerably weakened, however, by the fact that IBM permitted the federal government to use its own cards so long as the government agreed to pay a higher rental for IBM's machines.

The Supreme Court ruled 8–0 that the tying agreement violated section 3 of the Clayton Act. Justice Stone wrote the decision:

[IBM's] principal contentions are that its leases are lawful because the protection secured by the condition does not extend beyond the monopoly which it has acquired by patents on the cards and on the machines in which they are used and that in any case the condition is permissible under section 3 of the Clayton Act because its purpose and effect are only to preserve to appellant the good will of its patrons by preventing the use of unsuitable cards which would interfere with the successful performance of its machines. . . .

Appellant's patents appear to extend only to the cards when perforated, and to have no application to those which the lessees purchase before they are punched. The contention is thus reduced to the dubious claim that the sale of the un-punched cards is a contributory infringement of the patents covering the use of perforated cards separately and in combination with the machines. . . .

But we do not place our decision on this narrow ground. We rest it rather on the language of section 3 of the Clayton Act which expressly makes tying clauses unlawful, whether the machine leased is "patented or unpatented." . . .

Despite the plain language of section 3, making unlawful the tying clause when it tends to create a monopoly, appellant insists that it does not forbid tying clauses whose purpose and effect are to protect the good will of the lessor in the leased machines, even though monopoly ensues. In support of this contention appellant places great emphasis on the admitted fact that it is essential to the successful performance of the leased machines that the cards used in them conform, with relatively minute tolerances, to specifications as to size, thickness and freedom from defects which would affect adversely the electrical circuits indispensable to the proper operation of the machines. . . . [However, t]he Government, under the provisions of its lease, following its own methods, has made large quantities of the cards, which are in successful use with appellant's machines. The suggestion that without the tying clause an adequate supply of cards would not be forthcoming from competitive sources is not supported by the evidence. . . .

Appellant is not prevented from proclaiming the virtues of its own cards or warning against the danger of using, in its machines, cards which do not conform to the necessary specifications, or even from making its leases conditional upon the use of cards which conform to them. For aught that appears such measures would protect its good will without the creation of monopoly or resort to the suppression of competition. . . .

[W]e can perceive no tenable basis for an exception in favor of a condition whose substantial benefit to the lessor is the elimination of business competition and the creation of monopoly, rather than the protection of its good will.

Despite the 1936 decision, IBM continued to dominate the tabulating card market because its lessees continued to purchase their cards from IBM. In fact, IBM's card market share actually *increased* to 90 percent in 1954. In 1956, however, IBM agreed to a consent decree that required its market share in tabulating cards to be reduced to less than 50 percent. In order to meet the conditions of the decree, in 1963 IBM divested itself of approximately 3 percent of its tabulating card capacity [5].

United States v. American Can Company 87 F. Supp. 18
(1949) The *American Can* case dealt with the leasing practices of the
American Can Company and the Continental Can Company. American
Can and Continental Can both adopted a policy of leasing their can-
closing machines for a minimum of five years with the further restriction that the lessee purchase its can requirements during the five-year
period exclusively from its machinery supplier. Under no circumstances
did American Can or Continental Can offer machines for sale. These
leasing policies resulted in a two-firm concentration ratio of 80 percent
and had several possible anticompetitive effects. First, by placing approximately 80 percent of all can customers beyond the reach of competitors each year, the long-term leases reduced the potential market
available to new can manufacturers. Second, by refusing to sell their
machines, American Can and Continental Can eliminated any potential competition from a secondhand machinery market. Third, the
requirement that lessees purchase their requirements of cans from their
machinery supplier established a tie between machinery and cans.

These policies worked because the two firms produced superior
closing machinery. Their market power in machinery, therefore, was
responsible for their power in the can market. Under these conditions
potential entrants into the can market were virtually forced to produce
closing machinery as well as cans. This proved to be an almost impossible barrier, and American Can and Continental Can were able to control
both markets.

American Can's tying policy enabled it to increase its profitability
by practicing an interesting form of price discrimination in the machinery market. Market power was the result of superior machines, not
superior cans, yet American Can leased its machines at rentals *below
average cost!* This was possible because *can* prices were kept substantially above average cost. The cans, therefore, were used as a method of metering machine use. The more cans a firm used, the larger were
the profits it paid to American. A purchaser of 1 million cans paid ten
times more for the use of American Can's *machine* than the user of
100,000 cans.

The district court distinguished between the effect of a tying
arrangement and the effect of a requirements contract. It ruled that
although the tying agreement was illegal, a one-year requirements
contract for cans was reasonable. Judge Harris delivered the district
court opinion:

> The evidence herein discloses that American owns and controls more
> closing machines than the rest of the industry together, and demonstrates
> that defendant effectively ties the leasing of such machines to the sales of
> its cans. . . .
> It may be noted that the closing machines manufactured by American
> with slight adjustment, may be used to close the cans of the other can

manufacturers; that there are no basic patent rights involved as was the case in the International Salt controversy. . . .

It is manifest to this Court from the record herein that abundant proof has been supplied by the Government, and the Court accordingly finds that the leasing practices of can closing machines violate the said Act for they affect injuriously a sizable part of interstate commerce. . . .

In the instant case the Government's proof shows the use by defendant of approximately 4,000 requirements contracts involving 250 million dollars in business annually, and a domination in the canmaking industry for a period of almost 50 years. . . . [The] Government argues that domination and control having been demonstrated, this Court must hold as a matter of law, in the light of the contracts entered into and the business controlled under the contracts, implemented with the devices, means and methods already alluded to, that competition is foreclosed over a period of many years with respect to a sizeable segment of the can-making business, to wit, approximately 40 percent. . . .

Defendant contends that traditionally, in view of practices surrounding requirements contracts, this Court must undertake a comparative analysis in determining the merit or de-merit of such contracts; whether they are apt in their use in this particular industry; whether they are favored by the user-consumer, etc. . . .

The general reason assigned for requirements contracts was that canners wished to be assured of receiving containers when, as, and if needed, regardless of any contingency which might affect the raw material supply or the market. . . .

In its brief . . ., the Government takes the position that, by reason of the impingement of the machinery lease contracts upon the requirements contract the term of the requirements contract, be it fifteen years, ten years, five years or one day is immaterial. [The government contends t]hat the term requirements contracts perforce must be stricken as a whole. The basic answer to this contention is brief: The Government has intertwined the lease contracts with the requirements contract without giving recognition to the separate status of each. . . . Rather the question of reasonableness must to some degree be determined by the force and effect of the contract upon trade and commerce, and, when we take the requirements contract in and of itself and examine it in the light of its possible effect upon trade and commerce, it must be concluded that the *five year* term creates an unreasonable restraint in the light of all the facts, factors, circumstances and background.

In finding the five year requirements contract illegal, we are not thereby compelled to declare void any and all requirements contracts. We *cannot* ignore the testimony of countless witnesses who indicated the vital necessity of some sort of supply contract. . . . Others believed emphatically in a term not to exceed one year for, as it was pointed out, at the expiration date of such a period of time they could cast about in the open market.

Mindful that requirements contracts are not per se unlawful, and that one of the elements which should be considered is the length thereof, it is only fair to conclude after a careful review of the evidence, that a contract for a period of one year would permit competitive influences to operate at the expiration of said period of time and the vice which is now present in the five year requirements contracts would be removed. . . .

To strike down the requirements contracts and to declare them totally void as violative of the Sherman Act, without at the same time affording to the user-consumer a supply over a limited period of time would be destructive, illogical, unsound and not in consonance with the acute particular problems confronting the canning industry.

The district court decision eliminated most of the entry barriers created by American Can's policies. First, the maximum length of a lease or requirements contract was limited to one year. Second, American Can was required to offer all machines for sale at reasonable prices. Buyers were able to purchase machinery and free themselves to deal with any can manufacturer. Third, American Can was required to charge rental rates *above average cost*. This encouraged buyers to purchase rather than to rent machines and helped ease entry into the machinery market, but the welfare implications of increased machinery prices are unclear. Since the metering of machine use through can purchases was essentially a form of *first-degree* price discrimination, it *theoretically* enabled American Can to charge an effective price for the *least* used of its leased machines that approximated marginal cost. By raising effective rental rates, the court decision reduced the total number of machines leased or purchased and reduced access to can-closing machinery, particularly access by the smallest users of can-closing equipment. On the other hand, American Can's systematic price discrimination may have prevented entry into both the machinery and can markets and thereby reduced the level of effective competition and may have slowed the rate of technological advance in either or both markets.

Perhaps the most significant result of the decree was a dramatic increase in backward vertical integration into can production by major canners [6]. Between 1930 and 1946 only Campbell Soup had integrated backward by purchasing an entire can facility from Continental Can. After the decision self-manufacturing of cans became common. Within ten years of the decree many large packers (including California Packing; Hawaiian Pineapple; Green Giant; Stokley Van Camp; and Libby, McNeil, and Libby) had entered the can industry. Backward vertical integration greatly increased the major packers leverage in dealing with American Can and Continental Can since large vertically integrated packers could fight price increases by threatening to increase their self-manufacturing operations [7].

United States v. Jerrold Electronics Corporation 187 F. Supp. 545 (1960)   In December 1950 Jerrold Electronics installed America's first cable TV system in Lansford, Pennsylvania. After a short time, however, technical problems began to appear that required Jerrold to develop new equipment and techniques for cable installations. Because of these problems Jerrold's president, Milton Shapp (later the governor of Pennsylvania), decided that Jerrold would install community-wide systems only if the community agreed to purchase all of the necessary equipment from Jerrold and further agreed to purchase a Jerrold service contract.

The district court considered the technological necessity of the tying agreement and ruled that in the early years of the cable TV industry the tie was justified. The court also ruled that Jerrold could not continue indefinitely to sell only complete cable systems. District Judge Van Dusen wrote the decision:

> Jerrold's short and long-term well-being depended on the success of these first systems. It could not afford to permit some of its limited equipment to be used in such a way that it would work against its interests. A wave of system failures at the start would have greatly retarded, if not destroyed this new industry and would have been disastrous for Jerrold, who, unlike others experimenting in this field such as R.C.A. and Philco, did not have a diversified business to fall back on but had put most of its eggs in one precarious basket in an all out effort to open up this new field. . . . For these reasons, this court concludes that Jerrold's policy and practice of selling its community equipment only in conjunction with a service contract was reasonable and not in violation of section 1 of the Sherman Act at the time of its inception. . . .
>
> The court's conclusion is based primarily on the fact that the tie-in was instituted in the launching of a new business with a highly uncertain future. As the industry took root and grew, the reasons for the blanket insistence on a service contract disappeared. . . . In March 1954, it dropped the policy as a general rule and thereafter applied it on an area-by-area and case-by-case basis. . . . On the present record, it would be a matter of speculation to determine when Jerrold's policy was no longer justified in various areas of the country. . . . [T]his court makes no finding as to when this occurred. It is content to say that while Jerrold has satisfied this court that its policy was reasonable at its inception it has failed to satisfy us that it remained reasonable throughout the period of its use, even allowing it a reasonable time to recognize and adjust its policies to changing conditions. Accordingly, the court concludes that the defendants' refusal to sell [violated] the Sherman Act during part of the time this policy was in effect. . . .
>
> The difficult question raised by the defendants is whether this should be treated as a case of tying the sale of one product to the sale of another product or merely as the sale of a single general product. . . .

The record . . . establishes that the number of pieces in each system varied considerably so that hardly any two versions of the alleged product were the same. Furthermore, the customer was charged for each item of equipment and not a lump sum for the total system. Finally, while Jerrold had cable and antennas to sell which were manufactured by other concerns, it only required that the electronic equipment in the system be bought from it. . . .

There is a further factor, however, which, in the court's opinion, makes Jerrold's decision to sell only full systems reasonable. There was a sound business reason for Jerrold to adopt this policy. Jerrold's decision was intimately associated with its belief that a service contact was essential. . . . Jerrold could not render the service it promised and deemed necessary if the customer could purchase any kind of equipment he desired. The limited knowledge and instability of equipment made specifications an impractical, if not impossible, alternative. . . . As the circumstances changed and the need for compulsory service contracts disappeared, the economic reasons for exclusively selling complete systems were eliminated. Absent these economic reasons, the court feels that a full system was not an appropriate sales unit. . . .

The court concludes that the defendants' policy of selling full systems only was lawful at its inception but constituted a violation of section 1 of the Sherman Act and section 3 of the Clayton Act during part of the time it was in effect. . . .

In addition to initially selling its equipment only on a full system basis. Jerrold also imposed certain limitations on the equipment that could be added to the system in the future by means of certain provisions in its service contracts. One of these is the provision appearing in all of the contracts to the effect that the operator shall not install any unapproved, non-Jerrold equipment. . . .

An examination of the record discloses uncontradicted testimony concerning numerous systems which used non-Jerrold equipment without objection, although this fact was known to the defendants. On the other hand, no instances were brought to the court's attention in which it is clear that an operator considered himself unable to obtain non-Jerrold equipment because of the veto clause. The court finds that these provisions were not intended, and were not used, to prevent the use of competitive equipment in systems covered by a service contract.

The veto provisions were necessary to protect Jerrold in view of its maintenance obligations under the contracts and its financial interest in the success of the systems. Reasonable restraints are permissible for such purposes. . . . The restraint imposed by the requirement that Jerrold approve all equipment other than that it manufactured is reasonable in view of the meaning given to this provision as evidenced by Jerrold's conduct with respect to it.

In a separate section of the decision the district court permitted Jerrold's acquisition of ten cable TV systems because the acquisitions did not foreclose a *sufficient* portion of the market to violate section 7 of the Clayton Act. The court declared, however, that any additional purchases *might* violate the law, and Jerrold was ordered to refrain from further acquisitions for a period of three years.

Despite the fact that Jerrold had "won" the case, Jerrold was required

1. to stop tying service to equipment,
2. to stop tying its master antennas to other equipment,
3. to service non-Jerrold cable systems,
4. to permit customers to purchase other firms' equipment for connection with a Jerrold system.

Jerrold was permitted, however, to refuse to guarantee or warrant any cable system that connected equipment that Jerrold had not approved.

Prior to the *Jerrold* decision, it appeared that tying agreements were on the verge of being declared illegal *per se*. The Supreme Court, however, affirmed the *Jerrold* decision without comment and thereby established one acceptable defense in tying cases. Furthermore, in another case, *Fortner Enterprises v. United States Steel Corporation* [429 U.S. 610 (1977)], the Supreme Court established a second acceptable defense. Fortner accused U.S. Steel of tying prefabricated houses (the tied product) to the purchase of cheap credit (the tying product). The Supreme Court ruled unanimously that U.S. Steel had *no* market power in the credit market and, therefore, could not be guilty of violating the Clayton Act.

Susser v. Carvel Corporation 332 F.2d 505 (1964)   Carvel operated a chain of 400 retail stores that sold soft ice cream. Prior to 1955 Carvel had required its franchisees to sell Carvel products at prices specified by Carvel in its "Standard Operating Manual." Furthermore, prior to 1955 the franchisees were required to purchase their entire requirements of "supplies, machinery, equipment, and paper goods" from Carvel or Carvel-approved sources. In 1955 Carvel changed the standard agreement so that its dealers were required to purchase only supplies "which are a part of the end product" from Carvel. Under the new agreement franchisees were permitted to purchase machinery, equipment, and paper goods from independent sources. Furthermore, the new agreement only suggested retail prices and stated explicitly that dealers could sell Carvel products at any price.

In the first part of the circuit court decision, written by Chief Judge Lumbard, the court ruled that although it was illegal for Carvel to specify *required* prices in its operating manual, it was acceptable to suggest retail prices so long as no attempt was made to force franchisees to sell at those suggested prices.

With regard to the tying issue, Judges Friendly and Medina disagreed with Chief Judge Lumbard. The two-judge majority ruled that Carvel's practices were legal because the agreement helped to protect the Carvel trademark and an insubstantial amount of commerce was affected.

Judges Friendly and Medina wrote

> Here the facts to which plaintiffs were limited by the pre-trial order showed neither that Carvel has "sufficient economic power with respect to the tying product to appreciably restrain free competition in the market for the tied product" nor that "a not insubstantial amount of commerce is affected." Indeed, such figures as exist would prove the contrary. In 1960 there were in New York, Connecticut, and Massachusetts, 250 Carvel dealers out of a total of 125,000 outlets where ice cream cones could be purchased — amounting to one fifth of one per cent of the outlets and apparently doing about one per cent of the business. The other large Carvel states are New Jersey and Pennsylvania; the balance of a 1960 total of 400 Carvel dealers were scattered at one time over as many as 8 or 9 states from Maine to Florida and as far west as Wisconsin. These dealers competed not only with similar chains — Dairy Queen, Tastee Freez, Dari-Delite, King Kone, Dari-Isle, and others, but also with chains and independents utilizing mobile units, with chain stores and operations such as Howard Johnson. . . . Not only was the amount of commerce in these not consequential, but any damage to the plaintiffs was even less so. Eagle Cone's billings to Carvel averaged $460 per dealer per year, and Carvel's mark-up was slightly over 5% or about $25 per dealer; whether the dealers suffered even that much damage is questionable since the price Carvel charged them was less than they could have obtained if they bought in smaller quantities than Carvel. . . .
>
> The true tying item was rather the Carvel trademark, whose growing repute was intended to help the little band of Carvel dealers swim a bit faster than their numerous rivals up the highly competitive stream. . . .
>
> Tying arrangements differ from other *per se* violations, such as price fixing, in that they can be justified on occasion, as by proof that "the protection of goodwill may necessitate" their use "where specifications for a substitute would be so detailed that they could not practicably be supplied." . . . Since the value of a trademark depends solely on the public image it conveys, its holder must exercise controls to assure himself that the mark is not shown in a derogatory light. The record affords no sufficient basis for upsetting the finding of the District Judge that "To require Carvel to limit itself to advance specifications of standards for all the various types of accessory products used in connection with the mix would impose an impractical and unreasonable burden of formulation."

The *Carvel* case suggested that although franchisors could not fix their franchisees' prices, they could protect their trademark by taking actions to ensure the quality of the products sold at each outlet. In the 1971 *Chicken Delight* case, however, the Ninth Circuit Court of Appeals further restricted the right of the franchisor.

Siegel v. Chicken Delight 448 F.2d 43 (1971) The facts in the *Chicken Delight* case varied little from those in the *Carvel* case. Chicken Delight operated several hundred fast food chicken outlets. It required its franchisees to purchase a specified number of cookers and fryers and all of their supplies and mixes exclusively from Chicken Delight. Since Chicken Delight received no royalties or fees, its income was completely dependent on the revenues generated from selling the tied products to its dealers.

The circuit court ruled that the agreement violated the Clayton Act because Chicken Delight could have effectively specified quality standards for the purchase of cooking equipment and ingredients from independent suppliers. Judge Merrill wrote

> The relevant question is not whether the items are essential to the franchise, but whether it is essential to the franchise that the items be purchased from Chicken Delight. This raises not the issue of whether there is a tie-in but rather the issue of whether the tie-in is justified, a subject to be discussed below. . . .
>
> Chicken Delight maintains that, even if its contractual arrangements are held to constitute a tying arrangement, it was not an unreasonable restraint under the Sherman Act. Three different bases for justification are urged.
>
> First, Chicken Delight contends that the arrangement was a reasonable device for measuring and collecting revenue. There is no authority for justifying a tying arrangement on this ground. Unquestionably, there exist feasible alternative methods of compensation for the franchise licenses, including royalties based on sales volume or fees computed per unit of time, which would neither involve tie-ins nor have undesirable anticompetitive consequences.
>
> Second, Chicken Delight advances as justification the fact that when it first entered the fast food field in 1952 it was a new business and was then entitled to the protection afforded by *United States v. Jerrold Electronics.*
>
> We find no merit in this contention. Whatever claim Chicken Delight might have had to a new business defense in 1952 — a question we need not decide — the defense cannot apply to the 1963–70 period. To accept Chicken Delight's argument would convert the new business justification into a perpetual license to operate in restraint of trade.
>
> The third justification Chicken Delight offers is the "marketing identity" purpose, the franchisor's preservation of the distinctiveness, uniformity and quality of its product.

In the case of a trade-mark this purpose cannot be lightly dismissed. Not only protection of the franchisor's goodwill is involved. The licensor owes an affirmative duty to the public to assure that in the hands of his licensee the trade-mark continues to represent that which it purports to represent . . .

However, to recognize that such a duty exists is not to say that every means of meeting it is justified. Restraint of trade can be justified only in the absence of less restrictive alternatives. . . .

The District Court found factual issues to exist as to whether effective quality control could be achieved by specification in the case of the cooking machinery and the dip and spice mixes. These questions were given to the jury under instructions; and the jury, in response to special interrogatories, found against Chicken Delight. . . .

One cannot immunize a tie-in from the antitrust laws by simply stamping a trade-mark symbol on the tied product — at least where the tied product is not itself the product represented by the mark.

We conclude that the District Court was not in error in holding as a matter of law (and upon the limited jury verdict) that Chicken Delight's contractual requirements constituted a tying arrangement in violation of section 1 of the Sherman Act. Upon this aspect of the case judgment is affirmed.

Although the *Carvel* and *Chicken Delight* decisions may appear to be at odds with each other, the two decisions may simply reflect a justifiable Rule of Reason approach to franchise agreements. In the *Carvel* decision the court majority believed that it was *impossible* for Carvel to police the quality of ingredients used in its ice cream products effectively, while in the *Chicken Delight* case the court believed that it was *possible* for Chicken Delight to set the standards for the quality of its chicken effectively.

II   EXCLUSIVE-DEALING AGREEMENTS

Under an exclusive-dealing agreement, a buyer agrees to purchase its entire requirements of some product or service from one supplier. The potential anticompetitive effect of these arrangements is *foreclosure* of the market to competitors and potential competitors. Like tying arrangements, the anticompetitive potential of a requirements contract is highly dependent on the market power of the supplier. If a manufacturer with a small market share entered into a requirements contract, a relatively small share of the market would be foreclosed. On the other hand, if a dominant firm followed an exclusive-dealing policy, a great deal of foreclosure would occur, and entry barriers might be significantly increased. A Rule of Reason approach, therefore, is justified with respect to exclusive dealing.

Unlike tying agreements, which tend to benefit sellers but *not* buyers, exclusive-dealing arrangements often provide economic benefits to buyers and sellers alike. These potential benefits are discussed at length in the following cases.

***Standard Oil Company of California v. United States* 337 U.S. 293 (1949)**   The *Standard Oil* case concerned the use of requirements contracts in the oil industry. Under these contracts, independent gasoline retailers agreed to purchase their entire supply of gasoline from one company. Many of the contracts also required the retailer to purchase not only gasoline, but its entire supply of tires, tubes, batteries, and accessories from its gasoline supplier. All of the major oil companies used similar contracts; therefore, the outcome of the case concerned the entire oil refining industry.

Standard Oil had negotiated almost 6,000 requirements contracts with independent dealers in the Southwest. The government contended that these contracts foreclosed a substantial amount of the gasoline market and thereby created a barrier to entry in the refining sector. In the Justice Department's view, elimination of the contracts would encourage retailers to become split-pump stations, that is, stations carrying more than one brand of gasoline. It was hoped that the end of requirements contracts would open the market to new independent refiners, encourage price competition, and give the independent retailers more bargaining power vis-à-vis the major refiners.

Requirements contracts foreclosed some markets from independent refiners, but it is not clear that the overall effect of the contracts was to hinder competition. Requirements contracts provided both the refiner and the retailer with some benefits. They assured small independent retailers of a continuing supply of gasoline and afforded at least some short-run protection against unforeseen price increases. An independent retailer could, therefore, plan its competitive strategy on the basis of known costs and avoid the risk of storing a product with a fluctuating demand. From the independent refiners' viewpoint, the contracts lowered selling costs by reducing transaction costs and reduced uncertainty by protecting refiners from a rapid reduction in demand.

The Supreme Court recognized that the requirements contracts might have net economic benefits; nevertheless, it ruled that they violated the Clayton Act. According to a 5–4 majority, Standard Oil's foreclosure of 6.7 percent of the market indicated a reasonable probability that competition would be substantially reduced. Justice Frankfurter delivered the majority opinion:

> The issue before us . . . is whether the requirement of showing that the effect of the agreements "may be to substantially lessen competition" may

be met simply by proof that a substantial portion of commerce is affected or whether it must also be demonstrated that competitive activity has actually diminished or probably will diminish. . . .

[T]he showing that Standard's requirements contracts affected a gross business of $58,000,000 comprising 6.7% of the total in the area goes far toward supporting the inference that competition has been or probably will be substantially lessened. . . . Requirements contracts . . . may well be of economic advantage to buyers as well as to sellers, and thus indirectly of advantage to the consuming public. In the case of the buyer, they may assure supply, afford protection against rises in price, enable long-term planning on the basis of known costs, and obviate the expense and risk of storage in the quantity necessary for a commodity having a fluctuating demand. From the seller's point of view, requirements contracts may make possible the substantial reduction of selling expenses, give protection against price fluctuations, and — of particular advantage to newcomers to the field to whom it is important to know what capital expenditures are justified — offer the possibility of a predictable market. . . . They may be useful moreover, to a seller trying to establish a foothold against the counter-attacks of entrenched competitors. . . . Since these advantages of requirements contracts may often be sufficient to account for their use, the coverage by such contracts of a substantial amount of business affords a weaker basis for the inference that competition may be lessened than would similar coverage by tying clauses, especially where use of the latter is combined with market control of the tying device. . . .

We may assume, as did the court below, that no improvement of Standard's competitive position has coincided with the period during which the requirements-contracts system of distribution has been in effect. We may assume further that the duration of the contracts is not excessive and that Standard was a major competitor when the present system was adopted, and it is possible that its position would have deteriorated but for the adoption of that system. When it is remembered that all the other major suppliers have also been using requirements contracts, and when it is noted that the relative share of the business which fell to each has remained about the same during the period of their use, it would not be farfetched to infer that their effect has been to enable the established suppliers individually to maintain their own standing and at the same time collectively, even though not collusively, to prevent a late arrival from wresting away more than an insignificant portion of the market. If, indeed, this were a result of the system, it would seem unimportant that a short-run by-product of stability may have been greater efficiency and lower costs, for it is the theory of the antitrust laws that the long-run advantage of the community depends upon the removal of restraints upon competition. . . .

Before the system of requirements contracts was instituted, Standard sold gasoline through independent service-station operators as its agents, and it might revert to this system if the judgment below were sustained. Or it might, as opportunity presented itself, add service stations now operated independently to the number managed by its subsidiary, Standard Stations, Inc. From the point of view of maintaining or extending competitive advantage, either of these alternatives would be just as effective as the use of requirements contracts, although of course insofar as they resulted in a tendency to monopoly they might encounter anti-monopoly provisions of the Sherman Act. . . . So long as these diverse ways of restricting competition remain open, therefore, there can be no conclusive proof that the use of requirements contracts has actually reduced competition below the level which it would otherwise have reached or maintained. . . .

Though it may be that such an alternative to the present system as buying out independent dealers and making them dependent employees of Standard Stations, Inc., would be a greater detriment to the public interest than perpetuation of the system, this is an issue, like the choice between greater efficiency and freer competition, that has not been submitted to our decision. We are faced, not with a broadly phrased expression of general policy, but merely a broadly phrased qualification of an otherwise narrowly directed statutory provision. . . .

We conclude, therefore, that the qualifying clause of section 3 is satisfied by proof that competition has been foreclosed in a substantial share of the line of commerce affected.

Justice Douglas delivered a blistering dissent in which he argued that the majority's opinion would serve only to encourage the major refiners to operate their own service stations. In the long run it appears that Justice Douglas was correct. The major oil refiners all became much more vertically integrated into retailing after the *Standard Oil* decision. By the early 1980s the small independent service station appeared to be going the way of the dinosaur. Furthermore, there was no major development of split-pump stations. The elimination of requirements contracts was far from the only factor encouraging increased vertical integration; however, the Supreme Court decision added an additional incentive for oil refiners to integrate forward into retailing.

Federal Trade Commission v. Motion Picture Advertising Service Co., Inc. 344 U.S. 392 (1953)

The *Motion Picture Advertising Service* case is important from a legal standpoint because it suggested that requirements contracts could successfully be attacked not only under section 3 of the Clayton Act, but also under section 5 of the Federal Trade Commission Act *and* under the Sherman Act. Motion Picture Advertising Service was the leading producer and distributor of movie advertising films, which used to be commonly shown in motion-picture theaters. Most of its contracts contained an agreement to deal exclusively with Motion Picture Advertising Service for periods varying between one and five years. Motion Picture Advertising Service controlled 40 percent of its marketing area, and the top four firms controlled 75 percent of the national market.

Justice Douglas wrote the 7–2 majority decision:

> The Federal Trade Commission, the petitioner, filed a complaint charging respondent with the use of "unfair methods of competition" in violation of section 5 of the Federal Trade Commission Act[.] . . .
>
> The "unfair methods of competition," which are condemned by section 5 (a) of the Act, are not confined to those that were illegal at common law or that were condemned by the Sherman Act. . . . Congress advisedly left the concept flexible to be defined with particularity by the myriad of cases from the field of business. . . . It is also clear that the Federal Trade Commission Act was designed to supplement and bolster the Sherman Act and the Clayton Act — to stop in their incipiency acts and practices which, when full blown, would violate those Acts, as well as to condemn as "unfair methods of competition" existing violations of them. . . .
>
> The Commission found in the present case that respondent's exclusive contracts unreasonably restrain competition and tend to monopoly. Those findings are supported by substantial evidence. This is not a situation where by the nature of the market there is room for newcomers, irrespective of the existing restrictive practices. The number of outlets for the films is quite limited. And due to the exclusive contracts, respondent and the three other major companies have foreclosed to competitors 75 percent of all available outlets for this business throughout the United States. It is, we think, plain from the Commission's findings that a device which has sewed up a market so tightly for the benefit of a few falls within the prohibitions of the Sherman Act and is therefore an "unfair method of competition" within the meaning of section 5 of the Federal Trade Commission Act.

The Supreme Court affirmed an FTC order that required Motion Picture Advertising Service to limit the length of its exclusive contracts to one year. The case is important primarily because it relied on the FTC and Sherman Acts rather than on the Clayton Act to attack a requirements contract. Under the Clayton Act, the government was required to show an *injury* to competition. The FTC Act, however, did *not* require proof of competitive injury; therefore, the *Motion Picture Advertising Service* precedent made it easier for the government to attack requirements contracts.

***Tampa Electric v. Nashville Coal* 365 U.S. 320 (1961)**   In 1955 Tampa Electric, a regulated public utility, made plans to construct six additional generating facilities. Although all of the existing generating plants in peninsular Florida burned oil, Tampa Electric decided to use coal in the first two generators and contracted with Nashville Coal to supply its entire coal requirements for a period of twenty years. The contract set a minimum price of $6.40 per ton, and the future price was to be adjusted with changes in production costs. Tampa Electric spent $3 million more to build the coal-burning plants compared with the cost of building oil-burning facilities, and Nashville Coal spent $7.5 million preparing to meet the conditions of the contract.

In April 1957, right before the first scheduled coal delivery, Nashville Coal informed Tampa Electric that the contract violated the Clayton Act, and Nashville Coal would not fulfill its conditions. Tampa Electric was then forced to purchase coal from the Love and Amos Coal Company. The new contract called for a maximum price of $8.80 per ton and was cancelable on twelve months notice by either party. The new contract, therefore, failed to provide Tampa Electric with the long-term security it was seeking and was likely to result in a higher price. Tampa Electric then sued Nashville Coal to force compliance with the contract.

Both the district court and the circuit court of appeals declared the contract void. The Supreme Court, however, overturned the circuit court because the contract did not substantially lessen competition. The decision revolved around the definition of the market, with Justice Clark writing the 7–2 majority opinion:

> In practical application, even though a contract is found to be an exclusive-dealing arrangement, it does not violate the section unless the court believes it probable that performance of the contract will foreclose competition in a substantial share of the line of commerce affected. . . .
>
> In applying these considerations to the facts of the case before us, it appears clear that both the Court of Appeals and the District Court have not given the required [consideration] to a controlling factor in the case — the relevant competitive market area. This omission, by itself, requires reversal, for, as we have pointed out, the relevant market is the prime factor in relation to which the ultimate question, whether the contract forecloses competition in a substantial share of the line of commerce involved, must be decided. . . .
>
> Neither the Court of Appeals nor the District Court considered in detail the question of the relevant market. They do seem, however, to have been satisfied with inquiring only as to competition within "Peninsular Florida." It was noted that the total consumption of peninsular Florida was 700,000 tons of coal per year, about equal to the estimated 1959 requirements of Tampa Electric. It was also pointed out that coal accounted for less than 6% of the fuel consumed in the entire State. . . .
>
> We are persuaded that on the record in this case, neither peninsular Florida, nor the entire State of Florida, nor Florida and Georgia combined constituted the relevant market of effective competition. We do not believe that the pie will slice so thinly. By far the bulk of the overwhelming tonnage marketed from the same producing area as serves Tampa is sold outside of

Georgia and Florida and the producers were "eager" to sell more coal in those States. While the relevant competitive market is not ordinarily susceptible to a "metes and bounds" definition, . . . it is of course the area in which [Nashville Coal] and the other 700 producers effectively compete. . . . In point of statistical fact, coal consumption in the combined Florida-Georgia area has increased significantly since 1954. In 1959 more than 3,775,000 tons were there consumed, 2,913,000 being used by electric utilities including, presumably, the coal used by the petitioner. The coal continued to come from at least seven states [including parts of Pennsylvania, Virginia, West Virginia, Kentucky, Tennessee, Alabama, Ohio, and Illinois.] From these statistics it clearly appears that the proportionate volume of the total relevant coal product as to which the challenged contract pre-empted competition, less that 1%, is conservatively speaking, quite insubstantial. A more accurate figure, even assuming pre-emption to the extent of the maximum anticipated total requirements, 2,250,000 tons a year, would be .77%.

It may well be that in the context of antitrust legislation protracted requirements contracts are suspect, but they have not been declared illegal *per se*. . . . While $128,000,000 is a considerable sum of money, even in these days, the dollar volume, by itself, is not the test, as we have already pointed out.

The remaining determination therefore, is whether the pre-emption of competition to the extent of the tonnage involved tends to substantially foreclose competition in the relevant coal market. We think not. . . . On the contrary, we seem to have only that type of contract which "may well be of economic advantage to buyers as well as sellers." [*Standard Oil Company of California v. United States* 337 U.S. 293 (1949)] . . . In the case of the buyer it "may assure supply," while on the part of the seller it "may make possible the substantial reduction of selling expenses, give protection against price fluctuations, and . . . offer the possibility of a predictable market." The 20-year period of the contract is singled out as the principal vice, but at least in the case of public utilities the assurance of a steady and ample supply of fuel is necessary in the public interest. Otherwise consumers are left unprotected against service failures owing to shutdowns; and increasingly unjustified costs might result in more burdensome rate structures eventually to be reflected in the consumer's bill. . . . In weighing the various factors, we have decided that in the competitive bituminous coal marketing area involved here the contract sued upon does not tend to foreclose a substantial volume of competition.

The *Tampa Electric* decision set a Rule of Reason standard in requirements contracts cases, and limited the 1949 *Standard Oil* precedent. In the *Tampa Electric* decision the Supreme Court permitted a requirements contract that had little, if any, anticompetitive effect, and which tended to be mutually beneficial to buyer and seller. Despite this ruling, any supplier with a *significant* market share is still on shaky ground if it attempts to force requirements contracts on its dealers.

III TERRITORIAL AND CUSTOMER RESTRICTIONS

Manufacturers sometimes distribute goods through independent dealers who are required to sell only in a certain geographic area or only to certain types of customers. At first, these restrictions may appear to be obviously anticompetitive because they restrict competition between the manufacturer's dealers. They may, however, have some redeeming procompetitive effects [8]. In particular, territorial restrictions may enable manufacturers to obtain better-quality dealers and may reduce the costs of providing retailing services. The *net* effect of territorial restrictions is highly dependent on the market power of the manufacturer or manufacturers and whether the restriction increases the probability of collusion in either the manufacturing or the retailing sector. Territorial restrictions, therefore, call for a Rule of Reason approach.

White Motor Co. v. United States 372 U.S. 253 (1963)   Prior to the *White Motor* decision the Justice Department had taken the position that territorial customer restrictions were illegal *per se*, and based on this position, the department had negotiated a large number of consent decrees. The White Motor Company manufactured trucks and truck parts that it distributed through dealers who agreed to abide by a territorial restriction in their contract. The restriction specified that dealers would not sell trucks to any "individual, firm, or corporation" located outside of the dealer's exclusive territory.

White Motor defended the contracts on the ground that they enabled White to compete against larger truck manufacturers. The district court, however, agreed with the Justice Department and considered territorial restrictions a *per se* violation of the Sherman Act. The court granted a judgment for the government, without even considering the evidence. The Supreme Court, by 5–3, overturned the summary judgment and remanded the case to the district court for a full trial. Justice Douglas wrote the majority opinion:

> This is the first case involving a territorial restriction in a *vertical* arrangement; and we know too little of the actual impact of both that restriction and the one respecting customers to reach a conclusion on the bare bones of the documentary evidence before us. . . .
>
> Horizontal territorial limitations, like "[g]roup boycotts, or concerted refusals by traders to deal with other traders," . . . are naked restraints of trade with no purpose except stifling of competition. A vertical territorial limitation may or may not have that purpose or effect. We do not know

enough of the economic and business stuff out of which these arrangements emerge to be certain, they may be too dangerous to sanction or they may be allowable protections against aggressive competitors or the only practicable means a small company has for breaking into or staying in business . . . and within the "rule of reason." We need to know more than we do about the actual impact of these arrangements on competition to decide whether they have such a "pernicious effect on competition and lack . . . any redeeming virtue" . . . and therefore should be classified as *per se* violations of the Sherman Act.

There is an analogy from the merger field that leads us to conclude that a trial should be had. A merger that would otherwise offend the antitrust laws because of a substantial lessening of competition has been given immunity where the acquired company was a failing one. . . . But in such a case, as in cases involving the question whether a particular merger will tend "substantially to lessen competition" [*Brown Shoe Co. v. United States* 370 U.S. 294 (1962)] a trial rather than the use of the summary judgment is normally necessary.

A full trial based on the evidence was never held in the *White Motor* case because White Motor agreed to a consent decree under which it gave up its exclusive dealerships. Nevertheless, the issues raised by the Supreme Court in the *White Motor* case were important factors in the 1964 *Sandura* decision of the Sixth Circuit Court of Appeals.

Sandura v. Federal Trade Commission 339 F.2d 847 (1964)

Sandura was a relatively small manufacturer of vinyl floor coverings. Its first vinyl floor covering, Sandran, was initially marketed in 1949 and despite a quick sales start soon developed two major problems. Sandran usually began to yellow shortly after installation; even worse, many of the Sandran vinyls delaminated and broke apart. As a result of these problems, Sandura's sales declined from $7,126,000 in 1950 to just $3,557,000 in 1954, and the company was on the verge of bankruptcy.

Having established a terrible reputation with its original Sandran, Sandura finally perfected the product, but it could not obtain quality distributors to market its new, improved Sandran. In an effort to attract good distributors Sandura was forced to offer dealers exclusive territories. After establishing the exclusive territories Sandura was able to become competitive, and its sales grew to $24,001,523 in 1959. Its 1960 and 1961 sales, however, declined to $16,394,061 and $13,718,297, respectively. Furthermore, its market share remained small throughout the period, never exceeding 5 percent, and its share was dwarfed by the the Big 3 of the vinyl floor covering industry: Armstrong, Congoleum, and Pabco, which among them controlled over 75 percent of capacity.

The circuit court applied the Rule of Reason suggested by the *White Motor* decision and found the territorial restrictions were legal. Judge O'Sullivan wrote the decision:

> We believe, however, that the Commission was not justified in its rejection of the great body of uncontradicted testimony that the distributors would not have been willing to undertake the Sandura program without closed territories and would either drop the line or greatly alter their methods if deprived of their closed territories today. . . .
>
> We believe that the cumulative effect of the facts offered is legally sufficient to justify Sandura's use of closed territories. Unless vertical imposition of closed distributor territories were now to be declared illegal per se, it is difficult to imagine a basis for finding an unreasonable restraint of trade at the time Sandura instituted this scheme in 1955. While its spectacular success in the 1955–1959 period may be due to the novelty of its perfected product, it is clear that that product could not have been successfully marketed if Sandura had not been able to attract distributors by the promise of closed territories. . . .
>
> In summary, we feel constrained to uphold the legal sufficiency of the justification made by Sandura. We are of the opinion that the Commission's rejection of its sufficiency was without supporting factual foundation. We are satisfied that the record in this case is barren of credible evidence that the public would be benefited by requiring that Sandura distributors be allowed to intrude on each other's territory. The distributors, the dealers and the public will *best* be served by the continued economic health and competitive existence of Sandura as well as its distributors. We are of the opinion that *on this record,* the only justified conclusion is that elimination of the closed territory arrangement would impair competition, rather than foster it.

The *Sandura* decision made good economic sense. The competitive impact of Sandura's restrictions was positive. The territorial restrictions enabled Sandura to compete more effectively against giants like Armstrong and Congoleum. Just three years later, however, the Supreme Court handed down a decision, which if permanently upheld, would have overturned the *Sandura* decision.

United States v. Arnold Schwinn & Co. 388 U.S. 365 (1967)   In 1951 Schwinn was the leading U.S. manufacturer of bicycles with a 22.5 percent market share. In the next decade, however, Schwinn's share declined to 12.8 percent, and it lost its leadership position to the Murray Ohio Manufacturing Company. Murray sold primarily private-label bicycles to Sears, Montgomery Ward, and other large retailers. In contrast, Schwinn sold *some* of its bikes through twenty-two wholesale distributors, who in turn sold to a large number of independent retailers. Most of Schwinn's bikes, however, were sold directly to retailers on consignment, and under the so-called Schwinn plan. Under the Schwinn plan, Schwinn shipped its bicycles to retailers, but Schwinn maintained legal ownership, and the retailers were simply paid a commission on each sale.

The case revolved primarily around Schwinn's requirement that its twenty-two wholesalers sell only to franchised Schwinn dealers located in the wholesaler's exclusive territory. The wholesalers, however, were not restricted to selling only Schwinn bicycles, and many carried other bicycle brands. Each franchised Schwinn retailer was authorized to buy from only one wholesaler, and the franchised retailers were forbidden to sell to unfranchised bicycle retailers.

The Supreme Court drew a careful distinction between cases where Schwinn sold outright to wholesalers and cases where it sold on consignment or through the Schwinn plan. In cases of outright sale, a 5–2 majority held that it was illegal *per se* for a manufacturer to restrict its distributors' sales territories. In the cases where Schwinn maintained ownership over the goods, that is, under the consignment and Schwinn plans, the majority held that Schwinn could impose territorial restrictions under a Rule of Reason interpretation.

Justice Fortas delivered the majority opinion:

> The District Court here enjoined [Schwinn] from limiting the territory within which any wholesaler or jobber may sell any Schwinn product which it has purchased. It held that these are agreements to divide territory and, as such, are *per se* violations of section 1 of the Sherman Act. The court made clear that it confined its order to transactions in which the distributor *purchases* from Schwinn. As to consignment, agency and Schwinn Plan transactions, the court held that, in these instances "Schwinn has a right to allocate its agents or salesmen to a particular territory." . . .
>
> The [government] vigorously argues that, since this remedy is confined to situations where the distributor and retailer acquire title to the bicycles, it will provide only partial relief; that to prevent the allocation of territories and confinement to franchised retail dealers, the decree can and should be enlarged to forbid these practices, however effected — whether by sale and resale or by agency, consignment, or the Schwinn Plan. . . .
>
> We conclude that the proper application of section 1 of the Sherman Act to this problem requires differentiation between the situation where the manufacturer parts with title, dominion or risk with respect to the article, and where he completely retains ownership and risk of loss.
>
> As the District Court held, where a manufacturer *sells* products to his distributor subject to territorial restrictions upon resale, a *per se* violation of the Sherman Act results. . . . Such restraints are so obviously destructive of competition that their mere existence is enough. If the manufacturer parts with dominion over his product or transfers risk of loss to another, he may

not reserve control over its destiny or the conditions of its resale. . . . On the other hand, as indicated in *White Motors,* we are not prepared to introduce the inflexibility which a *per se* rule might bring if it were applied to prohibit all vertical restrictions of territory and all franchising, in the sense of designating specified distributors and retailers as the chosen instruments through which the manufacturer, retaining ownership of the goods, will distribute them to the public. Such a rule might severely hamper smaller enterprises resorting to reasonable methods of meeting the competition of giants and of merchandising through independent dealers, and it might sharply accelerate the trend towards vertical integration of the distribution process. But to allow this freedom where the manufacturer has parted with dominion over the goods — the usual marketing situation — would violate the ancient rule against restraints on alienation and open the door to exclusivity of outlets and limitation of territory further than prudence permits. . . .

As the District Court found, Schwinn adopted the challenged distribution programs in a competitive situation dominated by mass merchandisers which command access to large-scale advertising and promotion, choice of retail outlets, both owned and franchised, and adequate sources of supply. It is not claimed that Schwinn's practices or other circumstances resulted in an inadequate competitive situation with respect to the bicycle market; and there is nothing in the record . . . to lead us to conclude that Schwinn's program exceeded the limits reasonably necessary to meet the competitive problems posed by its more powerful competitors. In these circumstances, the rule of reason is satisfied.

We do not suggest that the unilateral adoption by a single manufacturer of an agency or consignment pattern and the Schwinn type of restrictive distribution system would be justified in any and all circumstances by the presence of the competition of mass merchandisers and by the demonstrated need of the franchise system to meet that competition. But certainly, in such circumstances, the vertically imposed distribution restraints — absent price fixing and in the presence of adequate sources of alternative products to meet the needs of the unfranchised — may not be held to be *per se* violations of the Sherman Act.

The legal and economic implications of the *Schwinn* decision are confusing. On the one hand, the decision was meant to clarify and simplify the law by placing a *per se* interpretation on most territorial restrictions. On the other hand, the *Schwinn* decision created an incentive for firms to avoid a *per se* ruling by merely setting up a consignment system of distribution and then taking a chance that the system would pass a Rule of Reason test in court. Furthermore, from an economic perspective it is hard to see how the Schwinn plan was any more or less restrictive than the condemned wholesaler-retailer system. Fortunately, in 1977, the Supreme Court came to accept this view and overturned the *Schwinn* decision.

Continental T.V. v. GTE Sylvania Inc. **433 U.S. 36 (1977)**   The confusion created by the *Schwinn* decision was clarified in the *Sylvania* case. Sylvania manufactured television sets, which it marketed prior to 1962 through a large number of independent retail stores and company-owned distributors. Prompted by a decline in its market share to between 1 and 2 percent, Sylvania decided to change its distribution system. Sylvania eliminated its wholesale distributors and decided to sell directly to a limited number of franchised dealers. In order to improve its position vis-à-vis the industry leader RCA, which controlled over 60 percent of the market, Sylvania decided to limit the number of franchisees in any given area and to permit its franchisees to sell only from the location or locations to which Sylvania gave permission. The new system was an effort to attract more aggressive and competent retailers, and the strategy worked. Under the new plan Sylvania increased its market share to 5 percent.

Continental T.V. was a San Francisco–based franchisee of Sylvania. In 1965 Sylvania decided to franchise another San Francisco dealer, Young Brothers, which was located approximately one mile from Continental T.V. Continental T.V. protested that this violated Sylvania's marketing policy. When Sylvania went ahead and franchised Young Brothers, Continental T.V. canceled a large Sylvania order and instead purchased a supply of televisions from one of Sylvania's competitors.

At approximately the same time that Sylvania franchised Young Brothers, Continental T.V. wanted to open another store, in Sacramento. Sylvania, however, refused to grant Continental T.V. a franchise in Sacramento because, according to Sylvania, the market was already adequately served by existing franchisees. Continental T.V. then informed Sylvania that it was going to move some Sylvania televisions from San Francisco to Sacramento and sell them from its Sacramento retail store regardless of its agreement with Sylvania. Two weeks later, Sylvania suddenly reduced Continental T.V.'s credit line from $300,000 to $50,000. In response to the credit reduction Continental T.V. withheld payments it owed on Sylvania televisions. Sylvania then terminated Continental T.V.'s franchise, and Sylvania's collection agency sued Continental T.V. in an effort to recover payment for the unpaid-for Sylvania televisions that were still in Continental T.V.'s possession.

A district court jury trial resulted in an award of $1,774,515 in treble damages to Continental T.V. The Ninth Circuit Court of Appeals, however, reversed the decision and held that Sylvania's restrictions were less harmful to competition than the restrictions used by Schwinn.

The Supreme Court ruled 6–2 in favor of Sylvania and, in the process, directly overturned the *Schwinn* decision. Justice Powell wrote

In the present case it is undisputed that title passed from Sylvania to Continental. Thus the *Schwinn per se rule* applies unless Sylvania's restriction on locations falls outside *Schwinn*'s prohibition against a manufacturer's attempting to restrict a "retailer's freedom as to where and to whom it will resell the products." . . . Unlike the Court of Appeals, however, we are unable to find a principled basis for distinguishing *Schwinn* from the case now before us. . . .

[W]e are convinced that the need for clarification of the law in this area justifies reconsideration [of the *Schwinn* decision]. *Schwinn* itself was an abrupt and largely unexplained departure form *White Motor Co. v. United States*, . . . where only four years earlier the Court had refused to endorse a *per se* rule for vertical restrictions. . . .

The market impact of vertical restrictions is complex because of their potential for a simultaneous reduction of intrabrand competition and stimulation of interbrand competition. Significantly, the Court in *Schwinn* did not distinguish among the challenged restrictions on the basis of their individual potential for intrabrand harm or interbrand benefit. . . . The pivotal factor was the passage of title: All restrictions were held to be *per se* illegal where title had passed, and all were evaluated and sustained under the rule of reason where it had not. . . .

Vertical restrictions reduce intrabrand competition by limiting the number of sellers of a particular product competing for the business of a given group of buyers. . . . Although intrabrand competition may be reduced, the ability of retailers to exploit the resulting market may be limited both by the ability of consumers to travel to other franchised locations and, perhaps more importantly, to purchase the competing products of other manufacturers. None of these key variables, however, is affected by the form of the transaction by which a manufacturer conveys his products to the retailers.

Vertical restrictions promote interbrand competition by allowing the manufacturer to achieve certain efficiencies in the distribution of his products. . . . Economists have identified a number of ways in which manufacturers can use such restrictions to compete more effectively against other manufacturers. . . . For example, new manufacturers and manufacturers entering new markets can use the restrictions in order to induce competent and aggressive retailers to make the kind of investment of capital and labor that is often required in the distribution of products unknown to the consumer. Established manufacturers can use them to induce retailers to engage in promotional activities or to provide service and repair facilities necessary to the efficient marketing of their products. . . .

We conclude that the distinction drawn in *Schwinn* between sale and nonsale transactions is not sufficient to justify the application of a *per se* rule in one situation and a rule of reason in the other. The question remains whether the *per se* rule stated in *Schwinn* should be expanded to include non-sale transactions or abandoned in favor of a return to the rule of reason. We have found no persuasive support for expanding the *per se* rule. . . .

> We revert to the standard articulated . . . in *White Motor.*

The present state of the law with regard to territorial restrictions applies the Rule of Reason to all cases. This makes economic sense since territorial restrictions of the type used by Sandura and Sylvania had a positive rather than a negative effect on competition.

IV   RESALE-PRICE MAINTENANCE

Resale-price maintenance (RPM) is the vertical counterpart of horizontal price-fixing. Under RPM agreements the manufacturer specifies the price that wholesalers and retailers can charge. These agreements are often initiated by retailers, rather than by manufacturers, and are particularly helpful to small retailers who cannot compete against low-priced discount houses. If one of the objectives of public policy is the preservation of the small local retailer, resale-price maintenance may be justified. On strict efficiency grounds, however, resale-price maintenance is almost never justified.

It is somewhat surprising that manufacturers *ever* agree to abide by RPM agreements. Once a manufacturer sets a product's price, it would normally be in the manufacturer's interest to have that product sell at the *lowest* possible retail price. Studies have shown that except in rare cases RPM results in *higher* retail prices and, therefore, *lower* sales for the manufacturer [9]. If RPM generally does not benefit manufacturers, why was RPM so popular prior to the 1970s in the United States?

Two main arguments have been advanced in support of RPM. First, and probably the most important reason for RPM's popularity, was the desire of small retailers to be able to compete with large discount stores. Small retailers put pressure on Congress, and under this pressure Congress legalized RPM with the passage of the Miller-Tydings Act in 1937. Second, there is one possible advantage of RPM to manufacturers. Resale-price maintenance might make tacit collusion between manufacturers easier to maintain. According to this argument, RPM can be used as a substitute for vertical integration into retailing [10].

In defense of RPM, manufacturers have argued that it prevents retailers from selling their products at low prices or as loss leaders. According to this theory, if a *high*-quality product is consistently sold at a low price, consumers will begin to think of the product as a *low*-quality product. If supermarkets continually sold Häagen-Dazs ice cream at cost, consumers might come to believe that Häagen-Dazs was not a high-quality ice cream. It is hard to believe that buyers are as simple minded as this argument implies, but even if they are, there are other ways of dealing with this problem. The manufacturer could simply *raise* the price of the product and thereby create an incentive for retailers to charge more.

Another argument used to justify RPM is similar to the argument advanced by Jerrold to justify its tying of service to cable TV systems. Some products may require high-quality service from the retailer. High-quality computer manufacturers (IBM, Apple) might *require* high-quality service from their retailers. By imposing RPM on their computer retailers, manufacturers could ensure that the dealers could not compete by charging lower prices. The dealers, therefore, would probably compete by attempting to provide better service. In the absence of RPM, some computer dealers would provide good, but costly, service and charge high prices, and other dealers would provide little or no service and charge low prices. Consumers could then shop around at the high-priced, good-service dealers, but purchase their computers at the low-priced dealers. The low-priced dealers would then obtain a free ride on the services provided by the high-priced dealers, and over time the high-priced, good-service dealers might be eliminated from the market. The prevention of a significant free-rider problem is the most reasonable economic justification for RPM, but there are probably few goods that actually require good service for technological reasons. It is hard to argue that Levi's jeans, an item that was sold under RPM for many years, must be sold in stores providing good service.

As the cases below indicate, the courts have generally been tougher on RPM than Congress has. In 1976, however, even Congress turned against RPM and repealed what were euphemistically called the fair-trade laws permitting RPM.

Dr. Miles Medical Company v. John D. Park & Sons Company 220 U.S. 373 (1911)

Dr. Miles produced proprietary medicines under a group of secret formulas. The drugs were sold to wholesalers and retailers under a written agreement that they would sell at prices set by Dr. Miles. Park & Sons was a wholesaler who refused to sign the price-maintenance agreement. Park induced a number of wholesalers who had signed the agreement to supply them with Dr. Miles medicines at cut-rate prices. When Park advertised and sold these drugs to retailers at reduced prices, Dr. Miles sued Park.

By 7–1, the Supreme Court ruled that the written agreements violated the Sherman Act. Justice Hughes delivered the majority opinion:

> That these agreements restrain trade is obvious. . . .
>
> But it is insisted that the restrictions are not invalid either at common law or under the act of Congress of July 2, 1890, . . . upon the following

grounds . . .: (1) That the restrictions are valid because they relate to proprietary medicines manufactured under a secret process; and (2) that, apart from this, a manufacturer is entitled to control the prices on all sales of his own products.

First. The first inquiry is whether there is any distinction with respect to such restrictions as are here presented, between the case of an article manufactured by the owner of a secret process and that of one produced under ordinary conditions. . . .

[Dr. Miles] has no [patent] statutory grant. So far as appears, there are no . . . patent[s] relating to the remedies in question. [Dr. Miles] has not seen fit to make the disclosure required by the statute and thus to secure the privileges it confers. Its case lies outside the policy of the patent law, and the extent of the right which that law secures is not here involved or determined. . . .

Second. We come, then, to the second question, whether the complainant irrespective of the secrecy of its process, is entitled to maintain the restrictions by virtue of the fact that they relate to products of its own manufacturer.

The basis of the argument appears to be that, as the manufacturer may make and sell or not, as he chooses, he may affix conditions as to the use of the article or as to the prices at which purchasers may dispose of it. The propriety of the restraint is sought to be derived from the liberty of the producer.

But because a manufacturer is not bound to make or sell, it does not follow that in case of sales actually made he may impose upon purchasers every sort of restriction. . . .

[T]his complainant can fare no better with its plan of identical contracts than could the dealers themselves if they formed a combination and endeavored to establish the same restrictions, and thus to achieve the same result by agreement with each other. If the immediate advantage they would thus obtain would not be sufficient to sustain such a direct agreement, the asserted ulterior benefit to [Dr. Miles] cannot be regarded as sufficient to support its system.

[W]here commodities have passed into the channels of trade and are owned by dealers, the validity of agreements to prevent competition and to maintain prices is not to be determined by the circumstance whether they were produced by several manufacturers or by one, or whether they were previously owned by one or by many. The complainant having sold its product at prices satisfactory to itself, the public is entitled to whatever advantage may be derived from competition in the subsequent traffic.

One of the major determining factors in the *Dr. Miles* decision was the use of a formal written agreement to maintain prices. Eight years later, the Supreme Court handed down a decision that appeared to limit the reach of the *Dr. Miles* decision to cases where a formal written agreement was used to enforce RPM.

***United States v. Colgate & Co.* 250 U.S. 300 (1919)**   Unlike Dr. Miles, Colgate had not resorted to written agreements to maintain its retail prices. Instead, Colgate announced a policy that it would not supply any wholesaler or retailer who refused to abide by Colgate's prices. In fact, a careful reading of the evidence suggests that Colgate went beyond simply announcing that it would not deal with price-cutters. Colgate at times used investigations to determine which companies were reducing prices and had even solicited information from dealers regarding which of its retailers were reducing prices. In any event, the Supreme Court ruled that Colgate's actions did *not* violate the Sherman Act. Justice McReynolds delivered the unanimous opinion of the Court:

> In the course of its opinion the trial court said:
>
> > "The pregnant fact should never be lost sight of that no [assertion] is made of any contract or agreement having been entered into whereby the defendant, the manufacturer, and his customers, bound themselves to enhance and maintain prices, . . . the defendant here refused to sell to persons who would not resell at indicated prices, and that certain retailers made purchases on this condition, whereas, inferentially, others declined so to do. No suggestion is made that the defendant, the manufacturer, attempted to reserve or retain any interest in the goods sold or to restrain the vendee in his right to barter and sell the same without restriction. The retailer, after buying, could, if he chose, give away his purchase, or sell it at any price he saw fit, or not sell it at all; his course in these respects being affected only by the fact that he might by his action incur the displeasure of the manufacturer, who could refuse to make further sales to him, as he had the undoubted right to do." . . .
>
> Considering all said in the opinion (notwithstanding some serious doubts) we are unable to accept the construction placed upon it by the Government. . . . And we must conclude that, as interpreted below, the indictment does not charge Colgate & Company with selling its products to dealers under agreements which obligated the latter not to resell except at prices fixed by the company. . . .
>
> In the absence of any purpose to create or maintain a monopoly, the act does not restrict the long recognized right of a trader or manufacturer engaged in an entirely private business, freely to exercise his own independent discretion as to parties with whom he will deal. And, of course, he may announce in advance the circumstances under which he will refuse to sell. . . . In *Dr. Miles Medical Co. v. Park & Sons Co.,* the unlawful

combination was effected through contracts which undertook to prevent dealers from freely exercising the right to sell. . . .

The judgment of the District Court must be *Affirmed.*

The *Colgate* decision appeared to create a large loophole in the Sherman Act with regard to RPM. Within three years, however, the Supreme Court had twice attempted to clarify the meaning of the *Colgate* decision. In both *United States v. Schrader's Sons* [252 U.S. 85 (1920)] and *Federal Trade Commission v. Beech Nut Packing Company* [257 U.S. 441 (1922)], the Supreme Court ruled that an express written agreement was *not* necessary for an RPM agreement to violate the Sherman Act. In both of these cases the Court ruled that because the defendants had made elaborate arrangements to police their RPM agreements, the plans violated the antitrust laws. These cases limited, without overturning, the *Colgate* decision and helped to create a movement among small retailers to legalize RPM. In 1937 this movement paid off with the passage of the Miller-Tydings Act.

The Miller-Tydings Act amended the Sherman Act to permit states to pass laws legalizing RPM agreements. The act also prevented the FTC from taking action against RPM as an unfair method of competition. By 1941, forty-five of the forty-eight states had passed so-called fair-trade laws permitting RPM. Only Texas, Missouri, Vermont, and the District of Columbia stood as exceptions.

Schwegmann Brothers v. Calvert Distillers Corp. 341 U.S. 384 (1951) The Miller-Tydings Act gave states the right to permit written RPM agreements, and Louisiana passed such a law. The Louisiana law, however, went beyond merely permitting RPM agreements. The law contained a provision whereby if *one* firm signed an agreement, all other retailers in Louisiana were forced to abide by the agreement. When Schwegmann Brothers, a large New Orleans retailer, refused to sign an agreement with Calvert Distillers and continued to sell Calvert's liquor at cut-rate prices, Calvert took Schwegmann to court.

By 6–3, the Supreme Court sided with Schwegmann and ruled that RPM agreements could not be enforced against nonsigners. Justice Douglas wrote the opinion:

> The omission of the nonsigner provision from the [Miller-Tydings Act] is fatal to [Calvert's] position unless we are to perform a distinct legislative function by reading into the Act a provision that was meticulously omitted from it. . . .
>
> [W]hen a state compels retailers to follow a parallel price policy, it demands private conduct which the Sherman Act forbids. . . . Elimination of price competition at the retail level may, of course, lawfully result if a distributor successfully negotiates individual "vertical" agreements with all

his retailers. But when retailers are *forced* to abandon price competition, they are driven into a compact in violation of the spirit of the proviso which forbids "horizontal" price fixing. . . .

The contrary conclusion would have a vast and devastating effect on Sherman Act policies. If it were adopted, once a distributor executed a contract with a single retailer setting the minimum resale price for a commodity in the state, all other retailers could be forced into line. Had Congress desired to eliminate the consensual element from the arrangement and to permit blanketing a state with resale price fixing if only one retailer wanted it, we feel that different measures would have been adopted — either a nonsigner provision would have been included or resale price fixing would have been authorized without [qualifications].

The *Schwegmann Brothers* decision greatly weakened the Miller-Tydings Act and probably would have effectively killed legalized RPM agreements if Congress had not acted to change the law again. In 1952 Congress voted to overrule the *Schwegmann Brothers* decision by passing the McGuire Act, which extended the Miller-Tydings Act to include nonsigners of a RPM agreement. Despite President Truman's opposition to the bill, it passed both houses by such large majorities that the president felt unable to veto it. It is interesting to note that President Franklin Roosevelt had opposed the Miller-Tydings Act as well, but was forced to sign the bill as a rider to the District of Columbia finance bill.

***United States v. Parke, Davis & Co.* 362 U.S. 29 (1960)**   After the passage of the McGuire Act, both Virginia and the District of Columbia failed to enact fair-trade laws. Parke, Davis announced a national policy of refusing to deal with wholesalers or retailers who sold below the Parke, Davis suggested prices. In the summer of 1956 drug retailers in Washington, D.C., and Richmond, Virginia, advertised and sold Parke, Davis drugs below the RPM prices. In order to enforce its prices, Parke, Davis informed its wholesalers that they would be cut off from supplies if they continued to supply price-cutting retailers. Parke, Davis also informed each of the cut-rate retailers that their supplies would be eliminated if they continued to cut prices. Furthermore, each wholesaler and retailer was informed that every other wholesaler and retailer was being informed of the Parke, Davis policy.

Even after being threatened by Parke, Davis, five retailers, including Dart Drug, refused to abide by Parke, Davis's prices, and these retailers were cut off from their supplies by Parke, Davis directly and by Parke, Davis wholesalers. Furthermore, supplies of *all* Parke, Davis drugs were eliminated, even prescription drugs that were never sold below RPM prices. When the five retailers persisted in selling drugs from existing stocks below the Parke, Davis list prices, Parke, Davis decided to modify its policy. Each of the five price-cutters was told that shipments would be resumed if the retailer simply stopped advertising Parke Davis drugs at cut-rate prices. When Dart Drug agreed to stop advertising, the four other price-cutters agreed to stop advertising, and Parke, Davis resumed shipments to all five firms. Within one month, however, several retailers were once again advertising Parke, Davis drugs at cut-rate prices. By this time the Justice Department, at the request of Dart Drug, had begun an investigation of Parke, Davis; therefore, Parke, Davis elected not to take any further action.

The district court held that the actions of Parke, Davis were legal under the *Colgate* doctrine. The Supreme Court, however, by 6–3, reversed this decision. Justice Brennan delivered the opinion:

> The program upon which Parke Davis embarked to promote general compliance with its suggested resale prices plainly exceeded the limitations of the *Colgate* doctrine. . . . Parke Davis did not content itself with announcing its policy regarding retail prices and following this with a simple refusal to have business relations with any retailers who disregarded that policy. Instead Parke Davis used the refusal to deal with the wholesalers in order to elicit their willingness to deny Parke Davis products to retailers and thereby help gain the retailers' adherence to its suggested minimum retail prices. The retailers who disregarded the price policy were promptly cut off when Parke Davis supplied the wholesalers with their names. . . . In thus involving the wholesalers to stop the flow of Parke Davis products to the retailers, thereby inducing retailers' adherence to its suggested retail prices, Parke Davis created a combination with the retailers and the wholesalers to maintain retail prices and violated the Sherman Act. Although Parke Davis originally announced wholesalers' policy would not under *Colgate* have violated the Sherman Act if its action thereunder was the simple refusal . . . to deal with wholesalers who did not observe the wholesalers' Net Price Selling Schedule that entire policy was tainted with the "vice of . . . illegality," . . . when Parke Davis used it as the vehicle to gain the wholesalers' participation in the program to effectuate the retailers' adherence to the suggested retail prices. . . .
>
> [I]f a manufacturer . . . takes affirmative action to achieve uniform adherence by inducing each customer to adhere to avoid such price competition the customers' acquiescence is not then a matter of individual free choice prompted alone by the desirability of the product. The product then comes packaged in a competition-free wrapping — a valuable feature in itself — by virtue of concerted action induced by the manufacturer. The manufacturer is thus the organizer of a price-maintenance combination or conspiracy in violation of the Sherman Act.

The *Parke, Davis* decision further eroded the importance of the *Colgate* precedent in states with no fair-trade laws. It was not antitrust policy, but economic factors that ultimately led to the death of RPM. The emergence of large discount houses throughout the United States and the existence of large mail-order houses in states with no fair-trade laws combined to make the fair-trade laws less and less effective. By 1975 only six states had fair-trade laws that were enforceable against nonsigners, and in 1976 Congress repealed the Miller-Tydings and McGuire Acts. At the present time, therefore, RPM agreements are effectively illegal *per se*. The *Colgate* precedent, however, has never been directly overturned by the Supreme Court.

V   GROUP BOYCOTTS

Group boycotts fall into one of two general categories. In some cases, a group of firms with market power over some product or service draws up a blacklist and refuses to deal with firms on the list. In other cases, a group of firms with control over a critical resource draws up a white list and supplies only firms on the list with the resource. The cases below illustrate both types of boycotts. If the group has market power, such boycotts will be clearly anticompetitive and should be illegal *per se*. The only reasonable exception to a *per se* rule would be in cases where the boycotting group has no market power.

***Fashion Originators' Guild of America Inc. v. Federal Trade Commission* 312 U.S. 457 (1941)**   The Fashion Originators' Guild of America (FOGA) was an association of designers, manufacturers, and distributors of women's clothing. Guild designers complained that after their original designs entered retail channels, nonmembers of the guild would copy the designs and market virtually identical garments. In order to stop this style piracy, FOGA combined to force retailers to stop marketing these copied fashions. All guild members agreed not to distribute garments to any retailer who marketed pirated styles. Furthermore, the guild managed to obtain signed agreements from more than 12,000 retailers not to sell pirated clothing.

Because the 176 manufacturers who were guild members controlled more than 60 percent of the women's garments that wholesaled at $10.75 and up, these manufacturers had considerable market power in the high-priced segment of the market. It was extremely important for retailers to have access to some garments produced by guild members.

In addition to organizing the boycott against retailers, the guild also prohibited its members from advertising, regulated the discounts its members could offer, prohibited members from selling at retail, regulated the days when sales could be held, and prohibited its members from selling to any retailer who conducted business from a private residence.

The FTC filed a complaint under section 5 of the FTC Act, and the Supreme Court ruled unanimously that the guild's actions violated the antitrust laws. Justice Black delivered the Court opinion:

> [A]mong the many respects in which the Guild's plan runs contrary to the policy of the Sherman Act are these: it narrows the outlets to which garment and textile manufacturers can sell and the sources from which retailers can buy . . .; subjects all retailers and manufacturers who decline to comply with the Guild's program to an organized boycott . . .; takes away the freedom of action of members by requiring each to reveal to the Guild the intimate details of their individual affairs . . .; and has both as its necessary tendency and as its purpose and effect the direct suppression of competition from the sale of unregistered textiles and copied designs. . . . In addition to all this, the combination is in reality an extra-governmental agency, which prescribes rules for the regulation and restraint of interstate commerce, and provides extra-judicial tribunals for determination and punishment of violations, and thus "trenches upon the power of the national legislature and violates the statute." . . .
>
> But petitioners . . . argue that their boycott and restraint of interstate trade is not within the ban of the policies of the Sherman and Clayton Acts because "the practices of FOGA were reasonable and necessary to protect the manufacturer, laborer, retailer and consumer against the devastating evils growing from the pirating of original designs and had in fact benefited all four." . . .
>
> [T]he unlawful combination [cannot] be justified upon the argument that systematic copying of dress designs is itself tortious, or should now be declared so by us. In the first place, whether or not given conduct is tortious is a question of state law. . . . In the second place, even if copying were an acknowledged tort under the law of every state, that situation would not justify petitioners in combining together to regulate and restrain interstate commerce in violation of federal law.

The *FOGA* decision made it clear that a group boycott could not be justified on the grounds that it was necessary to protect the group from the illegal actions of another firm or other firms. If the guild was concerned about pirating, it could have filed a law suit against the accused pirates, but it could not take the law into its own hands by violating the Sherman Act.

Associated Press v. United States 326 U.S. 1 (1945) In 1945 the Associated Press (AP) was a cooperative association of more than 1,200 newspapers in the United States. According to the AP bylaws, members were forbidden to supply news information to nonmembers and were given considerable power to block competitors from becoming AP members. If an applicant for membership did *not* compete with another

AP member, the applicant could become a member by a simple majority vote of the board of directors, with no financial payment to the AP. If, however, an applicant competed with an existing AP member, the applicant was required (1) to pay 10 percent of the total amount of the regular assessments received by the AP from members in the same competitive field during the *entire* period from October 1, 1900, to the time of the new member's election to the AP; (2) to relinquish all exclusive rights to any news or picture service, and to make all of its news sources available to its competitors upon the same terms as they were available to the applicant; and (3) to receive a majority vote of *all* regular members of the AP. Since the AP was the nation's largest supplier of news stories, these policies made entry into the newspaper business more difficult.

Despite the fact that competing news services existed, the Supreme Court held that the actions of the AP violated the Sherman Act. Justice Black delivered the 7–2 decision:

> Trade restraints of this character, aimed at the destruction of competition, tend to block the initiative which brings newcomers into a field of business and to frustrate the free enterprise system which it was the purpose of the Sherman Act to protect. . . . The Sherman Act was specifically intended to prohibit independent businesses from becoming "associates" in a common plan which is bound to reduce their competitor's opportunity to buy or sell the things in which the groups compete. . . .

> It is . . . contended that since there are other news agencies which sell news, it is not a violation of the Act for an overwhelming majority of American publishers to combine to decline to sell their news to the minority. But the fact that an agreement to restrain trade does not inhibit competition in all of the objects of that trade cannot save it from the condemnation of the Sherman Act. . . .

> [T]he argument is made that to apply the Sherman Act to this association of publishers constitutes an abridgment of the freedom of the press guaranteed by the First Amendment. . . . It would be strange indeed, however, if the grave concern for freedom of the press which prompted adoption of the First Amendment should be read as a command that the government was without power to protect that freedom. The First Amendment, far from providing an argument against application of the Sherman Act, here provides powerful reasons to the contrary. That Amendment rests on the assumption that the widest possible dissemination of information from diverse and antagonistic sources is essential to the welfare of the public, that a free press is a condition of a free society. Surely a command that the government itself shall not impede the free flow of ideas does not afford non-governmental combinations a refuge if they impose restraints upon that constitutionally guaranteed freedom. Freedom to publish means freedom for all and not for some. Freedom to publish is guaranteed by the Constitution, but freedom to combine to keep others from publishing is not.

Freedom of the press from governmental interference under the First Amendment does not sanction repression of that freedom by private interests. The First Amendment affords not the slightest support for the contention that a combination to restrain trade in news and views has any constitutional immunity.

The Supreme Court affirmed the district court decree and required the AP to furnish news on equal terms to both old and new AP members. The Court also ruled that members were free to furnish news to nonmembers.

Silver v. New York Stock Exchange 373 U.S. 341 (1963)   The major issue in the *Silver* case was whether government regulation could exempt an organization from the Sherman Act and permit it to carry out a group boycott. Harold Silver, who died before the final outcome of the case, was a municipal bond dealer located in Dallas, Texas. Silver installed private telephone lines that directly connected his Texas operations with several members of the New York Stock Exchange. During the summer of 1958 the exchange granted temporary approval of the telephone lines as well as a stock ticker service. In February 1959, however, without prior notice, the exchange's Department of Member Firms decided to cut off Silver's lines. By the beginning of March 1959 all of Silver's lines were gone. When Silver repeatedly asked for an explanation of the exchange's policy, he was told that the exchange would not disclose the reasons for its actions.

Shortly after the line cutoffs, Silver's business dropped dramatically, and he was forced to leave the bond business. When Silver sued, the New York Stock Exchange argued that it was regulated by the Securities and Exchange Commission and, therefore, was exempt from the Sherman Act. Furthermore, the New York Stock Exchange argued that section 6 of the Securities Exchange Act *required* the New York Stock Exchange to self-regulate its members' interactions with nonmembers. Specifically, section 6 required that any registered stock exchange must establish rules to provide for "the expulsion, suspension, or disciplining of a member for conduct or proceeding inconsistent with just and equitable principles of trade." Section 6 went on to state that the exchange's rules must be "just and adequate to . . . protect investors."

The district court ruled for Silver. The circuit court, however, held that the Securities Exchange Act permitted the New York Stock Exchange's actions.

By 7–2, the Supreme Court reversed the decision of the circuit court. Justice Goldberg wrote

> The fundamental issue confronting us is whether the Securities Exchange Act has created a duty of exchange self-regulation so pervasive as to constitute an implied repealer of our antitrust laws, thereby exempting the Exchange from liability in this and similar cases. . . .

It is plain, to begin with, that removal of the wires by collective action of the Exchange and its members would, had it occurred in a context free from other federal regulation, constitute a *per se* violation of section 1 of the Sherman Act. The concerted action of the Exchange and its members here was, in simple terms, a group boycott depriving petitioners of a valuable business service which they needed in order to compete effectively as broker-dealers in the over-the-counter securities market. . . .

The Securities Exchange Act contains no express exemption from the antitrust laws or, for that matter, from any other statute. This means that any repealer of the antitrust laws must be discerned as a matter of implication, and "[i]t is a cardinal principle of construction that repeals by implication are not favored." . . .

There is nothing built into the regulatory scheme which performs the antitrust function of insuring that an exchange will not in some cases apply its rules so as to do injury to competition which cannot be justified as furthering legitimate self-regulative ends. . . . Notwithstanding their prompt and repeated requests, petitioners were not informed of the charges underlying the decision to invoke the Exchange rules and were not afforded an appropriate opportunity to explain or refute the charges against them.

Given the principle that exchange self-regulation is to be regarded as justified in response to antitrust charges only to the extent necessary to protect the achievement of the aims of the Securities Exchange Act, it is clear that no justification can be offered for self-regulation conducted without provision for some method of telling a protesting nonmember why a rule is being invoked so as to harm him and allowing him to reply in explanation of his position. No policy reflected in the Securities Exchange Act is, to begin with served by denial of notice and an opportunity for hearing.

The *Associated Press* and *Silver* decisions suggest that in situations where a group of firms controls a resource that is considered *critical* to competition, the group must make the resource available to competitors on a more or less equal basis. Nevertheless, it is important to realize that a modified Rule of Reason still applies in group boycott cases. A small group of firms, with *no* market power, that bands together to form a buying or selling cooperative will usually be protected from the antitrust laws so long as alternative sources of supply are *easily* available to nonmember firms. If the cooperative effort confers a major competitive advantage on coop members, the cooperative may have to adopt an open-admissions policy.

VI SUMMARY

Unlike most horizontal agreements, certain types of vertical restraints of trade are not illegal *per se*. Requirements contracts and territorial restrictions come under a Rule of Reason standard. Tying arrangements, however, come close to being illegal *per se*, and resale-price maintenance is currently considered effectively illegal *per se* in most states.

It would be hard for most economists to criticize the current policy toward vertical restraints severely because it usually recognizes the potential benefits associated with certain types of vertical agreements while it recognizes the lack of economic justification for resale-price maintenance. Furthermore, the Supreme Court has not permitted the major types of anticompetitive vertical restraints, such as tying of nonpatented items to patented items or the use of requirements contracts by firms with market power. Current legal policy, however, can be criticized for failing to treat alike all vertical restraints that have essentially the same economic impact.

With regard to group boycotts, the Supreme Court has adopted a reasonable policy. There are no good economic arguments that can be advanced in support of group boycotts that either reduce the level of existing competition or make entry more difficult. With regard to boycotts, therefore, a tough standard is required, and a tough standard has been adopted.

On this rather positive note we complete our examination of the major antitrust cases in American history.

NOTES

1. For a rather unconvincing argument that tying agreements are *never* anticompetitive see D. T. Armentano, *Antitrust and Monopoly: Anatomy of a Policy Failure* (New York: Wiley, 1982), pages 198–203; for an excellent statement of the position that tying is rarely anticompetitive see R. A. Posner, *Antitrust Law: An Economic Perspective* (Chicago: University of Chicago Press, 1976), pages 171–184; see also W. L. Baldwin and D. McFarland, "Tying Agreements in Law and Economics," *Antitrust Bulletin,* September 1963, pages 743–778; for a summary see F. M. Scherer, *Industrial Market Structure and Economic Performance* (Chicago: Rand-McNally, 1980), pages 582–584.

2. D. E. Waldman, *Antitrust Action and Market Structure* (Lexington, Mass.: Heath, 1978), pages 143–150.

3. *International Salt Company v. United States* 332 U.S. 392 (1947).

4. *Siegel v. Chicken Delight* 448 F.2d 43 (1971); *Ungar v. Dunkin' Donuts of America,* no. 75-1625, appellants' brief filed 7/23/75 (3 cir. 1975).

5. Waldman, *Antitrust Action and Market Structure,* page 141.

6. Ibid., page 76.

7. C. H. Hessian, "The Metal Container Industry" in Walter Adams (ed.), *The Structure of American Industry* (New York: Macmillan, 1971), pages 323–324.

8. L. J. White, "Vertical Restraints in Antitrust Law: A Coherent Model," *Antitrust Bulletin,* Summer 1981, pages 327–345.

9. S. C. Hollander, "Summary of United States Experience with Resale Price Maintenance," in B. S. Yamey (ed.), *Resale Price Maintenance* (Chicago: Aldine, 1966), pages 67–100; M. Frankel, "The Effects of Fair Trade: Fact and Fiction in the Statistical Findings," *Journal of Business,* July 1955, pages 182–194; and J. F. Pickering, "The Abolition of Resale Price Maintenance in Great Britain," *Oxford Economic Papers,* March 1975.

10. See Chapter 4.

Index